THE HIDDEN MYSTERY OF THE BIBLE

Addington Books

THE HIDDEN MYSTERY
OF THE BIBLE

By
Jack Ensign Addington

DeVorss Publications
Camarillo, California

The Hidden Mystery of the Bible
Copyright © 1969 by Jack Ensign Addington

ISBN: 978-087516-696-4
Library of Congress Control Number: 70-93549
Tenth Printing, 2023

DeVorss & Company, Publisher
P.O. Box 1389
Camarillo CA 93011-1389
www.devorss.com

Printed in the United States of America

PREFACE

This book is not an attempt to interpret the entire Bible, but to show through examples how a secret code unlocks the hidden meaning thoughout the writings of the Bible.

In trying to understand the seemingly meaningless portions of the Bible, it became apparent to me that certain words, about one hundred to be exact, had been used over and over in identically the same way, often making no sense in or out of context, as one would use a secret code to hide a meaning that he did not wish exposed to the public. I tested this again and again and found it to be true. I found that once these code words were translated a door was opened to a whole new area of understanding.

The Bible is really an anthology, a collection of choice literary extracts from different authors, some relating to the spiritual side of life; some seeming to be written on the mental and physical. There is something of value for everyone at every level.

The material contained in the Bible is but a fraction of the original writings from which it was selected. The Biblical writings are revealed Truth which was preserved by word of mouth and gradually became written literature, the work of many spiritually minded authors. Later, groups of theologians made the selections which we think of as the Bible, deciding, according to their individual prejudices, what they judged worthy of keeping, what they would discard. For example, the Apocrypha, which is incorporated in the Vulgate, is generally omitted in Protestant versions of the Bible. The discovery of the Dead Sea Scrolls also gives evidence that much material was omitted from the Bible as we know it.

Various Bible concordances, encyclopedias, and dictionaries were used in researching the original meanings of the proper names. The secret code was revealed to me as a gradual unfoldment during twenty years of Bible teaching. I am particularly indebted to the Unity School of Christianity at Lee's Summit, Missouri, for their excellent *Metaphysical Bible Dictionary*.

Great credit goes to my wife, Cornelia, whose enthusiasm and persistence in pursuing this idea kept us working for the twelve years that it took to write this book. Without her endless work on the manuscript, it would not have been accomplished. I am also indebted to my many students who, year after year, begged for copies of the material presented in my classes and for a book on the subject, thus prompting me to put the material down in written form.

I wish to express grateful appreciation to Frances Brown who has been tireless in typing and retyping this manuscript and to Stella Terrill Mann whose encouragement, after carefully studying the manuscript, gave us a new incentive. Others who read the manuscript and gave helpful suggestions were Cornelia W. Sherman and Suzanne Huntzinger.

J.E.A.

Note: Unless otherwise noted, all scriptural references are to the King James Version of the Bible.

INTRODUCTION

This book had to be written. The need compelled it. The largest selling book in the English language is the Bible; and, yet, few people understand what it has to say. Because of this need, various translations have altered the original King James Version published in 1611. Some were helpful in certain areas, but mostly they tended to lose the beautiful mystical feeling underlying the words of the King James Version. In each generation there have been those who felt that the language of the Bible was archaic, that it should be modernized. Modernizing the language helped some to better understand the Bible in a literal, or historic, way, but left large areas completely misunderstood, especially those areas where an understanding of symbols, parables, allegories and such are required.

The Bible is a compilation of treatises on nearly every facet of man's life. Within its covers modern psychology will find all that it has to teach. It is the ultimate philosophy. It shows us how to commune with the unseen Power within each one of us. It shows us how to take dominion in our lives through the use of the Power. It is the story of every man in his journey through life, his mental and spiritual growth. The obstacles and problems he meets are presented in an understandable way.

The mystics of the ages have rather sensed than interpreted the deep esoteric meanings hidden within certain words of the Bible. Never before has a usable, workable key been presented. I humbly offer it here that the Bible may become a more understandable book, not just a book for the religious but a guidebook for every man. It may ultimately become man's greatest possession, the answer book for every problem that can ever come into his experience.

That which I have to offer began with the discovery that modern-day readers were completely overlooking the meanings behind certain proper names of people and places, continually featured in Biblical writing, meanings that the ancient writers had taken for granted and assumed would always be understood. I found that certain numbers and common words had a repetitious use and that when their symbolic or esoteric meaning was understood, they opened up entirely new avenues of wisdom and understanding. Herein lies the key to the hidden mysteries that have been concealed in the Bible for so many years.

The first five books of the Bible, known as the Torah or Pentateuch, contain the foundation for the teaching of the entire Book. Once a basis of understanding is found for these five books, the balance of the Bible can be understood easily.

I have felt absolutely driven to write this book. For years I had attempted to come to grips with the Bible. While I gained inspiration and insight from reading it, it was not until I found the key to the inner meaning that I began to grasp the wisdom contained there. I did not attempt to become a student of the Hebrew, Greek, or Aramaic, because I found that interpretations in Bible concordances, in Bible indexes, and Bible dictionaries, available to everyone, made this unnecessary. Once certain key words were understood, I found them to be used in the same way consistently throughout the books of the Bible. Thus, the interpretation for one story provided a backlog of understanding for others.

The Bible is presented on three levels. There is something

for everyone. On the obvious level there is history, rules of conduct, and beautiful literature; on the mental level there is enough philosophy to challenge the student forever; but on the spiritual level there is a whole new world of discovery awaiting the reader. Once the key to the deeper meaning is understood, one is able to enjoy the Bible without frustration. The stories of Job and Jehoshaphat interpreted in this book are found to be great psychological dramas.

I would not disturb anyone's thinking about the Bible, only open up new avenues for fresh discovery of the great Truths that lie therein. The Bible basically is a book of spiritual Truth. The things of the spirit are discerned by the spirit. There is something within each one that responds to the inner meaning, even though he may not know just what it is.

We cannot remove the mysteries from the Bible any more than we can remove the mystery of life. The Bible is the book of life—your life and my life. It exudes a beauty and vitality that cannot be explained in mere words. The mystery of the Spirit will always bring its power into those who are seeking Truth through the Bible. By understanding the true meaning of the words and symbols, this power becomes more readily available. The great Invisible gives us a strength and an understanding beyond our knowing. Who can ever explain completely the mystery of God undergirding the life in which we live? The Bible, once the deeper meanings are understood, even in a measure, shows us how the mystery of God unfolds in the life and experience of each one of us.

JACK ENSIGN ADDINGTON

CONTENTS

I WHAT THE BIBLE CAN MEAN TO YOU

The Bible is the most important book that has ever been published. It has had more influence on history and has affected more people's lives than any other book. It was not written by one person but, through divine Inspiration, it is the compilation of the thoughts and ideas of many whose words were passed down from generation to generation by mouth and by scroll. It did not receive publication for hundreds of years after the original words were conceived. Today we think of the Bible as being a part of the household of the Christian world. It is printed in many languages and each year more Bibles are sold than any other book, but few are read in comparison to the numbers sold. Many people feel that they ought to read it and try, but they give up because they do not understand it. Many of those who do read it take it literally, without knowing the inner meaning, and miss the best part.

How Some Have Studied the Bible

There are many people who devote their lives to studying the Bible. Some study it as history. Some try to prove its authenticity from an archeological viewpoint. Others can tell you just how many times a word appears in the Bible. Some have found certain passages that seem to foretell the modern freeways, automobiles, airplanes, and even space travel. To many, the end of the world is clearly foretold and modern wars predicted. As Jesus said about the Pharisees of his day who were also meticulous students, "verily . . . They have their reward." Their interest and their complete absorption in the subject is, in itself, a reward. But there are richer and greater rewards for those who are willing to seek them.

An Open Mind Is Necessary

Have you shied away from the Bible, considering it a series of genealogies, bloodthirsty battles, and "thou shalt nots" for the morally self-righteous? Have you considered that much of it was too colorful to be read aloud to the children? Do you have a casual acquaintance with the Psalms and a speaking acquaintance with the New Testament, but frankly never get around to reading the rest? Then, I would like to introduce you to the best guidebook to modern-day living that has ever been written. If you have thought that the Bible was dull, bewildering, contradictory, difficult and antiquated, I hope to show you in this book that the Bible is a storehouse of inspiration designed to fit every human need, a treasure trove of usable ideas, an infinite source of wisdom; most of all, a book of life, your life and my life.

Some of the Prejudices

It is important that we put aside all of our prejudices, our *preconceived notions.* Let's see what some of them are.

Some have thought that since the Bible was written many years ago, everything that needs to be said about it has already been said—and should be respected. This prejudice should be set aside immediately if we wish to gain an understanding of the greatest of all books. We have just as much right as anyone to dig into the true meanings in the Bible, letting our own inner Wisdom guide us into right understanding.

Another preconceived notion is that the Bible is old-fashioned, having no application to today's problems. Anything based on Truth is forever timely or applicable. Truth was revealed to the prophets of old just as it is revealed to us today and will always be revealed to all whose minds are open to receive it. The Bible is the best self-help textbook that has ever been written and its teaching applies to us today as if it were written for each one individually.

Another fallacy is that the Bible is contradictory. It is only contradictory on the exoteric side. To those who go beyond the physical and even the mental meaning into the hidden or esoteric meaning, there will be no contradiction. On the contrary, it will all be drawn together, interrelated as basic Truth always is.

There are those who say it is dull and bewildering. So would we if we were to read a letter written in a secret code. It would not make very much sense to us, would it? Once we are given the secret code, the clues that open to us the hidden meanings in the Bible, it becomes fascinating, an exciting adventure in self-discovery.

Some dispose of the Bible in one fell swoop. It couldn't have been written by God, they think, so there's nothing of Truth there at all.

The Bible has been written by God, through man. The men who brought us the inspiration contained in the Bible were men who were willing to let themselves be used by the Spirit within for this purpose. Thus, there were many scribes but only one Author—one Author writing about Himself as Creator, Creative Medium and Creation. As one understands this, the Bible turns out to be an autobiography, the Life of God in each one of us.

There are those, brought up in religions not acceptable to their intelligence, who became completely prejudiced. These people might even feel guilty about studying the Bible, in the light of discovering new meaning beyond that given by the parents, lest they somehow damage the image of the parents.

Let us put aside all of these prejudices. Take the Bible as if it were completely new to us. Pretend that we have never heard of it before and start from there.

What the Bible Actually Is

Actually, the Bible is the story of YOUR LIFE AND MY LIFE. It is the unfolding of the spiritual life of every man. As one grows in spiritual perception, he grows into a deeper understanding of the Bible. Each time he reads it, it contains a new and richer meaning. It is as if the pages come to life. What was once a gory battle becomes an allegory, giving the reader an insight into his own spiritual unfoldment. Jesus said that the enemies are all those of our own household.[1] They are enemy thoughts of our own mental households which can be overcome by Truth. The Bible is the story of man's journey from Paradise to Paradise. Along the way he meets all of the temptations and problems of everyday living. To quote from Judge Troward, a man with a deep understanding of the Bible:

> The Bible is the Book of the Emancipation of Man. The emancipation of man means his deliverance from sorrow and sickness, from poverty, struggle, and uncertainty, from ignorance and limitation, and finally from death itself.

1. Matthew 10:36; see also Micah 7:6.

This may appear to be what the euphuistic colloquialism of the day would call "a tall order," but nevertheless it is impossible to read the Bible with a mind unwarped by antecedent conceptions derived from traditional interpretation without seeing that this is exactly what it promises, and that it professes to contain the secret whereby this happy condition of perfect liberty may be attained.[2]

The Bible, which literally means THE BOOK, contains sixty-six books which tell in allegory, prophecy, epistle, parable and poem, man's generation, degeneration and regeneration. Over and over again, from every conceivable approach, we read of the experience of each one of us as he seeks to discover the Truth about himself and his relationship to Life.

The first two chapters of Genesis (meaning the beginning) and the last two chapters of Revelation, the final book, tell of the will of God for man. In the beginning we find man created in the "image" and "likeness" of God and given dominion ". . . over every creeping thing that creepeth upon the earth."[3] In Revelation we again have the vision of that perfection which rightfully belongs to man.[4]

All the rest of the Bible is concerned with the journey of the soul back to its original awareness of perfection, man as a child of God. It is the story of the struggle of man who, cheated by the senses into thinking that satisfaction comes from without, struggles to exert his will against God, the infinite Goodness and Perfection within him.

Story after story describes man's voluntary journey into bondage, the thing that happens to man when he chooses to become established in a consciousness apart from God. It is the story of the prodigal son; it is the story of the children of Israel, leaving their own lands, going down into Egypt into

2. Thomas Troward, *Bible Mystery and Bible Meaning,* New York: Dodd, Mead & Company, 1913, p. 1.
3. Genesis 1:26, 27.
4. Revelation 21, 22.

bondage and their great desire to get back to the promised land. This story is repeated over and over, like the theme in a symphony, in many different settings and circumstances so that each one wandering in the wilderness of unenlightened thought can find himself and his particular problem.

Through it all the Love of God seeks to reconcile man to Himself. God speaks through the prophets and all those who have ears to hear, offering to reclaim rebellious man and restore him to the Kingdom of Heaven, that divine order of perfection, that dominion which is man's rightful heritage as a child of God. This is the regeneration. It is not that man has really ever been lost; it is only that he has chosen to think of himself as separated from his Maker. It has seemed easier to him to trust in the evidence of his senses rather than the Truth of his Being.

Man's Divinity

The gift of God has already been given to man—absolute perfection, dominion over life. Made in the image and likeness of God, he has all of the attributes of God inherent within him—infinite Intelligence, omnipotent Power and omnipresent Love; but, given the power of choice, it is up to him to accept it for himself.

In the twenty-first chapter of Revelation the true state of bliss intended for man is revealed to John.

And I saw a new heaven [within] and a new earth [without]: for the first heaven and the first earth were passed away; and there was no more sea [former consciousness].

And I John saw the holy city [awareness of wholeness], new Jerusalem [inner peace], coming down from God out of heaven [within], prepared as a bride adorned for her husband.

And I heard a great voice out of heaven saying, Behold, the tabernacle of God is with men [God lives in men], and he will dwell with them, and they shall be his people [thought], and God himself shall be with them, and be their God.

And God shall wipe away all tears from their eyes; and there shall be no more death, neither sorrow, nor crying, neither shall there be any more pain: for the former things [state of halfness and imperfection] are passed away.

And he that sat upon the throne [*the God Self within that has dominion*] said, Behold, I make all things new. . . .

—Revelation 21:1–5

Spiritual rebirth makes all things new. Never again will anything seem the same. Through the dominion of God, the true Self within, man is given dominion, that dominion which is his birthright.

The Principal Character Throughout

Who do you think is the principal character in this marvelous Book to end all books; It is God. But how can that be when it is the story of *my* life? you ask. It is the story of God in *you*. The mountain tops, the wilderness, the Egypt, the flowering in the desert are all in you. To explain, we must start as the Book of Genesis starts, "In the beginning God. . . ." God is all there is, the only Cause, the only Creator, the only Substance, the only Intelligence. It was all made by God out of God, ". . . and without him was not any thing made that was made." [5] So let's start where everything starts, with God.

An Old Legend

There is an old legend that explains man's confusion regarding his divinity. It begins by asserting that mankind was created according to a divine pattern, a very special creation unlike any other; upright, endowed with Mind, given to understand and know the goodness, the perfection of Life and all created

5. St. John 1:3.

things; with eyes to perceive the good, the true, and the beautiful; with ears to hear the gorgeous symphony of the planets as they spin in their orbits, the songs of the birds and the sighing of the wind and the still small voice of his Maker; with speech to command and sing the praises of his God; with emotion and rapturous feelings of love and compassion; endowed with admiration for the marvelous beauty of the manifest universe and all it contains. The power of right action and unlimited accomplishments are his. All of these magnificent gifts were combined and many others were installed in a beautiful body temple of intricate and perfect design.

This masterpiece finished, the old legend goes, it remained to hide the eternal spark of divine Life. Should God hide the spark of life eternal in the outermost star of the universe, or in the uttermost depths of the ocean? And God decided that the place where man would be least likely to look, until he had grown in Grace to the stage where he could be trusted, was within the heart of himself. For when he would be wise enough to look within, he would be ready to receive the Imminence of God within himself.

Understanding the Meaning of the Christ

This is the meaning of the prophecy of Isaiah as quoted in Matthew:

> Behold, a virgin shall be with child, and shall bring forth a son, and they shall call his name Emmanuel, which being interpreted is, God with us.
>
> —Matthew 1:23; see also Isaiah 7:14

This is the Christ, God in us, Spirit individualized in and through man. In the Old Testament, God in man is called Jehovah God; in the New Testament, the Christ.

God and I in space alone
  And nobody else in view.
"And where are the people, O Lord?" I said.
"The earth below and the sky o'erhead
  And the dead whom once I knew?"

"That was a dream," God smiled and said,
  "A dream that seemed to be true,
There were no people, living or dead,
There was no earth and no sky o'erhead
  There was only myself—and you."
                    —Ella Wheeler Wilcox, "Illusion"

God in You Is Personal to You

If God is all in all, over all, and through all, the only Cause, the only Intelligence and, of necessity, the only Substance, then God at your point of awareness must be personal to you. Each person, each country, each battle is a state of consciousness which you encounter in Mind.

You will be hearing more about the nature of God in you, at your point of awareness, as we go along. You will come to know Him so intimately that you will at last understand why the personal pronoun is used to describe the Omnipresence.

At our house we read the Bible, not because it is the pious thing to do, but because we consider it the most interesting reading we have ever found. Once one discovers that God in you is the principal character in every one of the Bible stories, once one discovers the key to the hidden meaning of the Bible, he embarks on a treasure hunt. You will enjoy this treasure hunt more if you will look up the references given in your Bible so that we may explore them together. You will find it is like unscrambling exciting instructions leading to buried treasure.

Once we have found the secret, something happens. All of

a sudden the Bible is not just a series of disjointed writings, but an integrated study of man's spiritual journey from Paradise to Paradise. Man, created perfect in the beginning; seemingly dispossessed through his own ignorance; now, step by step, finding his own way back to his original perfection. At last he finds the New Jerusalem, *the possession of Peace,* or what we would call the awareness of Peace. The Bible comes to life when it is discovered that it is the story of our own individual spiritual growth here and now.

II   THE BIBLE SPEAKS TO US
IN FIGURATIVE LANGUAGE

Let us take a new look at the Bible. It is not history, although it contains many historical facts. It is not biography, although the lives of many are traced from the cradle to the grave. It is not a geographical study, although it does cover many interesting lands. It is, as Paul said in referring to Abraham and Sarah, primarily an allegorical writing.

> For it is written, that Abraham had two sons, the one by a bondmaid, the other by a freewoman.
> But he who was of the bondwoman was born after the flesh; but he of the freewoman was by promise.
> Which things are an allegory. . . . —Galatians 4:22–24

It is a good idea right here to see what the dictionary has to say in defining the word *allegory*. Webster says that it comes from the Greek word *"allēgoria"* meaning "description of one thing under the image of another." The definition is "The veiled presentation, in a figurative story, of a meaning metaphorically implied but not expressly stated. Allegory is prolonged metaphor, in which typically a series of actions are

11

symbolic of other actions, as in Bunyan's *The Pilgrim's Progress*." [1]

The Inner and the Outer Meaning

The Bible is one of the finest examples of the use of allegorical writing. Sometimes the stories make sense, more often they are confused in their outer meaning. Actually, the obvious or you might say the public, meaning, is the one which will baffle you. This is the reason that so many students turn away from the Bible in discouragement, deciding that it does not make sense to them.

Since the outer, or obvious interpretation, is all that most people know, they miss the inner meaning of the Bible. So far, most people have read the Bible as if it had only an exoteric, or outer, meaning. In so many instances in Bible writing there seems to be an obvious meaning, but within it is the inner one, carefully hidden down through the ages from the unenlightened ones who might have destroyed it to be preserved for us.

The thing that we have to be careful about is that we do not get caught up in the outer meaning. In every book of sacred writing there is an exoteric meaning and a hidden, or esoteric meaning. It is the only way that one can write spiritual truths and preserve them for all time.

For the sake of a better understanding, let us stop and define these terms. Exoteric is taken from the Latin *exotericus* and the Greek *exōterikos* meaning *outside*. Webster defines it: "External; exterior. Suitable to be imparted to the public. . . ."

Esoteric is from the Greek *esōterikos* meaning *inner*. And Webster defines it: "Designed for, and understood by, the

1. *Webster's New International Dictionary*, 2nd ed., Springfield, Mass.: G. and C. Merriam Company, 1957.

specially initiated alone. . . ." This is the concealed or hidden meaning. Down through the ages, this knowledge has been restricted to a select few because it would have been wasted on most people who were only interested in the exoteric, obvious interpretation.

Although one has to dig deep to find the esoteric meaning, it is there. It is not hidden from you in the sense that you cannot find it; it is just hidden from the casual view.

There are many esoteric writings. *The Prophet* by Kahlil Gibran is one, the *Bhagavad Gita* is another. The *Vedas,* the *Upanishads* and all of the writings that go to make up the Eastern scripture are esoteric writings.

For example, to look at the Garden of Eden story from the exoteric view is to look at the historical possibility of Adam being the first man. Literal-minded people have tried to do this and have found that science proves them wrong. An attempt to relate this event chronologically and to actually pinpoint the Garden of Eden on a map is equally baffling. A woman in one of my classes once asked me, "What kind of an apple did Eve offer Adam?" Now, it is obvious that this approach is not only going to get us into serious arguments with the scientific world and make us lose interest in a book that makes so little sense, but it is going to impede the spiritual growth we are all seeking. Many people have lost interest in the Bible at this point. "How can you say that the world was started 4,000 years ago," they ask, "when science has proved that primitive man existed millions of years before?" The outer meaning will always leave us confused, but the inner meaning holds together, proves itself with accuracy and precision.

The Garden of Eden story, which we will take up in more detail in a later chapter, is pure allegory with a deep and wonderful esoteric meaning. To try to look at it in any other way is like trying to place on a map the cities that Christian visited in his mythical journey in John Bunyan's book, *The Pilgrim's Progress.*

Suppose we were to translate *The Pilgrim's Progress* from English into French, but when we came to "the Slough of Despond" or "the City of Destruction" we left those words in English. In like manner, the characters, so aptly described in English by their names, Christian, Hopeful, Faithful, etc., in the English language. Having translated everything in between we would present the story to our French reader who, trying to make sense of the story, would say, "Why, this is silly. *Pourquoi?* This man is always travelling about from place to place, but why? What does it all mean?" Without the inner meaning of the characters and places, all of the significance of the story is lost. We know that this is an allegorical writing, that Christian's progress is the unfoldment of his character. As in the Bible, it is the story of the spiritual journey of every man.

Suppose a foreign agent receives a wire in secret code. The wire reads, "Give the box to Jane at the corner of Fifth and Manchester." If he has not been given the code, the wire means nothing for he does not know a Jane and there is no such address. But to the agent who is able to read the hidden meaning, the wire tells him at once, "The detailed instruction regarding the Jet Wing is ready for you at the usual place."

And so we find in the Garden of Eden allegory: "to eat" means to make one's own, to partake of mentally. Today the Adam and Eve of each one of us must choose whether "to eat" from the "tree of life," which means to partake of the truth about God and man in the garden of the soul, the kingdom of God within, called the "Garden of Eden" in the Bible; or whether we shall "eat" from the "tree of the knowledge of good and evil," our own false judgment in judging by appearances.

When we understand the inner meaning of the Bible, we

find that the things which appear to be physical directives have behind them definite spiritual meanings.

It is also helpful to understand something about the people who wrote the Bible. They were Orientals. The Oriental mind approaches things differently from the Occidental mind. Down through the years there has been this great difference. The Oriental mind is used to thinking in what we might consider *double talk;* that is, saying one thing, knowing that underneath there is a rich, hidden meaning. Thus, *to go up into a mountain,* an expression that is often found in both the Old and New Testaments, is to go up into a high state of spiritual consciousness. *To go into the desert* or *the wilderness* is to go into the wilderness of unenlightened or arid thought. The "streams in the desert" are streams of living water, streams of Truth, making the desert "blossom as the rose," making the consciousness beautiful. To "enlarge thy borders" is to expand the borders of one's own limited or temporary consciousness. The Bible is actually its own best interpreter and somewhere or other in this magnificent book, all of these terms are qualified.

The Bible Is an Oriental Writing

As we said before, the Oriental writing in the Bible is expressed in the terminology of the Orient. The Eastern mind is quite attuned to the idea of a spiritual truth being expressed as allegory or parable. The result is that on the surface you may seem to have a picture created, a moral rule of conduct expressed, or the adventures of a great people typified through battles, famines, romance, violence and intrigue; but, deep down underneath, there is a more satisfying meaning, a mystical, spiritual meaning that is of great help to the individual today and that is what everyone is seeking. When you discover this inner meaning, the Bible is found to be, in

Truth, THE WORD OF GOD, the Wisdom of the Infinite and this is the reason that the Bible lives on forever.

The big question that comes to so many is, "Why are mystical teachings given to us so often in allegory, parable and paradox?" The simple reason is that they cannot be stated in any other way and still retain their mystical meaning. In order to understand the great truths of the ages, it is necessary to have them presented from many angles, from many viewpoints, so that each person will have a viewpoint acceptable to him.

Why Use Figurative Language?

We find spiritual truths stated in many different ways. Jesus used the parable most effectively. The parable is a fictitious narrative, usually something that might naturally occur, from which a moral may be drawn. It was invented for the purpose of conveying Truth in a more engaging form than that of direct assertion. It is *figurative language*. The parable differs from the allegory in that it is short and direct and the emphasis lies on the lesson taught rather than upon the manner of presentation.

The Parable as a Teaching Method

We find Jesus presenting Truth in a very engaging manner, using illustrations in the form of parables and in the everyday language of the people which they could understand. These were timeless truths which we can understand and use today.

"And he spake many things unto them in parables . . .," saying "the kingdom of heaven is like unto . . ." and then he went on to compare it to many things, "one pearl of great price . . .," "a sower went forth to sow . . .," "a grain of mustard seed . . .," etc.[2] It is interesting to note here that nowhere does Jesus ever compare the kingdom of heaven to a city up in the sky with golden streets and pearly gates—not even as a parable. But let's let Jesus, himself, tell us why he used parables.

> And the disciples came, and said unto him, Why speakest thou unto them in parables?
>
> He answered and said unto them, Because it is given unto you to know the mysteries of the kingdom of heaven, but to them it is not given.
>
> For whosoever hath [understanding], to him shall be given. . . .
>
> Therefore speak I to them in parables: because they seeing see not; and hearing they hear not, neither do they understand. —Matthew 13:10–13

It is really not so different from our method of teaching Truth today. For the students who have a deep understanding of Truth, those who understand the working of the Mind, we can go on from there assuming they have a background, but for the beginners we use many illustrations, such as the illustration I often use of planting a seed (idea) in the fertile soil of the mind. There are many homely illustrations used today that bring home the message in various ways and that is what the prophets in Biblical times were doing in the language of their day. To farmers Jesus talked about farming, to fishermen he talked in the language which they understood. At all times, he was teaching his wonderful gospel ("good news") of Grace and Truth.

The allegory is like the parable in that both present a truth under the guise of fictitious narrative or description. However, an allegory is not confined exclusively to religious sub-

2. Matthew 13.

jects. It is developed to some length and adorned by such grace and beauty of style as is suitable.

To unlock the rich storehouse of treasure in the Bible, we are given certain keys that reveal the true meaning of the figurative language that has been used throughout the Scripture. It is impossible to explain absolute meanings in relative language. Therefore, the Bible makes use of figures of speech which are actually the only possible way to convey the hidden truths which must be received by the heart as well as the mind. The three keys which I will give you provide a secret code such as would be used by an underground movement to protect these valuable teachings from the crude touch of those who would not know or care that they be preserved. Through the use of figurative language another goal is accomplished. The Bible speaks to each one at his own level of awareness, so that, year after year as his understanding increases, he discovers richer and richer meanings, personal to him at that very moment of awareness. ARE YOU READY FOR THE KEYS?

The Three Keys to the Secret Code

The secret code is concealed in (1) the meanings of all proper names of persons and places, (2) certain other key words that appear over and over again, and (3) the concealed meanings of certain numbers that are used again and again.

The Bible is a guidebook to individual spiritual discovery. Priceless treasure, hidden from the harsh gaze of the unbelieving who might otherwise have destroyed it, awaits your discovery. Only those who have been given the secret code are allowed to belong to the spiritual underground. The possession of the code starts one out on a thrilling adventure, an adventure that is so personal that he feels that each new discovery is made by him for the first time. It is almost a shock to find that the enlightened of all ages have used the same code.

III   WHAT'S IN A NAME?

The First Key

Now, I am going to place in your hands three keys that will open doors that have heretofore remained locked to you. The first "key" is to be found in the meanings of proper names in the Bible. Name means *nature* in the Bible. "In His name" means according to His nature. Every Hebrew proper name, whether of a person or a place, will reveal to you a state of consciousness. You will find that as the state of consciousness changes in the story, the person's name will change. Thus, Abram become Abraham, Sarai becomes Sarah, Saul becomes Paul, etc. They cannot keep their names once their nature or character has changed because these proper names all have a deeper meaning than just a name.

Names Are States of Consciousness

One day, while looking in the index of my large reference Bible, King James Version, I noticed that following each and every Hebrew name there was, in parenthesis, an interpretation of that name. Each one was a state of consciousness or a description of an invisible quality. With high excitement, I began to reread some of the familiar Bible stories. To my great interest, I found that the battles were all between certain states of consciousness where the divine faculties in man made war with the human materialistic concepts of man. I read on avidly, half afraid that some of the names would spoil my theory. They never did. Like the names of the places in *The Pilgrim's Progress,* they gave a greater meaning, a meaning that made more sense. Each time the story proved out. No character was miscast. Each served a purpose in a story of consciousness unfolding in individual man. Even the genealogy of Jesus followed through as an orderly sequence of states of consciousness leading up to the birth of the Christ, the awareness of the Divine Sonship.

Thomas Troward tells us in *Bible Mystery and Bible Meaning:*

> The purpose of a name is to call up by a single word the complete idea of the thing named, with all those qualities and relations that make it what it is, instead of having to describe all this in detail every time we want to suggest the conception of it. The correct name of a thing thus conveys the idea of its whole nature. Accordingly, the correct name of God should, in some manner, be a concise statement of the Divine Nature. . . .[1]

Thus translation of names becomes the first KEY in unlocking the mystery of the Bible. Reread the Bible in the light of the meaning of proper names alone and a vast new import will be apparent.

1. Thomas Troward, *op. cit.,* p. 150.

The Nature of God

So when we are talking about a name, we are talking about the nature of the person or thing spoken about. We are talking about a total concept that is known and understood. As you open your mind to receive spiritual unfoldment, you will find that the nature of God is infinite. So we use that three letter word *God* to call to mind each time the nature of God, about which thousands and thousands of volumes have been written. When you read *God,* you call to mind what God has come to mean to you.

Thus every time we speak of *the name of God,* we are speaking of *the nature of God.* Look up some of the references to *name* with the aid of your concordance and you will feel almost as if you had discovered a secret code giving you access to buried treasure. Take Exodus 3:15 where we find the Lord saying to Moses, "this is my name for ever . . ." and read it *this is my nature for ever;* take Psalms 9:10, "they that know thy name [nature] . . . trust in thee . . ."; and Psalms 111:9, "holy and reverend is his name [nature]"; and Isaiah 42:8, "I am the Lord [law]: that is my name [nature] . . ."; and Micah 4:5, "we will walk in the name [nature] of . . . our God. . . ." This is only a beginning, but it will give you an idea of how to use the second Key.

In I Kings 8:17, we find Solomon saying, "And it was in the heart of David my father to build an house for the name of the Lord . . .," which then becomes to us who are seeking the inner meaning: *a consciousness of the nature of the divine Law.* It is the nature of God we are interested in for we are told that we are made in "the image and likeness of God." In the "name of the Lord" means in the nature of the divine Law. In the "name of Jesus Christ" means in the nature of the Christ in man. *We ask it in His name* no longer means that we are currying favor with God through Jesus, but that we are praying in the nature of the Christ which is Love and Peace and Trust and all that the Son implies.

The First Few Letters Give the Clue

In like manner, as your own understanding of spiritual things develops, each name will come to have deeper and deeper meaning for you. Jesse, the father of David, means *God exists.* But what do you know about God? Jesse now includes all that God has come to mean to you. God exists, where? If you have an awareness of God as Omnipresence, God exists everywhere and includes all within Itself. Therefore, you see that the Bible is talking about total living. God exists wholly and completely, to the same degree everywhere.

Looking down the index of a large Bible you see that many names start with JA, JE and JO.

A person versed in Hebrew would understand that Jahazia means *God revealed.* Jazarah means *God protects.* Jah is a contraction of Jehovah. Jair means *Jah enlightened,* Jalon means *Jah abides,* and Jamlack means *Jah rules;* Japhlet—*Jah causes to escape;* Jaharazia—*God is a couch (resting place).* I found as I checked back into couch that it means "to rest or bear the burden." Thus God is rest unto the soul and bears the burden. Jakolia means *Jah is able;* Jakonia—*Jah is establishing;* Jediah—*Jah is praise, Jah is knowing;* Jediael—*Jah knows;* Jedidiah—*Jah is a friend.* And so it goes, page after page. I am not going to give them all here, but you may look them up and find many interesting shadings of meaning in the Bible stories. These names and their meanings I have taken from *Analytical Concordance To the Bible* by Robert Young.[2]

Let us take some of the names which are better known to

2. Robert Young, L.L.D. *Analytical Concordance To the Bible,* 20th ed., New York: Funk and Wagnalls Co.

you. Jerusalem means *possession of peace*. Now what does Jesus mean? We have said this name for so many years without knowing that it has an inner meaning. It belongs with JE so it must relate to Jehovah God. Jesus means *Jah saves* and so does Joshua which is interchangeable with Jesus. Joseph means *Jah the increaser*. We will find in the story of Joseph that he was the increaser.

Let us take another prefix—Eli, from which we have Elijah, Elisha, and Elizabeth. Eli, in Hebrew, means *my God*. So when Samuel was studying under Eli, he was studying under God. And we are told that he drew his wisdom from Eli who taught him which means that Eli, God within, taught Samuel as He teaches each one of us. Samuel means *heard of God*. God calls to you according to your name or nature and you will answer when you are ready to hear. Eli also means unity, ascent, summit, apex, a going up, exaltation, supreme, the highest, the most high—my God. So we have Eli, not by accident, a high priest of Israel at the time of Samuel's birth. Elisha means *God is savior* and Elijah means Eli—(*God*) plus Jah—(*Jehovah*) *or God Himself;* therefore, the Presence of God.

Elijah, a Frequent Character in Jewish Folklore

The story of Nahum of Gamzo in the Jewish Talmud [3] is interesting in its reference to Elijah. It seems that Elijah often appeared throughout the Talmud and Jewish folklore. Often in times of emergency, Elijah would appear. In the story, Elijah appeared as one of the men in the court. Elijah means *God Himself*. To you and me, the text would read *Elijah appeared,* but he who reads from the original Hebrew would read *God, Himself, appeared*—the Presence was there.

3. Rev. Dr. A. Cohen, *Everyman's Talmud,* New York: E. P. Dutton & Co., Inc., 1949, p. 80.

Do you see how all this ties in? There is no mystery of names to the Hebrew. Therefore, to get the real meaning of Hebrew writings, it is important for us to know the meaning of the names we are using. Elhanan means *God is gracious;* Elean means *God is founder of people;* Eliacean means *God is setting up;* Eleabah, *God hides.*

When Jesus, in Gethsemane, said "Abba, Father, all things are possible to Thee," he spoke to the *Father.* Whenever we have the prefix *Ab,* it is referring to Father. Abram is the father of height, or exalted father. But his name was changed to Abraham as his spiritual nature unfolded. When God told him—at the age of 105 with a wife, Sarai, in her nineties—how to overcome his apparent lacks and limitations and that he could have children, then his name was changed and God called him the *father of multitudes* or *Abraham.* Sarai also had her name changed, an interesting sidelight which I shall tell you about in a moment. Do any of you have the name Abigail? If you do, you have a wonderful name for it means *father of joy, cause of delight.* If your name is Abner, it means *father of light, father of enlightenment.* Abidan—Ab means *father* and Dan means *judgment,* so we have *father of judgment* or source of judgment.

Name Means Nature

If the Bible is complicated to us, it is because we don't know the Hebrew language. We just don't know what the Scriptures are sometimes talking about. This is what we miss when we try to make these stories into historical documents. When we use the true names, signifying natures, then real meaning is revealed to us. The stories are not just about ancient peoples, but stories of direct meaning for each one of us.

Take any of the Bible genealogies and trace them back, taking each name and looking up its Hebrew meaning. By putting in the meaning rather than the names, you will find that the genealogies are an unfoldment of ideas.

Do you wonder that I say that reading the Bible is a treasure hunt? It is an exciting adventure. I have found that the *Metaphysical Bible Dictionary* [4] is a wonderful help in tracing Bible meanings. Also, many large Bibles give the Hebrew meanings of proper names, as do Bible encyclopedias. Even if you know just a few of these key names, the Bible will take on a new meaning for you.

The Names on Bible Maps Mean More Than You Think

As we go along, we will get into the names of places which have tremendous significance. You will find Jacob, after he awakens from his dream in which he sees the angels ascending and descending on the ladder to heaven, calling the name of the place where he rested Peniel: "for I have seen God face to face." Peniel means *the presence of God* or *the recognition of God*.

An interesting sidelight concerns the pineal gland, sometimes called the *Third Eye*. The Yogi approaches his meditation by directing his attention to a point in the center of the forehead just above and between the eyes where the "third eye" or mystic eye is said to be located, to him the center of Light. It is interesting to note that this is the location of the gland that directs the body functions and is called the pineal gland. Webster describes the pineal gland as having the structure of an eye "with a more or less distinct retina and lens, and is then called the pineal eye, or median eye. . . . It was formerly, by some philosophers, supposed to be the seat of the soul." [5]

4. *Metaphysical Bible Dictionary*, Lee's Summit, Missouri: Unity School of Christianity, 1953.

5. *Webster's New International Dictionary*, 2nd ed., *op. cit.*

I believe that the Eastern religions continue today to believe that the third eye is the seat of spiritual insight. Somewhere along the line, the spelling has been slightly altered since the Bible spells the word Peniel or Penuel, but the similarity of meaning suggests that they are related. Peniel means *recognition of God.* Meditation is for the purpose of recognizing God, our spiritual Source. To this we direct our attention. Is this not the seat of the soul, spiritual insight, the union of man with his infinite Source?

Each Place Is a Place in Consciousness

Egypt signifies *bondage;* Eden, *delight or bliss;* Bethel stands for the *house of God, consciousness of the all Good;* the tower of Babel or Babylon, as you can guess, means *confusion.* The people who dwell in these lands represent the kind of consciousness from which they originate; their children are always thoughts springing from the parent thought.

To the Hebrew storyteller, each story had a deeper meaning. Do you begin to see WHAT'S IN A NAME?

In the next chapter we will explore the second key, a glimpse at the special vocabulary through which the Bible conveys an endless stream of variations on the theme of Consciousness unfolding—subtle differences and gradations of meaning made possible through the ingenious use of a secret code.

IV   WHAT'S IN A WORD?

It makes no difference what you are studying, you are going to find that there is a vocabulary particular to that subject. If you are studying law, you will find that there is a vocabulary for law, words that are used exclusively in connection with that subject. If you pick up a book on music, you soon discover that it has nothing to do with the study of law, for in music the words *octaves, sharps, flats, allegro* and *fortissimo* have meaning, while in law the student is concerned with words such as *torts, felony, depositions* and *contracts.* A woman who becomes interested in dressmaking will soon discover that it has its own exclusive vocabulary. She will start using such terms as *bias-cut, darts, tucks, gathers, pleating, hemlines* and *bustlines.* Electronics is developing a language all its own. Each subject has its own unique vocabulary. The meaning of the words is particular to that study.

In semantics, the study of words, we learn that different words call up different feelings and prejudices in each person according to his past experience and conditioning. One word suggests volumes of thoughts and feelings relating to that word.

Let's Define Our Terms

An old college professor of mine used to say before any discussion of a subject, "Let's define our terms." There are certain words used in the Bible that are always used figuratively to give meanings that are far from literal.[1] This is the second key that unlocks the mystery of the Bible.

Consciousness Is the Only Reality

Take the word *land.* *Land,* in the Bible, is used to refer to consciousness. *Land* is consciousness unfolding at different levels from the invisible to the visible. Consciousness is the only reality. It is the substance of life. Out of it form evolves. Every reference in the Bible to *land* has to do with various stages of awareness within the individual—*plains, wilderness, desert, plateaus, far country, mountains, caves, islands, firmament, hills* and *valleys.* Once you start thinking of these words as states of consciousness rather than physical places, you begin to see why they are used and why the happenings in the stories are woven around certain key words.

When Abram was talking to God, after he had separated himself from Lot who represents his *negative thinking,* God said to Abram,

Lift up now thine eyes, and look from the place where thou art northward, and southward, and eastward, and westward:
For all the land which thou seest, to thee will I give it, and to thy seed for ever. —Genesis 13:14, 15

Here the Lord, the divine Law, is teaching Abram, whose name means faith in the invisible power of God, to lift up his vision and from this uplifted state of consciousness, get a

1. See Glossary.

well-balanced perspective. In Bible symbolism, he is told to look in every direction, a balanced perspective.

In the Bible, the east always refers to the within, the west to the without. The north is above as on a map and the South is below; the north is the conscious mind and the south is the subconscious mind. An interesting reference to this is found in Isaiah:

> Fear not: for I am with thee: I will bring thy seed [ideas] from the east [within], and gather thee from the west [outer-appearances];
>
> I will say to the north [conscious mind or outer appearances], Give up; and to the south [the within or subconscious mind], Keep not back. . . . —Isaiah 43:5, 6

Therefore looking to the east, west, north, and south, would be bringing every facet of the mind into harmonious balance.

And now Abram is told, "For all the land which thou seest, to thee will I give it, and to thy seed forever." The *seeds* are the thoughts springing from faith in the invisible power of God (Abram) and the *land* is the invisible Substance or consciousness. But now the divine Law gives Abram further instructions. He is to do more than just look.

> Arise, walk through the land in the length of it and in the breadth of it; for I will give it unto thee. —Genesis 13:17.

Abram was here being told by God within him that that which he could conceive of, believe in, confidently expect, and accept for himself, was his. That is the way it is for each one of us. That which we can *walk in,* that which we can experience in consciousness, is ours, first in the invisible inner experience and then outpicturing (showing itself outwardly, on the surface, etc.) for all the world to see. That which we can accept in the within is bound to come into our experience. Our only problem is that we sometimes walk in *land* that we do not really want.

Wilderness, desert, waste places are *kinds* of *land,* states of consciousness within the individual. They are dry, arid, places in our mind which have not yet been watered by the *river of Life,* the *flow of Truth.* These are the undisciplined or uncultivated thoughts in the mind of man. We move out of these wastelands of the mind through meditation and prayer. Through treatment and affirmation, we cultivate and enrich the soil of the mind, digging out the weeds of negative thinking and watering the land with the living water of Truth.

We find Jesus going into the *wilderness* to pray, going into an arid region of consciousness where there was no *living water,* consciousness of Truth. There he would *fast,* abstain from thoughts of separation from God, and spend his time in communion with the Presence. You will find that after such a period of building spiritual consciousness, Jesus would always go up "into a mountain." This did not mean that he dug a hole into a mountain of rock and earth, but he entered into a state of high spiritual consciousness. When Jesus went up "into a mountain" to deliver his famous Sermon on the Mount, he entered into such a state of high consciousness preparing himself to deliver the ideas that came to him out of this high awareness of the Presence of God.

The Mystical Topography of Isaiah

Isaiah used many references to the topography of the terrain in his colorful way of pointing up spiritual truths. No other part of the Bible sparkles with poetic originality quite like Isaiah where even the trees clap their hands.

> The voice of him that crieth in the wilderness, Prepare ye the way of the Lord, make straight in the desert a highway for our God.

Every valley shall be exalted, and every mountain and hill shall be made low: and the crooked shall be made straight, and the rough places plain: —Isaiah 40:3, 4

It becomes obvious now with this insight that Isaiah is not speaking of an earth-moving operation, but about the movement of Truth in the mind of man.

Desert refers to that seeming waste area in the consciousness, that area that has no fruitage, the thinking that is not productive of good. And then, in the beautiful style of Isaiah there come "streams in the desert," that movement of Truth in Mind, which causes the "desert" to "blossom as the rose."

for in the wilderness shall waters break out, and streams in the desert.

And the parched ground shall become a pool, and the thirsty land springs of water. . . .

. . .

and the desert shall . . . blossom as the rose.

—Isaiah 35:1, 6, 7

How better could these desert people, who knew full well the need of moisture, have described the blessing of Truth that welled up in their parched souls. And thy soul shall be as a watered garden was the nicest thing that they could possibly imagine.

Bible Lands Denote More Than a Map Can Show

Beulah land means the consciousness of unity or oneness. *Beulah* means *married*, *Beulah land* signifies the perfect union with God, infinite Goodness within which constantly awaits the Israelites, *children of God*. Beulah land is the consciousness of the individual who has consciously entered into a union with the Perfect Power within himself which is God.

The Land of Judah is the consciousness of praise, for Judah means *praise*. It is that place in consciousness where we recognize and praise God. This explains why there are so many references in the Bible to the Land of Judah which are out of context to the rest of the story that is being told.

The Land of Israel is the consciousness of Sonship, children of the Most High, the chosen *thought people* within all of us.

There are so many interesting references to land that one could write a book just tracing this one word through the Bible. I attempted to count the references to *land* in Young's *Concordance* and finally gave up at fifteen hundred! I mention this to show what an important word this is in our Bible vocabulary.

All of the peoples of the Bible are *thought people*. The various places are states of consciousness. The experiences that the *people* encounter along the way are the experiences that we encounter as we find spiritual unfoldment in our daily lives.

Trust in the Lord, and do good; so shalt thou dwell in the land, and verily thou shalt be fed. —Psalms 37:3

Trust in the divine Law of Life and express this infinite Goodness in your life, and you shall abide constantly in the consciousness of Good and truly you will partake of spiritual food or divine ideas which become all that you need on every level of life.

Each One Builds His Own House

The word *house* means consciousness as mind, body and affairs. We dwell in the invisible *house* of the mind.

Except the Lord build the house, they labour in vain that build it. . . . —Psalms 127:1

Through wisdom is an house builded; and by understanding it is established. —Proverbs 24:3

These references are to the *house* that we build in consciousness. The Bible speaks of the *house* of prayer, the *house* of mourning, the *house* of feasting. These could only mean the consciousness that is described. The Father's *house* or the *house* of the Lord is the consciousness of oneness with God, the Source of all Being.

The word *house* has different meanings or shadings of consciousness—consciousness as mind, body, or affairs. The roof over our heads is the outpicturing of our consciousness, our larger *house,* as is the body of our affairs. We have all known people who move many times and yet the moment we walk into their current home, we know it is theirs. It reflects their personalities. "It looks just like them," we say. In the same manner, people repeat the same patterns or experiences over and over until they change their inner thinking. The body of their affairs is the outpicturing of the inner *house.* "In my Father's *house* [my italics] are many mansions. . . ." [2]

In the infinite Mind, there are many states of consciousness, many stages of awareness, facets of understanding, evolving from the invisible into the visible. "The body is the part of the soul that shows." The larger body or affairs is also "the part of the soul that shows."

The word *tent,* a temporary house easily moved, means a temporary state of consciousness as when one is evolving from one state of growth to another. Abram was said to remove his *tent* after he had enlarged his vision.

Enlarge the place of thy tent, and let them stretch forth the curtains of thine habitations. —Isaiah 54:2

We are told in Genesis "such as dwell in tents . . . have

2. St. John 14:2.

cattle." Those who do not abide in spiritual consciousness, but continue to wander in temporary consciousness or with an awareness that is not established in Truth, will *have cattle,* depend on the thoughts of sensation or animal strength.

More Code Words

In the Glossary of this book, you will find the meanings of various other words which are used over and over in the Bible. *To eat* means to partake of mentally and spiritually, to make something one's own—you might say to digest mentally. *Water* is the fluidic, ever-changing movement of the mind. "Up into a mountain, the mountain of God," etc., means up into a high state of exalted consciousness. *Bread* is the substance of life, the spiritual food. *Heaven* is the realm of divine ideas, the conscious awareness of God within. *Earth* is the outer manifestation of the *within.* "As in heaven, so on earth" means as *within, so without,* the unformed substance of the mind made manifest as earthly effect.

Every form of light, stars, moon, sun, candles are used to indicate spiritual illumination in one form or another. To me, "the bright and morning star" identified as the Christ in Revelation is that enduring light which is still there after the night, the darkness of human experience, is gone. It continues to shine as the new day of experience starts.

You will find these words and other key words to understanding the Bible in your Glossary. Perhaps as you study the Bible, the meanings of still other words will be revealed to you. I find it is a never-ending process. I am continually experiencing the thrill of new discovery.

Those who think that the Bible is dull and bewildering have not discovered the keys words that reveal the hidden meaning.

You Discover a Secret Document

Suppose you were to read a message written in a secret code that almost made sense to you, but kept seeming rather foolish and unimportant. You would soon put it down in exasperation. But now suppose that you were to realize that it was a very important secret document containing highly important information absolutely vital to your welfare. All at once, you discover a word from the secret code, one word leads to another and soon the entire code is revealed to you. Now you are able to read the message that before seemed rather stupid. All of a sudden it has come to life. Your excitement knows no bounds. You have discovered something of great value, hidden treasure, and there is more where this comes from. In fact, it is endless and every word will be just as important, of vital interest to you and your personal welfare. This describes the revelation of the secret meaning of the Bible. Once given the secret code, the hidden meaning is revealed, providing fascinating reading, an exciting adventure in Self-discovery.

Truth the Same Wherever You Find It

Those who study other mystical writings of the East, such as Buddhist or Hindu scripture, soon discover that they share the same secret code used in the Bible. Once a person understands the code, all sacred writings reveal their secrets to him. What was formerly a blurred picture suddenly comes into focus. The writers of the Bible and other sacred scripture use the same words to reveal ageless Truth. Our excitement mounts as the answer comes with brilliant clarity—there is only one Writer, *the Spirit of Truth.*

> Howbeit when he, the Spirit of truth, is come, he will guide you into all truth. —St. John 16:13

The Spirit of Truth that comes to each one is the eternal Writer and this is why the words and meanings all agree.

The Bible, being an Oriental writing, is expressed in the terminology of the Orient. The Eastern mind is quite attuned to the idea of spiritual Truth being expressed as allegory or parable through the use of certain words that seem to denote things but really denote states of consciousness. The result is that on the surface we may seem to have a picture created, a moral rule of conduct expressed, or the adventures of a great people typified through battles, famines, romance, violence and intrigue, but, deep down underneath, there is a more satisfying meaning, a mystical, spiritual meaning that is of great help to the individual today.

The Guidebook for Today

We have thought of the Bible as going back into antiquity when, in Truth, it is the bringing of the Truths of antiquity into our present-day living for the purpose of meeting today's problems. It becomes the answer everyone is seeking, a Guidebook for today. Once we discover the hidden inner meaning of the Bible, it is found to be truly THE WORD OF GOD, the Wisdom of the Infinite revealed in many ways, at many different times, through many teachers. It is eternal Wisdom. This is why the Bible lives forever.

V   THE MYSTERY OF NUMBERS

In the Bible several mystical numbers are used again and again. These numbers are used in exactly the same way in other sacred writings of the East. As one understands the mystical meaning of these numbers, he is given the third *key* unlocking the mystery of the Bible.

The Mystical Seven

Seven is the mystical number most often used in Biblical writings. By actual count, I found that the number seven appears 494 times. It is used from the first chapter of Genesis through the sixty-six books of the Bible. We find it many times in the last book, Revelation. As you read the various references to *seven,* you soon see that the Bible, itself, is its own best interpreter. It is soon seen that seven is used to indicate perfection; that which is finished, completed and perfect. Thus the Lord blessed the seventh day.

In six days (according to Bible symbolism), God made heaven and earth. The work finished, He rested on the seventh.

And God saw every thing that he had made, and, behold, it was very good. And the evening and the morning were the sixth day.

Thus the heavens and the earth were finished, and all the host of them.

And on the seventh day God ended his work which he had made; and he rested on the seventh day from all his work which he had made.

And God blessed the seventh day, and sanctified it: because that in it he had rested from all his work which God created and made. —Genesis 1:31; 2:1–3

Here we have completion. Furthermore, we are told to complete our work in like manner.

Six days shalt thou labour, and do all thy work:

But the seventh day is the sabbath of the Lord thy God: in it thou shalt not do any work, thou, nor thy son, nor thy daughter, thy manservant, nor thy maidservant, nor thy cattle, nor thy stranger that is within thy gates:

For in six days the Lord made heaven and earth, the sea, and all that in them is, and rested the seventh day: wherefore the Lord blessed the sabbath day, and hallowed it.

—Exodus 20:9–11

Sabbath means to rest from labor. It is the *it is finished* consciousness. It is the most important step in prayer in which we completely release our prayer to God. It means that we are to finish that which is given to us to accomplish, the necessary human footsteps, and then to rest in the Lord, the divine Law of Life, trusting and knowing that *it is done, finished, perfect, and complete.*

Yes, all of the thought people in our consciousness are to rest, even "thy stranger that is within thy gates", the thought that is new and strange to us. It is the blessed time. All is to be released to the Creative Process that knows how to bring it about.

We are told to forgive—not seven times, but seventy times seven—that is, unlimited, complete forgiveness. We are to perfectly forgive, be *finished* with our resentment, leaving no loose ends. What an interesting study it would be, just to follow up and analyze the uses of seven and the multiples of seven in the Bible and other mystical writings where seven is so often employed!

Twelve Is the Ultimate

The next most prevalent mystical number in the Bible is twelve. Let us see how it is used. Twelve is the number of spiritual fulfillment, spiritual completion. Seven means we finish the work in Mind, but twelve is spiritual realization or completion, divine perfection, the perfect will of God for man. Twelve, according to Young's *Concordance,* is used 161 times.

There are twelve pillars, twelve years of service, twelve silver bowls, twelve golden spoons, twelve kids for an offering, twelve fountains, twelve tribes, and twelve disciples.

There were twelve tribes of Israel and twelve disciples. If you investigate the meanings of their names, you will soon see for yourself that they represent the different spiritual qualities or faculties in man.

After the multitude was fed, we find, "And they did all eat, and were filled: and they took up of the fragments that remained twelve baskets full." [1] Here the number twelve signifies the spiritual fulfillment derived from even the "fragments" of the *bread of Life* which is the *word of God.*

In Revelation we find twelve used often. There are twelve stars, *divine fulfillment through illumination;* twelve angels, *divine fulfillment through the messengers of God* or our own spiritual thoughts; and the wall of the city, referring to *the*

1. Matthew 14:20.

new Jerusalem or the consciousness of Peace, had twelve foundations. This consciousness is established as a consciousness of divine fulfillment. I could go on and on, but let's get on to another mystical number which is often used in the Bible and other inspired writings.

That Magic Number—Forty

The number *forty* is used so many times that we immediately see that there must be a symbolical meaning. It is used to indicate *an indefinite but completed period of time.* It is as if one said in referring to himself, "I went through a period of indecision or confusion which is over. Now I am experiencing a period of spiritual growth." Forty indicates periods, or stages of spiritual growth in consciousness.

Each of the three periods in the life of Moses was forty years. Each time Moses went "up into the Mount" (a high state of exalted spiritual consciousness), it was for forty days and forty nights—a completed period of meditation in high consciousness. Elijah was forty days and forty nights on Mount Horeb, and he was the same number of days and nights on Mount Carmel. The children of Israel were in the hands of the Philistines for forty years; and for forty years, the children of Israel ate manna. Of course, we also find that Jesus went into the wilderness for forty days and forty nights and was seen by the disciples forty days after his resurrection, *a completed period of spiritual unfoldment.*

Other Numbers Used

Other numbers in the Bible are meaningful but are not as prevalent. "Hear, O Israel: The Lord our God is one Lord." [2] One means indivisible, unity, all encompassing, undivided.

2. Deuteronomy 6:4.

The number six indicates the working period in the cycle of creation. *Six days shalt thou labour.* We work spiritually as we progress and then we release, or rest on the seventh day, which indicates completion or perfection accepted.

And Moses went up into the mount, and a cloud covered the mount.

And the glory of the Lord abode upon Mount Sinai, and the cloud covered it six days: and the seventh day he called unto Moses out of the midst of the cloud.

And the sight of the glory of the Lord was like devouring fire on the top of the mount in the eyes of the children of Israel. —Exodus 24:15–17

Moses means *drawn out.* In the spiritual consciousness that is drawn out we go up into the mount, meaning high spiritual awareness, and there we work (six) in Truth and having done the spiritual work we rest (seventh day) realizing the glory of the divine Law which heretofore has been invisible to us (under a cloud).

Three indicates wholeness of life or the threefold nature of being which is the trinity—Spirit, Mind and Body. Spirit expressing through Mind manifests as body (outward form). All of Life is a Trinity, three aspects of the One. Some of the trinities of Life are: *man, woman, child; masculine, feminine, offspring; idea, creative medium, effect;* and many more. "And now abideth faith, hope, charity, these three; but the greatest of these is charity." [3]

3. I Corinthians 13:13.

VI   THE SECRET CODE IS BORN

And now came the time of putting it all together. Having discovered the three keys outlined in chapters three, four, and five, I began to see that I had stumbled upon something tremendously important. I shall never forget that day! It dawned upon me that I had uncovered something of great value; something that had been there all of the time, yet new to me, for I was seeing it for the first time.

The Great Day of Discovery

All of a sudden it came to me that the three keys with which we had been working constituted a code, literally a secret code which would reveal the true meaning of the Bible. My wife and I were sitting in my study at home surrounded by reams and reams of notes relating to the Bible; the work of many classes I had given; the work of months of patient research. There were lists of names with their hidden meanings from the Hebrew; lists of places with their inner meanings; and words, words defined—some even scribbled on the backs of envelopes. It seemed like a maze, but now we could see it all fitting together. With the three keys that had been handed to us, we could develop a secret code which would unlock the mystery of any story in the Bible!

We looked at each other, communicating as husbands and wives do. Words could not describe our excitement. We didn't need words to describe it for the air was full of the thrill of discovery. Here we had been working for years without realizing this vast treasure that had been right where we were, unnoticed. It was buried treasure right in our own backyard!

We had always known that such books as Ezekiel and Revelation were written in symbols. We had commented that there must be some significance in the fact that these symbols tallied so closely, but to see that there was a hidden, yet discernible, meaning running throughout the Bible behind such simple words as *land,* such commonplace names as *Bethel,* opened a new world of discovery.

Which Bible to Use

We have a rather fine collection of Bibles at our house which includes various translations as well as some very old and some unusually beautiful Bibles. Picture us then, literally surrounded by Bibles, in our eagerness, jumping from one to another as we compared the translations at hand. We had the King James Version, the Moffat translation, Smith-Goodspeed, the Revised Standard Version, the Revised English Version, and the beautiful Lamsa translation. For the most part they didn't vary too much although we discovered that by checking each version and putting them all together, we could often dig out a more complete meaning. We finally decided that for our purposes the King James Version was best; for the same verses that formerly seemed inconsistent now turned out to best illustrate the hidden, inner meaning.

Thus, all references in this book are to the King James Version.

We Start on the Code

Having reached this decision, we set to work on the secret code. It all seemed simple, too simple to be true, as one word led to another. It was unbelievable! This was the vocabulary of the Bible, hidden from all but a select few for thousands of years. Yet, this special vocabulary bridged the gap for us today, making us one with the mystics of long ago. We were so excited that we could think of little else for days. Some of the first words that came to light I have already given you—land, mountains, valleys, caves, water, etc. Now others came as fast as popcorn once it has started to pop.

Having opened the door, it was surprising how fast the three keys led us into an organized code. The words seemed to come in families or series and each new category led us on to the next. I will not attempt to give you all of the words here,[1] but a sampling of each group will illustrate how the code fits together and becomes the esoteric vocabulary of the Bible.

A FEW PROPER NAMES MOST OFTEN USED AND THEIR DEEP SIGNIFICANCE

> Adam—generic man; the son of man or human man.
> Christ—Spirit individualized in man as spiritual man.
> Abraham—faith in the invisible Power of God.
> Lot—dark negative thinking.
> Esau—red; hairy; the material or physical side.
> Jacob—the supplanter; the mental, intellectual step upward.
> Israel—the spiritual rebirth; prince of God; awareness of sonship.

1. See Glossary.

Elijah—God is; the Presence of God.

Moses—drawn out; the Truth which is continually drawing us out of bondage.

SAMPLING A FEW NAMES OF PLACES THAT REVEAL HIDDEN MEANING

Eden—bliss; the Garden of Eden is the garden of the soul; the kingdom of God within; living by Grace where all is provided.

Judah—consciousness of praising God; recognition of God.

Egypt—false sense of bondage; serving the physical and the psychical.

Bethel—house of God; God Consciousness.

Jerusalem—city of peace; awareness of the peace of God.

Canaan—low land or material existence.

Horeb—mountain of God; exalted state of consciousness.

WORDS THAT REFER TO CONSCIOUSNESS UNFOLDING FROM INVISIBLE TO FORM

land—the outpicturing or forming of consciousness; the land emerges out of the water or fluidic substance of Mind.

mountain—a high state of spiritual consciousness; as, to go up into a mountain to pray.

cave—hidden thoughts; concealed thinking; pressed down into the subconscious mind.

sea—the unformed thought; universal Mind; the deep subconscious mind.

water—unformed, fluidic consciousness.

rivers, streams—the movement of Truth in Mind; as, and there shall be "streams in the desert."

desert—unillumined consciousness; the wilderness of thought; ignorance.

fish—ideas drawn out of the deep (subconscious mind).

birds—liberated thought; ideas in conscious mind.

creatures—thoughts.

creeping things—subtle thoughts that tempt.

sheep—pure, unadulterated thoughts.

angels—spiritual thoughts; inspiration from God, therefore messengers of God.

food—the spiritual thought by which we are fed; such as, "I have meat to eat that ye know not of."

bread of Life—the word of God; divine Inspiration; spiritual food.

to eat—to partake of mentally and spiritually; to receive into one's consciousness.

THE MOST SIGNIFICANT NUMBERS USED THROUGHOUT THE BIBLE

one—unity; wholeness; that which cannot be divided.

three—three aspects of being; the trinity; unity of oneness; spirit, mind and body.

six—the working cycle; such as, ". . . Six days shalt thou labour."

seven—it is finished; perfection; release; used to indicate completion.

twelve—spiritual fulfillment; spiritual completion.

forty—a completed cycle; any indefinite, but completed period of time; a period of unfoldment or spiritual growth; a finished experience.

(Multiples of numbers are used for emphasis.)

SYMBOLS USED TO SHOW ILLUMINATION

day—a degree of unfoldment in consciousness; illumined consciousness.

morning—the light that comes when the period of darkness is over; the new inspiration; such as, "joy cometh in the morning."

light—divine illumination; such as, "the Lord is my light."

sun—conscious awareness of spiritual understanding.

moon—the reflected light; the intellectual understanding.

stars—bright spots of spiritual illumination; revelations of Truth.

bright and morning star—the Christ Consciousness, that Light that endures all through the night of seeming darkness and is still there when morning comes.

candle—the individual understanding that should not be hiddren, such as, "Neither do men light a candle, and put it under a bushel" (let your light shine).

OTHER SYMBOLS THAT ARE MOST PREVALENT

stone—intellectual or spiritual Truth.

rock—the enduring Truth.

sand—rock that has been pulverized and does not hold together; therefore, unstable or shifting thought.

blood—the circulation of Life; the Life Principle.

wine—spiritualized thought.

tree—the connecting link between earth and heaven; our thinking rooted in the earth but reaching toward heaven.

heart—emotional or feeling side of life; subconscious mind.

feet—the understanding; that which we stand upon.

VII   THE LAW OF GOD AND
          THE LAW OF MAN

Genesis, Chapters 1–3
St. John, Chapter 1: 1–3

love is the fulfilling of the law. —Romans 13:10
O how love I thy law! it is my meditation all the day.
                                        —Psalms 119:97
Open thou mine eyes, that I may behold wondrous things
out of thy law. —Psalms 119:18
All's love, all's law. —Robert Browning.

God is Love and God is all. Love is the nature of God, Law
is the way God works or the action of God. It is in the area
of Law, God in action, that all of the mystery lies.

The great Law that encompasses all law on the mental and
physical level is the law of cause and effect. When we go to
First Cause which is God, we are speaking of the divine Law.
The principle is always the same; the difference lies in
whether we start with First Cause or secondary cause. For
instance, First Cause is Love and Love begets love. Hate and
fear have nothing to do with First Cause. They, too, beget
thought children after the law of cause and effect. The divine
Law is the Law of Love and divine right action, the Law
that transcends all other laws.

Let's Define Our Terms

My dictionary defines cause as:

> that which occasions or effects a result; the necessary antecedent of an effect; that which determines the condition or existence of a thing, esp. that which determines its change from one form to another. . . . The Scholastics held that there is a hierarchy of causes, the supreme or first cause being the divine mind.[1]

Every Thought Produces an Effect

Down through the ages, scientists have understood the action of the law of cause and effect as it applied to the physical sciences, but have not understood how the same law applied to the mental realm. Every time one thinks a thought, he is bringing the law of cause and effect into action. Around the turn of the century, William James told us that every thought is motor in its consequences. That is to say that invisible thought has its visible counterpart in the world of visible expression. This explains the common expression "thoughts are things." Each thought is a cause producing a corresponding effect.

Since man has the power of choice, he has the right to choose which thoughts he will entertain in mind. Since he can choose the kind of thoughts that will produce undesirable effects in his life, he is then free to part company with his Creator and the perfect plan provided for him. Even God cannot assure him that he will have desirable effects, free agent that he is. Even God cannot compel man to enjoy the bliss he could enjoy were he to keep his thoughts God-centered.

1. *Webster's New International Dictionary*, 2nd ed., *op. cit.*

Two Ends of the Same Stick

For every cause there is an effect and that effect is in accord, like unto the cause. Cause and effect are two ends of the same stick. The cause is like the effect; the effect is like the cause. Cause is invisible. Effect is visible. Cause is in the realm of unconditioned Mind. Effect is in the realm of form, where the unconditioned becomes conditioned, the invisible Substance takes form. Thought is the channel through which this action takes place. Thought is the connecting medium through which the effect is produced. The Power that produces the effect is invisible. We see only the effect. The invisible Power working through the creative medium produces the effect.

The Bible speaks of the law of cause and effect as sowing and reaping and tells us again and again that *everything reproduces after its kind.* The way the law works remains a mystery. Jesus in speaking of this mystery, said, "I can of mine own self do nothing" . . . and "the Father that dwelleth in me, he doeth the works." [2]

Planting the Seed

The best illustration of the law is found in the planting of a seed in the ground. You see at once from this comparison why the Bible calls the law of cause and effect, "sowing and reaping." If you plant a carrot seed in the ground, you know that you will harvest a carrot. If you plant a cucumber seed, it will produce a cucumber. When you plant a seed in the ground, there is within that seed the Life Power, a spark of energy that under given circumstances will go through the process of germinating and reproducing itself.

Did you ever take your thumb nail and open a seed to see

2. St. John 5:30;14:10.

what makes it grow? You found nothing. The Power and the Intelligence that knows exactly how to produce the intricate design of the plant is invisible. Yet it is there. Certain kinds of leaves if placed in water or a dark place will produce out of themselves tiny plants exactly following the mother plant. All through Life everything reproduces after its kind. The seed is planted and then it draws to itself that which it needs from the elements—the sun, the moisture, the soil, and gradually something happens. The roots go down and the stalk comes up and eventually the seed itself disappears and becomes part of the plant it has created.

Verily, verily, I say unto you, Except a corn of wheat fall into the ground and die, it abideth alone: but if it die, it bringeth forth much fruit. —St. John 12:24

The very same thing occurs with an idea that falls into the creative soil of the Mind. There is a Creative Medium working through Mind that takes an idea planted in Mind and reproduces it.

Reaping the Harvest

For as he thinketh in his heart [sub-conscious mind—feeling nature], so is he. . . . —Proverbs 23:7

As with the tiny seed that produces a large plant, the thought is insignificant compared to the outer experience which is often exaggerated. The subconscious mind, the creative medium of life, goes by feeling. The subconscious mind has no sense of humor. It is continually aware of what is being given to it and goes to work to produce effects like the seed thoughts which have been given it. When a seed idea is planted in mind, it will germinate and bear fruit. It is nurtured by the amount of feeling that accompanies it. For every thought that we think in mind, there will be some kind of reaction in our lives. I cannot tell you how this happens any more than I can break a seed open and see the Life Force there. I only know that It is there and that the Law of Life is always at work with unerring accuracy reproducing the seed that is planted in the creative soil of the mind. "I have planted, Apollos watered; but God gave the increase." [3]

The Bible Explains Creation

There are three different creation stories in the Bible, two in Genesis and one in the Gospel according to St. John. Does this surprise you? Two of these stories have to do with the Law of God, the divine Law. The other points out how man distorts the divine Law and reaps suffering in this life. It is, you might say, man's misuse of the divine Law that gets him into all the trouble. Without conflict, there is no plot in a story. It is man's conflict, brought about by his own misuse of the Law, that provides the plot for the Bible. Had man been content to abide in bliss, living by Grace under the divine Law, he would have no problems, no sickness, no suffering. He would live happily everafter, dwelling in the kingdom of God (within), abiding by First Cause and experiencing perfect effect. The story would end with the second chapter of Genesis—and *he lived happily everafter.* Most of the Bible has to do with man's innate desire to return to the perfect life God provides for him.

God's Perfect Plan

"Thou Great First Cause, least understood!" wrote Alexander Pope. First Cause is Absolute, the eternal verity. God's

3. I Corinthians 3:6.

perfect plan for man is brought out in two of the creation stories. The third shows how man, being endowed with the power of choice, chooses his own problems.

"Every plant, which my heavenly Father hath not planted, shall be rooted up," [4] said Jesus. Only God's creation is true and enduring. This is why healings are possible. The divine Law transcends the lesser law. Now, let's take a look at God's creation and see how this works out.

The First Creation Story

In the beginning God created the heaven and the earth.
—Genesis 1:1

In the beginning there is nothing but God, for God is all there is. Therefore everything created by God must be created out of God, the only Substance. "The heaven and the earth" refer to the creative process. *As within, so without.* The heaven is the consciousness within, it is outpictured as the form, the earth or the part that shows. The invisible becomes the visible.

And the earth was without form, and void; and darkness was upon the face of the deep. And the Spirit of God moved upon the face of the waters.
And God said, Let there be light: and there was light.
—Genesis 1:2, 3

In the beginning of the creative process there is that which is without form, the substance of Life which Sir Arthur Eddington referred to as *mind stuff*. The dictionary defines *mind stuff* as:

4. Matthew 15:13.

> The elemental material, internally of the nature of mind, externally, or as it appears to us, in the form of matter, which is assumed to be the ground of reality.[5]

Therefore, the earth (outer manifestation) appeared to be without form and void. In the beginning of every creative process there is only the raw material—*undifferentiated mind stuff.*

"And the Spirit of God moved upon the face of the water" (the surface mind or conscious mind). ". . . The face of the deep" represents the deep subconscious mind. Together, "the face of the deep" and "the face of the waters" represent Universal Consciousness. Thus, the spirit of Creativity is continually expressing Itself in and through all of Life. Life desires to express Itself to the fullest. Man is given a choice. He may live abundantly, letting God live through him fully; or, he may hold back the creative process by suppressing Life at his point of awareness.

God Creates through Man

God, in man as man, accomplishes His great creative work. The creative Spirit moves man. This is the beginning of desire. Desire is the first step. It must precede any creation. Then, what happens? God, divine Love, the creative Spirit, moves across that which is formless. This is the specialization, the bringing into form which takes place through the speaking of the word. Here, the creative *word* is "and God said, let there be light. . . ."

When we plant the carrot seed, we are saying *let there be a carrot.* We know that the carrot seed we plant will produce a carrot. We have faith in the Life in the carrot seed. We do not say, "Now look here carrot seed, I'm going to put you in

5. *Webster's New International Dictionary,* 2nd ed., *op. cit.*

the ground, and if you come up a cucumber plant, I'm going to cut off your little head!" We plant the seed and we say, "let there be a carrot," and a carrot is created. The *word* is the idea that we entertain in mind. It is the mental seed that we plant in mind. It need not be a verbal word that is spoken aloud.

The Key Word in Creation: Let

". . . Let there be light: and there was light." In Chapter VI, we talked about the vocabulary of the Bible, the unique meaning of certain key words. We said that *light* means divine illumination (wisdom and understanding). So we have the first step in the divine creation, *Let there be wisdom and understanding.*

Solomon sought to align himself with the will of God, the divine plan when he asked for understanding. He asked for an understanding heart and was given wisdom, which means the ability to make right choices, choices in accord with the divine plan, the First Cause. The Lord (divine Law) by wisdom and understanding establishes the heavens (consciousness within) which produces through the creative medium the earth (outer form).

Happy is the man that findeth wisdom, and the man that getteth understanding.

For the merchandise of it is better than the merchandise of silver, and the gain thereof than fine gold.

She is more precious than rubies: and all the things thou canst desire are not to be compared unto her.

Length of days is in her right hand; and in her left hand riches and honour.

Her ways are ways of pleasantness, and all her paths are peace.

She is a tree of life to them that lay hold upon her; and happy is every one that retaineth her.

The Lord by wisdom hath founded the earth; by understanding hath he established the heavens. —Proverbs 3:13–19

"Happy is . . . the man that getteth understanding" because out of understanding comes all that he needs in the outer world.

And God said to Solomon, Because this was in thine heart, and thou hast not asked riches, wealth, or honour, nor the life of thine enemies, neither yet hast asked long life; but hast asked wisdom and knowledge for thyself, that thou mayest judge my people, over whom I have made thee king:

Wisdom and knowledge is granted unto thee; and I will give thee riches, and wealth, and honour, such as none of the kings have had that have been before thee, neither shall there any after thee have the like. —2 Chronicles 1:11, 12

It is interesting to note at this point that the name Solomon means in Hebrew: whole; entire; complete; integral; peace; concord; integrity.

So there was light (wisdom and understanding) and the Bible says "it was good. . . ."

Again the creative principle is applied.

And God said, Let there be a firmament in the midst of the waters, and let it divide the waters from the waters.
—Genesis 1:6

Firmament means to make firm, to make solid, a foundation. The literal Bible reader who looks only to the obvious meaning considers it the arch in the sky. We find a much richer meaning, a deeper meaning. It is a firm unwavering place in consciousness. It is faith in Mind Power. The establishing of the firmament is the establishing of faith. Dividing the waters from the waters brings in selectivity, selecting the specific idea from the midst of the multiplicity of ideas (waters).

Each day for six days God specialized the divine idea which was then acted upon in Mind and became manifest form. This is the creative process. In each instance that for which the word was spoken came to pass. Each time "God saw that it was good."

Spiritual Man—the Offspring of God

On the sixth day, God said, "Let us make man in our image, after our likeness. . . ." "Male and female created he them." The masculine and the feminine aspects of life, Love and Wisdom, combine to be the *parents* of spiritual man. *Everything reproduces after its kind.* Spiritual man is the offspring, the *image* of his Father Creator, out of the very essence of God. Spiritual man is the product or outpicturing of First Cause. God and spiritual man are one. Spiritual man is the extension of God as the rays of the sun are the extension of the sun. ". . . Male and female created he them." Just as there are two aspects of the nature of God, so are there two sides to each one's nature, the masculine (wisdom, directing mind) and the feminine (love, subjective mind).

> So God created man in his own image, in the image of God created he him; male and female created he them.
> And God blessed them, and God said unto them, Be fruitful, and multiply, and replenish the earth, and subdue it: and have dominion over the fish of the sea, and over the fowl of the air, and over every living thing that moveth upon the earth. —Genesis 1:27, 28

Here, man, the least prepared physically to conquer and subdue the earth, is endowed with mental dominion. The fish of the sea are ideas deep in Mind, the fowl of the air are conscious thoughts of Mind, and every living thing that moveth upon the earth is the movement or outpicturing of these ideas, the world that man makes for himself. Since he has dominion within, he has dominion without. The dominion comes through understanding. In the Bible, feet denote understanding, that which we stand upon. In the beautiful mystical words of the Psalmist, "Thou hast put all things under his feet."

O Lord our Lord, how excellent *is* thy name [nature] in all the earth [outer manifestation]! who hast set thy glory above the heavens.

.   .   .

When I consider thy heavens [super-conscious Mind], the work of thy fingers, the moon and the stars [illumination], which thou hast ordained;
What is man, that thou art mindful of him? and the son of man, that thou visitest him?
For thou hast made him a little lower than the angels [God's thoughts], and hast crowned him with glory and honour.
Thou madest him to have dominion over the works of thy hands; thou has put all things under his feet [understanding]:
All sheep and oxen, yea, and the beasts of the field [sensuous or material thoughts];
The fowl of the air [liberated thoughts], and the fish of the sea [ideas deep in mind], and whatsoever passeth through the paths of the seas [minds].
O Lord our Lord [our divine Law], how excellent is thy name [nature] in all the earth! —Psalms 8:1, 3-9

Isn't it thrilling how this ties in with Genesis 1? Let us now consider this in the light of the vocabulary that we already know. It is as if to say: O divine Law, the divine Law of my own being, how excellent is Thy nature in all of the manifest world. Thy glory precedes all consciousness. When I consider the divine Consciousness, the Light that we are able to perceive, has already been established, I am humble indeed to be a part of it all and to be visited by Thy thoughts. Man is only lower than the angels in that man can elect to think thoughts of separation from God. But You have given him the dominion of a king and the glory and honour that goes to a king. Having given him dominion through consciousness, all things are subject to his understanding of Truth. All of the thoughts in the conscious and subconscious mind, every idea that moves through Mind is subject to his understanding. O divine Law, how excellent is Thy nature as it is expressed in all the manifest universe!

What a plan! What an endowment, what a heritage man has! We join with the Psalmist in a feeling of wonder and awe. We are ecstatic in our praise of this wonderful plan!

It Is Finished and Perfect

The six days represent the working cycle and now we come to the rest period when the work is complete—"and he rested on the seventh day from all his work which he had made." This is the Shabbath of the Jews, the Sabbath sacred to the Christians, the time of rest and release.

> Thus the heavens and the earth were finished, and all the host of them.
> And on the seventh day God ended his work which he had made; and he rested on the seventh day from all his work which he had made.

And God blessed the seventh day, and sanctified it: because that in it he had rested from all his work which God created and made.

These are the generations of the heavens and of the earth when they were created, in the day that the Lord God made the earth and the heavens. —Genesis 2:1–3

Here we are told very definitely that the heavens (consciousness within) and the earth (manifestation of that consciousness), including a male and female created in God's own image, were complete, finished and very good. The six days symbolize the cycle of work, the creative cycle, and the seventh day, perfection, the *it is finished and perfect*. Nothing can be added to or taken away from this finished creation.

The Second Creation Story

And now we skip over to the fourth verse of the second chapter of Genesis and what do you know, we start all over again!

These are the generations of the heavens and of the earth when they were created, in the day that the Lord God made the earth and the heavens.

And every plant of the field before it was in the earth, and every herb of the field before it grew: for the Lord God had not caused it to rain upon the earth, and there was not a man to till the ground. —Genesis 2:4, 5

The term "Lord God" means *the divine Law is the Creator.* We see why it is said that the plants and the herbs were created before they were in the ground and before they grew; for everything that is created in the manifest universe must first be created in the invisible realm of Mind. This must be a repetition of the creation story in Genesis 1 for we were told there, in great detail, of the creation of the plants and herbs. Heaven (divine consciousness) was the firmament (a firm foundation of faith) and out of the waters (the unformed moving consciousness) had come everything reproducing *after its kind.* It was all finished and completed and pronounced very good, including man, His very own image and likeness. So, when we are told "there was not a man to till the ground," we cannot help but wonder where were the two that He had brought into being. "But there went up a mist from the earth, and watered the whole face of the ground." [6]

Here we are given the clue. Since the Bible is its own best interpreter, let us take another verse here that may explain.

> Every good gift and every perfect gift is from above, and cometh down from the Father of lights, with whom is no variableness, neither shadow of turning.
> Of his own will begat he us with the word of truth, that we should be a kind of first fruits of his creatures.
> —James 1:17, 18

The true creation wrought by God is "from above." It is stepped down into visible manifestation from the higher consciousness which the Bible calls heaven. Thus, if a mist goes up "from the earth . . ." and waters the whole face of the ground, we can only deduce that it was an illusion of the senses, originating solely in the outer manifestation. Thus begins the allegory of the creation that explains how man misuses his God-given power of choice, and elects to separate himself from the life of Grace, which the Bible calls the Garden of Eden. "Much of your pain is self-chosen." [7] So through man's own choice, begins the long journey in Self-Discovery

6. Genesis 2:6.
7. Kahlil Gibran, *The Prophet,* New York: Alfred A. Knopf, Inc., 1958, p. 52.

which ends with John's vision of paradise regained, the New Jerusalem of Revelation.

> And the Lord God formed man of the dust of the ground, and breathed into his nostrils the breath of life; and man became a living soul.
> And the Lord God planted a garden eastward in Eden; and there he put the man whom he had formed.
> And out of the ground made the Lord God to grow every tree that is pleasant to the sight, and good for food; the tree of Life also in the midst of the garden, and the tree of knowledge of good and evil.
>
> .   .   .
>
> And the Lord God took the man, and put him into the garden of Eden to dress it and to keep it.
> And the Lord God commanded the man, saying, Of every tree of the garden thou mayest freely eat:
> But of the tree of the knowledge of good and evil, thou shalt not eat of it: for in the day that thou eatest thereof thou shall surely die. —Genesis 2:7–9; 15–17

The Garden of Eden—Allegory or Fact?

The Garden of Eden story is an allegory, artistic and ornate. Like every allegory, it brings us a lesson that has to do with ideas. People are used as characters in the story and they seem to live in certain places, but all of this is a device to point up a certain lesson. As such it has rich meaning for us to use in our own spiritual unfoldment. Since it is an allegory and is used to convey hidden meaning we shall have to see if there are certain key words that will give us a clue.

Let's see what *Eden* means first. The Hebrew word *Eden* actually means *delight*. A garden is cultivated, well-cared for land (fertile soil of the mind) where seeds are growing and flowering. To the desert people of the Bible land, a garden was a delight, just about the nicest thing they could think of. As Jeremiah put it, "and their soul shall be as a watered garden." *Eastward* or *east,* in the Bible, always indicates *the within.* So here we have the *garden of the soul,* a garden of *delight,* a garden *planted* or *established by God in consciousness.*

Thus it can be seen that only the most limited and restricted viewpoint would reduce the Garden of Eden to a small *hedged in* area in Asia. When people start talking about the Garden of Eden as identified between the Euphrates and the Tigris, they have missed the entire point. The Garden of Eden is a state of consciousness. It is really the kingdom of Heaven within, a state of consciousness in which there is perfect bliss, divine harmony, attunement with God.

The tree is the connecting link between the heaven and the earth, the invisible and the visible. ". . . To eat of the tree of life" is to *partake of the fruit of the Absolute.* Absolute means complete, entire, unconditional. It is First Cause. There is no opposite to the Absolute because the Absolute is all in all. Absolute is pure Spirit and the fruit of the Absolute is the fruit of Spirit.

> But the fruit of the Spirit is love, joy, peace, longsuffering, gentleness, goodness, faith.
> Meekness, temperance: against such there is no law.
> —Galatians 5:22, 23

As we partake of, or live in accord with, the attributes of God, here called the fruit of the Spirit, we live by First Cause which is living by Grace. We dwell in the Garden of Eden (delight). Therefore, we do not come under the law of cause and effect and its subsequent suffering.

Eating the Forbidden Fruit

When we *eat* of the "tree of the knowledge of good and evil . . .," we introduce human judgment and we come under the law of cause and effect. This is living in the realm of sensation, the human or relative. Paul was pretty strong in his description of the "fruits" of the "tree of knowledge of good and evil . . ." which he designated "the works of the flesh. . . ."

> For all the law is fulfilled in one word, even in this; Thou shalt love thy neighbour as thyself.
> But if ye bite and devour one another, take heed that ye be not consumed one of another.
> This I say then, Walk in the Spirit, and ye shall not fulfil the lust of the flesh.
> For the flesh lusteth against the Spirit, and the Spirit against the flesh: and these are contrary the one to the other: so that ye cannot do the things that ye would.
> But if ye be led of the Spirit, ye are not under the law.
> Now the works of the flesh are manifest, which are these; Adultery, fornication, uncleanness, lasciviousness,
> Idolatry, witchcraft, hatred, variance, emulations, wrath, strife, seditions, heresies,
> Envyings, murders, drunkenness, revellings, and such like: of the which I tell you before, as I have also told you in time past, that they which do such things shall not inherit the kingdom of God. —Galatians 5:14–21

Do all of these strong words seem to apply to somebody else? "They do not apply to me," you say? Perhaps not indeed, but if you will examine your heart you will find that if you partake of human judgment, that is partake of the "fruits" of the "tree of the knowledge of good and evil . . .," you are mentally experiencing some measure of the above. And as Jesus said, it is not your actions that betray you but what is in your heart. These are "the little foxes, that spoil the vines." Do you see why the divine Law gives man the ultimatum about *eating* (partaking mentally) of the "tree of the knowledge of good and evil . . ."? To do so is to give up Absolute bliss and be under the law of sin and death. "But if ye be led of the Spirit, ye are not under the law."

A Psychiatrist Examines the Tree

To me the most correlation between the religious postulations of our culture and our psychodynamic formulation occurs with reference to the conceived basis of man's human difficulties. Religion bases the separation of man from God and from Paradise (the good life) on the allegorical or symbolic story of Adam and Eve in the Garden of Eden as related in Genesis. This story says that Adam "ate of the fruit of the tree of the knowledge of good and evil" and as a consequence was immediately and henceforth banished from Paradise. To me this says simply that man took into himself or incorporated (ate) the fruits or the results of "the knowledge of good and evil"—or the knowing of right from wrong, or moral judgment—and that it resulted in his being shut out from the good life. Whereas this interpretation is not one that I have ever seen expounded, it appears to me that not only does "authority" say that the separation of man from Paradise is by reason of his having incorporatetd moral judgment, but it harmonizes completely with what I have found to be true clinically.

Anyone having read the foregoing chapters will be clearly aware that the theory of psychodynamics presented postulates that man's propensity for moral judgments—his naïve assumption that he has the capacity for determining such judgments—is the basis of all his human trouble. His judgmental attitudes alienate him from his fellow man as well as from his true self; they make him incognizant of reality, and deprive him of mental health or the good life.

Even though the truth of this postulate may be seen by anyone who cares to look at himself or at human ills, it is difficult for people to accept it because they are convinced (they assume or believe) that all good and desirable behavior is the product of a moral value system essentially comparable to their own. It would be almost inconceivable for most people to look at their moral judgments as the real factor which keeps them out of Paradise. Yet we have seen that it is these which produce the fears, the half-lives, the cruelties, the symptoms, and the unhappiness of human beings.

According to the story in Genesis, it was suggested to Adam that to incorporate moral judgment and thereby to be able to account things as right and wrong was to have made him "like God," but, as the story goes, it merely complicated and impoverished his life. Actual experience with people demonstrates the truth of this point of view. Man, through his moral judgmental propensities, tries to "play God"—deciding that this is good and that the other is bad—when it takes the perspective or wisdom of God or of the ages to make such determinations. The more judgmental a person is, the more trouble he has and the more impoverished is his life. It is better for man to be tentative and to reserve judgment than to act as though he can know for sure. The more perspective he has, the closer he can approximate the wisdom of God, but perspective is noticeably lacking wherever a morally judgmental attitude prevails.[8]

Adam Names His World

So, Adam, generic man, is warned by the divine Law, the Lord God, not to partake of human judgment. Let's see what happens.

> And the Lord God said, It is not good that the man should be alone; I will make him an help meet for him.

8. Camilla M. Anderson, M.D., *Beyond Freud*, New York: Harper & Brothers, 1957, pp. 265, 266.

And out of the ground the Lord God formed every beast
of the field, and every fowl of the air; and brought them unto
Adam to see what he would call them: and whatsoever Adam
called every living creature, that was the name thereof.

—Genesis 2:18, 19

All these had been created before but now the mist of the
earth shows them through the eyes of man.

Name means nature. He called each one according to its
nature. This is all the judgment man ever needs. He may
describe things according to the nature—this is hot, and that
is cold; this is wide and that is narrow. This mountain is high
and that hill is low. This animal is an anteater because it eats
ants. This is not moral judgment, but descriptive judgment
for the purpose of a mental filing system or clarification. If
we say this man is a brown man because his skin is brown
and this man is a white man because his skin is white, this
is not conditioned judgment because there is no emotional
feeling about it.

Everything is good because it is all created by God. So as
Adam names the things in his life, it is impersonal judgment
without condemnation, for Adam has not yet eaten of the
"tree of the knowledge of good and evil." He labels them, but
does not judge them.

His Help Meet Arrives

And the Lord God caused a deep sleep to fall upon Adam,
and he slept: and he took one of his ribs, and closed up the
flesh instead thereof;

And the rib, which the Lord God had taken from man,
made he a woman, and brought her unto the man.

And Adam said, This is now bone of my bones, and flesh
of my flesh: she shall be called Woman, because she was taken
out of Man.

Therefore shall a man leave his father and his mother, and shall cleave unto his wife: and they shall be one flesh.

And they were both naked, the man and his wife, and were not ashamed. —Genesis 2:21–25

The feminine or feeling side of Adam (generic man) is symbolized by Eve. The masculine, Adam, is the conscious mind. The feminine, Eve, is the subconscious mind. Eve was taken out of Adam in a deep sleep because that is the domain of subconscious mind. The subconscious never sleeps. She is made out of the very substance of Adam because she is part of his very being. There is a masculine and feminine side to every person. This is the marriage within, the perfect union of the conscious and subconscious mind—"and they shall be one flesh."

Each one of us has at times reached that state of spiritual oneness in which he is in tune with all Good and is completely free. "And they were both naked . . ." in the Garden of Eden completely unencumbered by moral judgment, uninhibited, free in their spiritual awareness. They knew only Good and therefore they were unashamed. There was no sense of sin, condemnation or guilt.

The Perfect Life

Here we have the masculine and the feminine derivatives of the one life, in the garden of the soul—the completely balanced life—in a state of bliss. Adam and Eve had everything that they needed provided for by God, infinite Wisdom and Intelligence, everything free for them *to eat,* to partake of or make their own. They were sustained and nourished by Spirit, their every need anticipated and met by Spirit. This is the life of Grace that God makes available to each one of us so long as we continue to *eat* from the *tree of life.*

Up to this point, we have the divine Law or all of life proceeding out of First Cause. First Cause was reproducing Itself upon the direction of Itself. No secondary causes had been introduced through false thinking. Man was the image and likeness of God and, behold, everything was very good.

That Old Serpent—Moral Judgment

Now the serpent was more subtle than any beast of the field which the Lord God had made. And he said unto the woman, Yea, hath God said, Ye shall not eat of every tree of the garden?

And the woman said unto the serpent, We may eat of the fruit of the trees of the garden:

But of the fruit of the tree which is in the midst of the garden, God hath said, Ye shall not eat of it, neither shall ye touch it, lest ye die.

And the serpent said unto the woman, Ye shall not surely die:

For God doth know that in the day ye eat thereof, then your eyes shall be opened, and ye shall be as gods, knowing good and evil.

And when the woman saw that the tree was good for food, and that it was pleasant to the eyes, and a tree to be desired to make one wise, she took of the fruit thereof, and did eat, and gave also unto her husband with her; and he did eat.

And the eyes of them both were opened, and they knew that they were naked; and they sewed fig leaves together, and made themselves aprons. —Genesis 3:1–7

The serpent represents that subtle thought of temptation that comes to all of us, thinking not from high ideas but from the very lowest level of appearance, sensual thinking that promises great satisfaction but ends in pain. It is looking to outer effects for fulfillment. Their eyes were opened to outer appearances. This is the beginning of the shifting of the attention from the real value of spiritual understanding to the false value of material gain. It is the beginning of judging by the world's standards instead of inner Guidance which comes through understanding. It is judging by appearances. It is moral judgment. "Judge not according to the appearance, but judge righteous judgment." [9]

Judging righteous judgment is eating from the "tree of life." Judging by appearances is eating from the "tree of the knowledge of good and evil."

The Results of Eating Forbidden Fruit

The temptation is always there, lurking in the underbrush of our thinking. Any time that anyone passes moral judgment on another, he assumes the prerogative of being as gods, knowing good and evil. He tries to play God and, for the moment, feels important because of his judgment. A false feeling of exhilaration comes and for a little while his ego is inflated. But, always this judgment takes its toll. He ceases to have peace of mind. He feels miserable and the end result is that he condemns himself even as he has condemned the other.

In Truth, we judge ourselves when we judge another for how could we see the evil in another were it not in ourselves. Any sense of duality is the temptation of the serpent. We are tempted also when we trust in outer effects for our security, such as our bank accounts, our stocks and bonds, our property holdings, and even what our friends think of us. God is the Source of our good. Our security is in God. It does not depend upon outer conditions.

We "eat" from the "tree of the knowledge of good and evil" when we think that we have to experience evil in order to know good by contrast; when we think that we must experi-

9. St. John 7:24.

ence poverty in order to appreciate wealth; ill health to appreciate health; drunkenness to appreciate sobriety; false appetites to appreciate freedom; unhappiness to appreciate happiness; selfishness to appreciate generosity. Evil is not the Truth at all. There is no power in it whether we think we see it in ourselves or another. It is only the temptation of the serpent.

Now, the woman *Eve, the feminine or feeling side,* is easily tempted because she does not reason but acts entirely on feeling or emotion. Man lets his feelings lead him to destruction. And so Adam and Eve were cast out of the beautiful garden of the soul because they could not accept their good.

"Passing the Buck"

And they heard the voice of the Lord God walking in the garden in the cool of the day: and Adam and his wife hid themselves from the presence of the Lord God amongst the trees of the garden.

And the Lord God called unto Adam, and said unto him, Where art thou?

And he said, I heard thy voice in the garden, and I was afraid, because I was naked; and I hid myself.

And he said, Who told thee that thou wast naked? Hast thou eaten of the tree, whereof I commanded thee that thou shouldest not eat?

And the man said, The woman whom thou gavest to be with me, she gave me of the tree, and I did eat.

And the Lord God said unto the woman, What is this that thou hast done? And the woman said, The serpent beguiled me, and I did eat. —Genesis 3:8–13

Here we have a little Biblical humor for the discerning. These verses succinctly point up a trait of which we are all guilty—shifting the blame or "passing the buck." Not only did Adam place the blame on Eve, but he slyly blamed God for giving him his temptress. Eve, of course, blamed the serpent.

And who told Adam he was naked? After eating of the forbidden fruit, *human judgment,* he developed a guilt complex. Now he was completely exposed. He saw himself for the first time in the eyes of the world's judgment. It is only after we develop moral judgment that we start being concerned over the judgment of others.

The Lord God is the Spirit of Truth within each one of us that will reveal to us the Truth about ourselves for our own growth if we will but hear it. But, like all of us, the characters in this allegory refused to face the Truth about themselves. It seemed perfectly natural to have eaten from the "tree of the knowledge of good and evil" just so long as they could blame somebody else for it. We all do it. If we can just find somebody a little bit worse than we are and point up their folly, it seems to lighten our load of guilt a bit. As with Adam and Eve, it gets us nowhere in the long run.

It brings to my mind a conversation I once had with a man who was on the Prison Board of the State of California. Part of his work was to visit the prisons every month. He talked to hundreds of the inmates there. He laughingly said, "I have yet to talk to a guilty man!"

Why the Serpent Was to Blame

Adam blamed Eve, Eve blamed the serpent. The serpent, I suppose, just blamed his serpent nature. And well he might —the serpent stands here for false beliefs, another name for that old devil Satan whom Jesus called "the liar." False beliefs have only the power we give them, but they are always getting us into trouble. God blamed the serpent.

And the Lord God said unto the serpent, Because thou hast done this, thou art cursed above all cattle, and above every beast of the field; upon thy belly shalt thou go, and dust shalt thou eat all the days of thy life. —Genesis 3:14

Adam and Eve in us will always try and blame some secondary cause for our downfall. "I sat in a draft and *it* gave me the cold;" "My family was hungry so I had to rob the bank;" "Times are bad all over and so my business is poor;" and on and on, refusing to face the fact that the problem is in our own negative thinking. But God does not tarry with secondary causes. God, the divine Law being First Cause, does not recognize secondary causation.

This is an interesting place to digress for a moment and trace a word through the Bible so that you may see that the Bible is its own best interpreter. Serpent is used throughout to denote false beliefs or false thinking. In Revelation we have:

And the great dragon was cast out, that old serpent, called the Devil, and Satan, which deceiveth the whole world: he was cast out into the earth, and his angels [thoughts] were cast out with him. —Revelation 12:9

The serpent, the dragon, the Devil, Satan, call it what you will, is that which is not true, false thinking and all that goes with it. It deceives those who live according to appearances, judging by human intellect and all false standards. It is interesting to note that false thinking is cast into the earth (outer experience) taking even the angels (thoughts) that surround it.

Jesus spoke of serpents in his figurative language several times. He said, *if you ask your father for a fish* (idea) *will he give you a serpent* (erroneous thought?) Then we have the mystical references to serpents as Jesus is talking to the eleven remaining disciples just before he leaves them. He is giving them instructions.

> In my name shall they cast out devils; they shall speak with new tongues;
> They shall take up serpents; and if they drink any deadly thing, it shall not hurt them; they shall lay hands on the sick, and they shall recover. —Mark 16:17, 18

In the nature of the Christ, as portrayed so beautifully by Jesus, shall the true disciples, or enlightened ones, cast that which is false out of their thinking. They shall speak with the new tongue of Truth, and they shall take up problems and meet them and if, in the past, they have drunk (taken into consciousness) any false thinking, it shall be neutralized and have no power to hurt them. And every one they touch in Mind with this uplifted consciousness shall be healed.

And he said to the seventy:

> And the seventy returned again with joy, saying, Lord, even the devils are subject unto us through thy name.
> And he said unto them, I beheld Satan as lightning fall from heaven.
> Behold, I give unto you power to tread on serpents and scorpions, and over all the power of the enemy: and nothing shall by any means hurt you. —Luke 10:17–19

Here we have devils, Satan, serpents and scorpions used interchangeably to denote false thinking. The Christ Truth witnesses Satan falling from consciousness as lightning. When Truth comes in, that which is not true leaves like lightning. There is absolutely no power in it. There is only power in God—Truth.

The Punishment of Adam and Eve

Unto the woman he said, I will greatly multiply thy sorrow and thy conception; in sorrow thou shalt bring forth children; and thy desire shall be to thy husband, and he shall rule over thee.

And unto Adam he said, Because thou hast harkened unto the voice of thy wife, and hast eaten of the tree, of which I commanded thee, saying, Thou shalt not eat of it; cursed is the ground for thy sake; in sorrow shalt thou eat of it all the days of thy life;

Thorns also and thistles shall it bring forth to thee; and thou shalt eat the herb of the field;

In the sweat of thy face shalt thou eat bread, till thou return unto the ground; for out of it wast thou taken: for dust thou art, and unto dust shalt thou return.

.   .   .

Therefore the Lord God sent him forth from the garden of Eden, to till the ground from whence he was taken.

—Genesis 3:16–19, 23

What worse punishment could come to these two—that woman should bring forth her children in sorrow and be ruled by her husband; and that man should labor in sorrow amidst thorns and thistles to produce his bread! The revolt against this ultimatum goes on year after year. Many women resent their portion as childbearers; other women try to be equal to men, resenting every act of man. Men struggle to get riches without labor. By their acceptance of the Bible curse, they have taken the Bible literally and missed the great meaning.

We Can Stop Eating the Forbidden Fruit

Suffering in childbirth that has been thought to be inevitable is a fiction. It is an attitude of mind that causes a woman to be cast out of the Garden of Eden. Like Adam and Eve, in the allegory, we each have the right to name every sensation and every attitude in our life experience. So long as women call the sensation accompanying childbirth *labor pains,* the nature of these sensations will be painful.

But along came a man called Dr. Grantly Dick Reed who renamed the whole procedure and called it "Natural Childbirth" or "Childbirth Without Fear," [10] and the whole experience is changed for the women who try it. The reason this transformation takes place is because the woman is taught to agree with childbirth instead of fearing it as a so-called ordeal. Through agreement, she *eats* of the "tree of life" instead of *eating* of the "tree of the knowledge of good and evil."

I have counselled with many women who have, with their doctor's help, followed the *Natural Childbirth* method. These women have proved beyond a doubt that it is not necessary to suffer in childbirth. One woman told her doctor in the midst of having her baby, "This is so easy, I would have a baby every year if you doctors didn't charge so much!" Recently, one of the young women made a tape recording of the entire birth which is now being used in *Natural Childbirth* classes. This woman had given birth to two children with travail and complications. Through the old thinking which produced undue tension, she had suffered pain. Now she has had three children through *Natural Childbirth* without any suffering. The sensations that she had before considered pain were now understood to be contractions, a perfectly natural part of an experience for which she was thoroughly prepared through exercise and right thinking. I know of no better example of an application of the Garden of Eden allegory in everyday living.

10. Dr. Grantly Dick Reed, *Childbirth Without Fear,* New York: Harper & Brothers, 1953.

Going Back to First Cause

When we turn from the false appearances of sin and suffering and go back to First Cause which is Absolute Good, we go back and eat from the "tree of life" and are privileged to return to the garden of bliss.

A good example of this is whether one's work is a chore or a fulfillment. When one really loves his work and feels that he is being creative and expressing his true nature through it, then he is *eating* from the "tree of life." Each one is given a gift of expression and when he is using that gift, looking to the divine Law for the ways and means of expression, he lives in the garden of bliss. Work need not be labor or struggle. It can be done so effortlessly that it is pure joy and seems hardly to be work at all. But if one resists his work and in his heart considers it evil, then ". . . Thorns also and thistles shall it bring forth to thee" and "in sorrow shalt thou eat of it." Man is given a choice. The result depends on his own attitude.

> Work is love made visible.
> And if you cannot work with love but only with distaste, it is better that you should leave your work and sit at the gate of the temple and take alms of those who work with joy.[11]

Living by Grace Is Living in the Garden of Eden

As long as one lives by comparisons, by relating one thing to another, as "this is good, that is evil," there is going to be a sense of separation. Trusting and relying upon mental power and material things instead of Spirit will only bring forth sorrow "all of the days of thy life."

We live in the Garden of Eden when we live intuitively,

11. Kahlil Gibran, *op. cit.*, p. 28.

from the inside out, trusting in the Power and Intelligence of God within. Jesus taught this. He said, "the kingdom of heaven is at hand." The "kingdom of heaven" and the "garden of Eden" are one and the same. It was just as if Jesus came saying, "The Garden of Eden is now at hand."

Jesus accepted the Old Testament teaching of one God, "the Lord, our God, is one Lord," one Good and the only Good. Love the Lord thy God "with all thy mind," all thy strength, all thy understanding, with your total self. He taught that duality was destructive, bringing sorrow and pain; that we should love God within our fellow man as being the same God within us. His message was a recognition that there was no duality whatsoever. That there was only one Life, one Truth, one "tree of life" from which to eat, if we would abide in the *garden of bliss,* that state of perfect everything which was and is today man's heritage.

Evil Makes the Headlines but Truth Prevails

It is interesting to note that evil, or what appears to be evil, seems to get the headlines today as it did in the Garden of Eden allegory.

Much emphasis was put on the "tree of the knowledge of good and evil" because that was the great temptation. To live in peace and harmony, love and understanding, is normal and natural. The way of judgment and condemnation is unnatural and great emphasis is made to warn us that we should stay away from the "tree of the knowledge of good and evil" lest we suffer the consequences of Adam, "man, whose breath is in his nostrils," man who looks to materiality for pleasure and satisfaction. We are given the warning that life is to be lived according to the divine plan, according to divine Law. "Be ye therefore perfect, even as your Father which is in heaven is perfect." [12]

12. Matthew 5:48.

The Third Story of Creation

In the first story of creation given in the Bible, we found that each act of creation came through the specializing of Mind through the speaking of the word. Now let us turn to the New Testament and see what we find there:

> In the beginning was the Word, and the Word was with God, and the Word was God.
> The same was in the beginning with God.
> All things were made by him; and without him was not any thing made that was made.
> In him was life; and the life was the light of men.
> And the light shineth in darkness; and the darkness comprehended it not.
>
> .   .   .
>
> And the Word was made flesh, and dwelt among us, (and we beheld his glory, the glory as of the only begotten of the Father), full of grace and truth. —St. John 1:1–5, 14

The first creation story began: "In the beginning God created the heaven and the earth." [13] In the third version, we have, "In the beginning was the Word, and the Word was with God. . . ." Is it not the same thing? "The same was in the beginning with God," verse two, is simply a repetition to emphasize that God is all in all. Here we are told again that all life comes through light (wisdom and understanding), that everything is created by God out of Himself.

The Essence of Life

"The Divine Essence is Love and Wisdom," said Sweden-

13. Genesis 1:1.

borg.[14] The light (divine illumination) which shines amidst ignorance is not overcome by this darkness.

Energy is the substance from which everything is made. Einstein discovered that energy and mass are equal and interchangeable, $E = mc^2$. There is no dead matter, all is Spirit in everchanging form.

The Christ is Spirit individualized in each one of us. As we behold the Christ made visible in each other, we are beholding the glory of the only begotten of the Father, which Meister Eckhart said is constantly being begotten, full of grace (love) and truth (understanding). Through the Christ within us, we have the essence of Life Itself—love and wisdom. It creates out of Itself the manifest world. God acting through man is manifested as creation, by means of the creative process of life.

Spinoza calls the underlying reality of all life *substance.* By this he does not mean the material, as the substance of a chair, but literally, that which stands beneath. Spinoza took the term from the Greek philosophers who took the term from the Greek word *ousia* which means the inner being or essence. To quote from the correspondence of Spinoza:

> I take a totally different view of God and Nature from that which the later Christians usually entertain, for I hold that God is the imminent, and not the extraneous, cause of all things. I say, All is in God; all lives and moves in God.[15]

Spinoza agreed with Paul and why not? Paul told the men on Mars Hill that he was quoting their own poets, the same Greek philosophers from whom Spinoza drew his reasoning

14. Emanuel Swedenborg, *Foundation Truths of the Christian Religion,* London: Swedenborg Society, 1901.
15. Will Durant, *The Story of Philosophy,* New York: Simon and Schuster, Inc., 1926, pp. 188–189.

of the substance of all life. No wonder Spinoza agreed with Paul who said, "For in him we live, and move, and have our being; as certain also of your own poets have said, For we are also his offspring."

VIII FAITH IS THE BEGINNING
OF EVERYTHING

THE STORY OF ABRAHAM AND SARAH

Genesis, Chapters 12–24

But without faith it is impossible to please him: for he that cometh to God must believe that he is, and that he is a rewarder of them that diligently seek him. —Hebrews 11:6

Faith is the beginning of everything. Faith is the beginning of every gain, every step of unfoldment, every bit of spiritual growth that we make in this life. ". . . Without faith it is impossible to please him . . .," that is, put ourselves in harmony with the divine Law. The Bible tells us, "The Lord [divine Law] he is God. . . .[1] It is obvious that in order to put our trust in the divine Law, we must believe that It is and that It is all powerful in our lives.

The story of Abraham is the story of the growth of faith in our lives and the tests that we draw to ourselves to make us grow. As we move through the life of Abraham, step by step, we see the unfolding of faith, we see the importance of complete and total surrender to the direction and guidance

1. Deuteronomy 4:35.

of God from within. Faith is trusting in infinite Wisdom, the perfect Power, the abiding Love of God within us.

Was Abraham a Real Person?

Do not be misled. The story of Abraham is an allegory. Paul emphasizes this in his Epistle to the Galatians.

> But he who was of the bondwoman was born after the flesh; but he of the freewoman was by promise [faith].
>
> Which things are an allegory: for these are the two covenants [promises]; the one from the mount Sinai, which gendereth to bondage, which is Agar [Hagar].
>
> For this Agar is mount Sinai in Arabia, and answereth to Jerusalem which now is, and is in bondage with her children.
>
> But Jerusalem which is above is free, which is the mother of us all. —Galatians 4:23–26

Paul was subtle here. I cannot help but wonder how many of his students got his meaning. Before Abraham had his miraculous son of his old age by his beloved Sarah, he had a son by Sarah's handmaid, Hagar. Here, Paul is interpreting this allegory just as we are in this book.

When God told Abraham and Sarah that they would have a child when they were well past the age of childbearing, at first they could not believe it and so did the obvious—Sarah gave her handmaid, Hagar, who was young, to Abraham to bear the child. The tendency with all of us is to look to the thing that seems to make sense, that is, be reasonable to our materialistic thinking. We try to find the answers in the outer world before we are willing to rely on the spiritual Power within. We attempt to find satisfaction in the lesser and miss the greater.

Hagar means *stranger* in Hebrew, and the materialistic thought is always a stranger to the spiritual thought. The reference to Mt. Sinai is a reference to living under the law of the Ten Commandments, the law of a people in bondage. And wasn't it clever of Paul to differentiate between *the Jerusalem which now is* and is in bondage (to the Romans) and *the Jerusalem which is above which is free and is the mother of us all.*[2] The obvious Jerusalem, the city in bondage to the Romans, is all that most people see. The Jerusalem which is above is the consciousness of Peace that comes from complete reliance on God. This consciousness is always free and is the mother of us all, the faith that is the beginning of everything.

Man's Extremity Is God's Opportunity

About 1691 John Flavel opened a door to the understanding of faith when he said "man's extremity is God's opportunity."[3] Often it is only in our extreme need that we are willing to stop struggling with life and give God an opportunity.

The Bible does not teach these truths in a lukewarm fashion, but is always dramatic in presenting them. Therefore, we find that Abraham's test of faith required a most radical reliance upon God. Where we are tightest, there we need stretching. Even with you and me, the tests that we draw to ourselves must always be the thing that will force us to grow. The challenge comes where we are most protective of our cherished misconceptions, those little fears and foibles that we hide away.

Abram became known as Abraham. His wife Sarai was later renamed Sarah. As their nature changed, their names were also changed. Name always means nature. This is the story of

2. Galatians 4:25, 26.
3. John Flavel, *Faithful and Ancient Account of Some Late and Wonderful Sea Deliverances.*

the unfolding of faith in each one of us. Each test that Abraham faced was the most dramatically difficult assignment that could be imagined. Do you know why we are always given the most difficult assignments? Because nothing else would force us to put radical trust in God and without this complete surrender, God cannot act through us.

It Takes Implicit Trust

The Bible is a book of faith. Omnipresent, omniscient and omnipotent God is not perceptive to the senses. Jesus expressed this clearly when he said, "The kingdom of God cometh not with observation: Neither shall they say, Lo here! or, lo there! for, behold, the kingdom of God is within you." [4] The Bible is an account of the Power of God unfolding in the life of man. Every story emphasizes that man must have implicit trust in the Power for it to be effective in his life, and that fear and doubt obscure the Power.

This trust is not to be continually subject to test. Suppose you had a month of overcast sky with the sun never shining. You would know the sun was still there. You would have faith in the sun. In the same way, we must have faith in the unseen Power of God.

The stories in the Bible go to great extremes to show that the Power of God must be trusted implicitly. Too often man feels that God is to be trusted part of the way, not all the way. This is a mistake. To trust wholly in the mind's interpretations of the sense perceptions is a mistake that will lead to destruction. To trust in the Power of God leads to life abundant.

The story of Abraham reveals a life of absolute faith in God. Here was a man who never faltered, although he was

4. Luke 17:20, 21.

faced with situations that seemed to be impossible. Abraham portrays faith in the invisible Power of God.

The Abraham Story

For those of you who are not too familiar with the story of Abraham as told in Genesis twelve through Genesis twenty-four:

Abram was his name in the beginning. He was the son of Terah. After his brother Haran died, Abram and his father took Haran's son, Lot, with them and moved to a place called Haran.

After Abram's father died, the Lord said to Abram who was then seventy-five years old: "Get thee out of thy country, and from thy kindred, and from thy father's house, unto a land that I will show thee. . . ." [5]

Abram Disowns Sarai for the Sake of Security

After Abram left Haran, taking Sarai and Lot with him, he passed through Canaan on his way to Sichem. There was a famine in the land of Sichem and Abram went down into Egypt. Because he feared what would happen to him, he asked Sarai to pretend to be his sister. The Egyptians found Sarai very fair and she was taken into Pharaoh's house and Abram was given sheep, oxen and he asses, menservants and maid-servants, and she asses and camels because of Sarai. But the Lord plagued Pharaoh and his house with great plagues because of Sarai; and Pharaoh asked Abram why he did not tell him that Sarai was his wife. He sent Abram away with his wife and all that he had.

5. Genesis 12:1.

What This Story Means to Us

In order to understand what this story means to us, we must first understand the meaning of some of the key names.

Abram stands for faith in the invisible, invincible Power of God. Sarai, his wife, means the feeling or emotional side. Every wife in the Bible stands for the subjective side of the consciousness represented by the husband. Sarai here stands for emotions that faith is afraid to acknowledge. The Hebrew name, Sarai, actually means contentious. So we have faith taking along negative thoughts: contentious feelings and dark negative thinking represented by Lot.

> And Abram took Sarai his life, and Lot his brother's son, and all their substance that they had gathered, and the souls that they had gotten in Haran; and they went forth to go into the land of Canaan; and into the land of Canaan they came.
> —Genesis 12:5

Faith, the consciousness of trust in the invisible, invincible Power of God, takes with it in the beginning stages, contentious feelings and related dark, negative thinking, as well as the spiritual awareness that it has gathered in Haran (an exalted state of mind). Faith and its not yet purified thoughts depart for Canaan (the lowlands of materiality). In Sichem, which means *burden bearing,* there was a famine, as there always is in this kind of thinking. Famine means a state of mind where there is no spiritual inspiration upon which faith can be nourished. It is in this impoverished state of mind that we look to Egypt for our good; the fleshpots of Egypt in the Bible stand for bondage to materiality. The Egyptians represent the thoughts that dwell in this state of mind.

Abram had built up his soul consciousness to an exalted state (Haran), yet shortly thereafter, he entered into a state of famished consciousness and went so far as to look to Egypt (bondage to materiality) for his good. It is interesting to note that he was not sent here by the guidance of God, but by his own confused thinking.

And there was a famine in the land: and Abram went down into Egypt to sojourn there; for the famine was grievous in the land.

And it came to pass, when he was come near to enter into Egypt, that he said unto Sarai his wife, Behold now, I know that thou art a fair woman to look upon:

Therefore it shall come to pass, when the Egyptians shall see thee, that they shall say, This is his wife: and they will kill me, but they will save thee alive.

Say, I pray thee, thou art my sister: that it may be well with me for thy sake; and my soul shall live because of thee.

And it came to pass, that, when Abram was come into Egypt, the Egyptians beheld the woman that she was very fair.

The princes also of Pharaoh saw her, and commended her before Pharaoh: and the woman was taken into Pharaoh's house.

And he entreated Abram well for her sake: and he had sheep, and oxen, and he asses, and menservants, and maidservants, and she asses, and camels.

And the Lord plagued Pharaoh and his house with great plagues because of Sarai Abram's wife.

And Pharaoh called Abram, and said, What is this that thou hast done unto me? why didst thou not tell me that she was thy wife?

Why saidst thou, She is my sister? so I might have taken her to me to wife: now therefore behold thy wife, take her, and go thy way.

And Pharaoh commanded his men concerning him: and they sent him away, and his wife, and all that he had.

—Genesis 12:10–20

How It Relates to Us

Briefly this story means that we are continually taking our faith, as yet unproven, together with our feeling side and our remaining negative thoughts, back into bondage to fear. In turning to the Lord, we give lip service *only* to our awareness of God and have within us a heap of rubbish that comes from putting our faith in the little ego self. This kind of conflict always causes a famine in the land, a state of consciousness where there is no spiritual inspiration.

The entire story of Abram becoming Abraham is the story of the unfolding of faith in individual consciousness and the various experiences that come through proving faith.

God had promised Abram (faith in the invisible Power) that he would be blessed forever and his seed (ideas) would inhabit the world. But with his negative thoughts and feelings, faith seeks the security of sense consciousness (Egypt).

As we go about proving our faith, it is important that each one of us understand some of the pitfalls along the way. In the beginning, we come to a place where there is a famine, that is, we seem to lack the spiritual inspiration that we have had in our exalted state of mind. The answers to our prayers just aren't coming through as we would like and we are inclined to doubt. We do not trust our spiritual inspiration and, fearful that our faith will not stand up, we are subject to the hypnotism of race consciousness. We permit our feeling side (here portrayed as the wife) to be taken over by the ruling thought in sense consciousness (Pharaoh). This ruling thought may be a belief in contagion, a belief in hard times, or any other sense of separation from our highest good. The feeling or emotional side is always receptive to the intellect. We cannot at any time forsake our direction over the subconscious mind. To do so is to hand over our dearest possession to the dominant thought in sense consciousness. Great troubles come of this. To let someone else take charge of our thinking is the most dangerous thing we can do. It leads only to destruction. When faith loses control in us, we are in bondage to race consciousness. We have to take all that we have and get out of that land.

Every time Abram moves his family from one place to another, *one state of mind to another,* he *pitches his tent and then removes his tent.* The tent here stands for *a temporary or easily moved house.* Since house stands for *a kind of consciousness,* it is clear that these stages in the spiritual journey of faith (Abram) stand for *temporary states of consciousness along the way.*

> And Lot also, which went with Abram, had flocks, and herds, and tents.
> And the land was not able to bear them, that they might dwell together: for their substance was great, so that they could not dwell together.
> And there was a strife between the herdmen of Abram's cattle and the herdmen of Lot's cattle. . . . —Genesis 13:5–7

The strife between the herdmen indicates that the thoughts belonging to such different states of mind just cannot agree.

> And Abram said unto Lot, Let there be no strife, I pray thee, between me and thee, and between my herdmen and thy herdmen; for we be brethren.
> Is not the whole land before thee? separate thyself, I pray thee, from me: if thou wilt take the left hand, then I will go to the right; or if thou depart to the right hand, then I will go to the left. —Genesis 13:8, 9

The time had come at last when faith in the invisible Power (Abram) must part with its erstwhile companion, dark negative thinking (Lot). Faith can afford to be generous and so it gives Lot first choice. Lot looked on both sides before making his choice. On one side was the lowlands of Canaan and on the other, the lush well-watered plains of the Jordan. Lot chose the latter. His land looked good according to appearance by which Lot's thinking always judges, but his land contained Sodom and Gomorrah, wicked (thought) people who were later destroyed. This land was watered by the Jordan, *meaning race consciousness.*

Abram, on the other hand, dwelt in the land of Canaan (meaning lowlands), but even here he was able to look up to a higher state of consciousness:

> And the Lord said unto Abram, after that Lot was separated from him, Lift up now thine eyes, and look from the place where thou art northward, and southward, and eastward, and westward:
>
> For all the land which thou seest, to thee will I give it, and to thy seed forever.
>
> And I will make thy seed as the dust of the earth: so that if a man can number the dust of the earth, then shall thy seed also be numbered.
>
> Arise, walk through the land in the length of it and in the breadth of it; for I will give it unto thee. —Genesis 13:14–17

Do you see why *Abram, faith in the Unseen,* and *Lot, faith in materiality,* came to a parting of the ways? However, once *Abram* was separated from his negative thinking, it was possible for him to lift his consciousness from the place where he was, *the lowlands of consciousness,* and get *a balanced perspective*—look North, South, East, and West.

We must continually remember that each story relates in some marvelous way to a guide for our everyday living. The Bible is a textbook of practical Truth, an encyclopedia of spiritual wisdom. It may appear to be talking about material things, but always there is a hidden message of profound spiritual significance.

What We See Becomes Our Experience

To see in the Bible means *to comprehend, to understand, to discern.* All of the *land (consciousness)* which we understand belongs to us and to our *seed (thoughts)* forever. But, what are we seeing? Are we seeing trouble on every side, inharmony, lack, imperfection of body and affairs? Or are we seeing wholeness, abundance, and divine right action? What we are seeing becomes very important because "all the land which thou seest, to thee will I give it. . . ."

Because Lot could see only material gain, he settled for the area in which the principal cities were Sodom and Gomorrah. Eventually he was taken captive by the wicked people (thought people) of Sodom and had to be rescued by his uncle (faith).

O, it is so important what we are seeing for ourselves! Are we always looking for trouble? A woman was seated in a crowded restaurant. A man went by and accidentally stumbled against her foot. He told me later that he could not imagine how it had happened as he didn't see her foot anywhere near him. As he went back to apologize, he heard her muttering to herself, "Somebody kicked me! Someone is always kicking me!" She had a consciousness of being kicked. This was all that she could *see.*

Have you ever heard a person say, "Life is just one blow after another!" Since that is what they are *seeing* for themselves, it will be so.

I know a woman who has a champagne taste and a beer pocketbook. This is hard on her because she cannot accept enough out of life to provide for herself in the style in which she would like to be accustomed. Here is a person with tremendous potential, talent, ability, charm; and yet, she has never been able to earn more than fifty dollars a week, and each position that starts out in high enthusiasm soon ends with disappointment for herself and her employer. This has become a habit, all that she can see.

Abraham Meets the Test of Faith

In chapter fifteen of the book of Genesis, we find the key to Abraham's success.

> After these things the word of the Lord came unto Abram in a vision, saying, Fear not, Abram: I am thy shield, and thy exceeding great reward.
> And Abram said, Lord God, what wilt thou give me, seeing I go childless, and the steward of my house is this Eliezer of Damascus? —Genesis 15:1, 2

Here the *Lord,* the *divine Law of Good,* tells Abram that It is his "shield" (protection), and his "reward"—an "exceeding great reward"—all that he needs and more. But Abram at first finds it hard to accept this good news. To him, as to any Hebrew patriarch, to be childless was to be a complete failure, and Abram says the "steward of my house [the keeper of my consciousness] is this Eliezer of Damascus?" "Eliezer" means *God of help* and "Damascus," *sack of blood.* He therefore says to the Lord that he is just a human being trusting in God to help him. Ah, but this humility is the beginning of faith.

With this step in the direction of an expanding faith, the Lord promises that he will not go childless and verse six is the key verse in the entire chapter: "And he believed in the LORD; and he counted it to him for righteousness." [6]

6. Genesis 15:6.

He believed in the divine Law of Life and that the right use of the Law was working for him to bring right action into his affairs.

The Lord Renames Abram and Sarai

Because Abram had been faithful in following God's Guidance and walking in the light as it had been given to him, the Lord came to him in a vision and changed his name and that of his wife (subconscious or feeling side) from Abram to Abraham and from Sarai to Sarah.

> Neither shall thy name any more be called Abram, but thy name shall be Abraham; for a father of many nations have I made thee.
> And I will make thee exceeding fruitful, and I will make nations of thee, and kings shall come out of thee.
>
> .   .   .
>
> And God said unto Abraham, As for Sarai thy wife, thou shalt not call her name Sarai, but Sarah shall her name be.
> And I will bless her, and give thee a son also of her: yea, I will bless her, and she shall be a mother of nations; kings of people shall be of her. —Genesis 17:5, 6, 15, 16

Since *name* in the Bible always refers to *nature,* we see at once that *the nature has changed.* Abram and Sarai have, you might say, won their spurs, passed the test, graduated to a new level of awareness. They are now entitled to be called *Abraham* which means *father of the multitude,* and *Sarah* which means *princess,* and the Lord tells them that kings shall come out of their union. Their nature, both conscious and subconscious, has now been raised, and they portray the faith that is the beginning of a multitude of powerful thoughts. *Kings* denote *ruling thoughts* or *thoughts of dominion,* as do *princesses.* Abraham and Sarah now show forth the faith that moves mountains, and anything can happen with such faith. Still, they can't quite accept the miracle that is to follow. What a challenge to anyone's faith! Shall a couple almost a hundred years old have a child of their own?

Abraham Laughed, Sarah Laughed, and God Laughed

So the Lord tells them that they are going to be blessed with a son. Abraham, the Bible tells us, fell on his face—he must have laughed pretty hard!

> Then Abraham fell upon his face, and laughed, and said in his heart, Shall a child be born unto him that is an hundred years old? and shall Sarah, that is ninety years old, bear?
> And Abraham said unto God, O that Ishmael might live before thee! —Genesis 17:17, 18

How like all of us! We want to trust God, to believe that with God all things are possible, still it seems simpler and easier to trust in the things that we can perceive with the five senses. Abraham already had Ishmael by the obvious means of taking Sarah's young handmaid Hagar. Furthermore, maybe Abraham had misunderstood God, maybe God meant Ishmael. Ishmael represents personality or judging by human standards, but the son that is promised stands for the Christ consciousness, or spirit individualized through faith.

> And God said, Sarah thy wife shall bear thee a son indeed; and thou shalt call his name Isaac: and I will establish my covenant with him for an everlasting covenant, and with his seed after him.
> And as for Ishmael, I have heard thee: Behold, I have blessed him, and will make him fruitful, and will multiply

him exceedingly; twelve princes shall he beget, and I will make him a great nation.

But my covenant will I establish with Isaac, which Sarah shall bear unto thee at this set time in the next year.

—Genesis 17:19–21

Which is to say, that the role of personality is not to be condemned or belittled. It has its place, too, as the son of man; the true son is the son of God, spiritual man, who is the heir to the kingdom, the Christ consciousness.

So Abraham had a son by Hagar, the handmaid, but God explains that He didn't mean it that way. God meant that Abraham was to have a son, a thought springing from his true spiritual union. In the story, this is almost too much for Abraham to accept.

Abraham laughed. Shall I, Abraham, who is an hundred years old and Sarah, who is ninety, have a son? Then Sarah was visited by the Lord, the Voice, which came to her and told her that she was to give birth to a son, and Sarah laughed, too. Sarah had to be convinced. Three angels (messengers of God, spiritual thoughts) had to visit Sarah and Abraham before they would believe that this impossible thing could come to pass. Well, you know, this is the way it happens with us. These allegories are for the purpose of showing, in a highly dramatic way, how God can do the impossible through us. Finally, one of the angels said again that Sarah was to give birth to a son and again Sarah laughed.

And he said, I will certainly return unto thee according to the time of life; and, lo, Sarah thy wife shall have a son. And Sarah heard it in the tent door, which was behind him.

Now Abraham and Sarah were old and well stricken in age; and it ceased to be with Sarah after the manner of women.

Therefore Sarah laughed within herself, saying, After I am waxed old shall I have pleasure, my lord being old also?

And the Lord said unto Abraham, Wherefore did Sarah laugh, saying, Shall I of a surety bear a child, which am old?

Is any thing too hard for the Lord? At the time appointed I will return unto thee, according to the time of life, and Sarah shall have a son.

Then Sarah denied, saying, I laughed not; for she was afraid. And he said, Nay; but thou didst laugh.

—Genesis 18:10–15

Nothing Is Impossible to God

How many times our desires seem impossible. We fail to see how they can be fulfilled because of the way things appear in the relative world. Then we hear God say to us, "is anything too hard for me?"

Jesus emphasized this: "With men this is impossible; but with God all things are possible"; and "If thou canst believe, all things are possible to him that believeth." [7]

Many times we are tempted to think that miracles are just coincidents, that they would have happened without God's help. So the Bible makes it so farfetched that there can be no doubt that divine intervention has taken place.

God Has the Last Laugh!

A son is born to Abraham and Sarah as God promised and is named, guess what? *God laughed!* The meaning of Isaac is *God laughed!*

And the Lord visited Sarah as he had said, and the Lord did unto Sarah as he had spoken.

For Sarah conceived, and bare Abraham a son in his old age, at the set time of which God had spoken to him.

7. Matthew 19:26; Mark 9:23.

And Abraham called the name of his son that was born unto him, whom Sarah bare to him, Isaac.

And Abraham circumcised his son Isaac being eight days old, as God had commanded him.

And Abraham was an hundred years old, when his son Isaac was born unto him.

And Sarah said, God hath made me to laugh, so that all that hear will laugh with me. —Genesis 21:1–6

You know, when we start thinking about these seemingly impossible challenges, about things being insurmountable, we get so deadly serious. If we could just laugh about them. If we could just take this attitude—all right, they say it can't be done and to all appearances it can't be done, but divine Intelligence knows it can be done. The bumble bee, scientifically, is judged not able to fly, but it does. I know women who, according to medical science, were supposed to have been unable to bear children, but they did. I have known people who were in the last stages of terminal cancer, supposed to pass on in a matter of days, and all of a sudden they were healed and all evidence of the disease had left them. I know of so many miracles that they have ceased to astound me. I know, from experience, that nothing is too hard for God.

We see the impossible today all around us, that which would have seemed impossible just a few years ago. Who would have thought thirty years ago that we, in the United States, would be sitting in our living rooms watching an event taking place in England! Imagine, pictures taken simultaneously in London; transmitted in such a way as to bounce the impulses off Telestar, a man-made satellite in orbit several hundred miles above the earth. To think that the impulses could be picked up at a receiving station in this country! They are then transmitted by cable to sending stations throughout the country so that people in the United States can witness a great event taking place in England via Telestar. God must have laughed again. To men, it was impossible just a short time before, to God it was possible all of the time.

Isaac was circumcised, according to Jewish tradition, but circumcision has a rich spiritual meaning and much is said throughout the Bible of its spiritual significance. It means the cutting off of mortal tendencies and is indicative of purification. It signifies turning away from the materialistic concept and that the regeneration is of the spirit, not the flesh. Therefore, we have the word used thusly:

> And the Lord thy God will circumcise thine heart, and the heart of thy seed, to love the Lord thy God with all thine heart, and with all thy soul, that thou mayest live.
> —Deuteronomy 30:6
>
> Circumcise yourselves to the Lord, and take away the foreskins of your heart, ye men of Judah and inhabitants of Jerusalem. . . . —Jeremiah 4:4
>
> Circumcise therefore the foreskin of your heart, and be no more stiffnecked. —Deuteronomy 10:16

Abraham's Great Moment of Faith— Faith Made Perfect

". . . Faith, if it hath not works, is dead. . . ." [8] Abraham not only trusted God, but was willing to act on his faith. Too often people give lip service to their faith, but are not willing to do something about it. Faith without works is dead, for faith and works are two ends of the same stick.

> Even so faith, if it hath not works, is dead, being alone.
> Yea, a man may say, Thou hast faith, and I have works:

8. James 2:17.

shew me thy faith without thy works, and I will shew thee my faith by my works.

Thou believest that there is one God; thou doest well: the devils also believe, and tremble.

But wilt thou know, O vain man, that faith without works is dead?

Was not Abraham our father justified by works, when he had offered Isaac his son upon the altar?

Seest thou how faith wrought with his works, and by works was faith made perfect?

And the scripture was fulfilled which saith, Abraham believed God, and it was imputed unto him for righteousness: and he was called the Friend of God.

Ye see then how that by works a man is justified, and not by faith only. —James 2:17–24

It seems that Paul wasn't the only one who was impressed by the dramatic story of the proving of Abraham's faith.

By faith Abraham, when he was tried, offered up Isaac: and he that had received the promises offered up his only begotten son,

Of whom it was said, That in Isaac shall thy seed be called.
—Hebrews 11:17, 18

Did ever a man have a greater test of faith? Here was Abraham called upon to sacrifice Isaac as a burnt offering, Isaac the son of his old age, whose birth was a miracle. How dearly Abraham must have loved this boy, and the promise was that through Isaac, Abraham would be the father of nations. Abraham did not question. He did not stand back and say, "Wait a minute, this is carrying this trust and faith business a little bit too far." The story is fraught with tension and emotion. Picture the boy following his father up the mountain, the wood for the fire strapped to his back. And then he asks his father, "Where is the lamb for the burnt offering?"

And it came to pass after these things, that God did tempt Abraham, and said unto him, Abraham: and he said, Behold, here I am.

And he said, Take now thy son, thine only son Isaac, whom thou lovest, and get thee into the land of Moriah; and offer him there for a burnt offering upon one of the mountains which I will tell thee of. —Genesis 22:1, 2

So Abraham, obedient in his faith, rose early the next morning and saddled his ass and took two young men and Isaac with him. He departed without any question as God had instructed him. On the way, he cut the wood. And "on the third day Abraham . . . saw the place afar off" that God had designated. So Abraham told the young men to wait there while he and Isaac went to worship. Now he strapped the wood on Isaac's back and "he took the fire in his hand, and a knife. . . ."

And Isaac spake unto Abraham his father, and said, My father: and he said, Here am I, my son. And he said, Behold the fire and the wood: but where is the lamb for the burnt offering?

And Abraham said, My son, God will provide himself a lamb for a burnt offering: so they went both of them together.

And they came to the place which God had told him of; and Abraham built an altar there, and laid the wood in order, and bound Isaac his son, and laid him on the altar upon the wood.

And Abraham stretched forth his hand, and took the knife to slay his son.

And the angel of the Lord called unto him out of heaven, and said, Abraham, Abraham: and he said, Here am I.

And he said, Lay not thine hand upon the lad, neither do thou any thing unto him: for now I know that thou fearest God, seeing thou hast not withheld thy son, thine only son from me.

And Abraham lifted up his eyes, and looked, and behold behind him a ram caught in a thicket by his horns: and Abraham went and took the ram, and offered him up for a burnt offering in the stead of his son.

And Abraham called the name of that place Jehovah-jireh [the Lord will provide]. . . . —Genesis 22:7–14

Once one starts out to trust God completely, he has to be willing to follow where God leads and to know that God will provide the right answer. The great temptation is to feel that you have to know the end before you start out on the journey, the result being that the journey in faith is never even begun. Each one of us has some protective area in his life, something that is just as important to him as Isaac was to Abraham and sooner or later, he must be willing to sacrifice it if necessary. Just as with Abraham, once he has put his treasure second to God, he is not called upon to sacrifice it.

This story may seem to you to be just another one of those gory Bible stories. If so, you have missed its inner meaning. The key is that it shows a radical, total trust in the infinite Intelligence and Power within us. Too often we say, "I will believe *if,* I will trust *if,* I will accept this *if.*" But if we can reverse that and say, "All right, I know that there is That within me which knows, That within me which is able to do all things and is everywhere present. I trust It implicitly to do the right thing in the right way for my highest good and that of everyone else," we have the faith that taps the great Power.

In the New Testament we find, by way of contrast, the story of what happens to one who refuses to trust God all the way. The rich young man seemed to have faith but was not willing to act upon it. He trusted his wealth more than he trusted God.

A young man came to Jesus and asked him what good thing

he should do to have eternal life. Jesus told him to keep all of the Commandments.

> The young man saith unto him, All these things have I kept from my youth up: what lack I yet?
>
> Jesus said unto him, If thou wilt be perfect, go and sell that thou hast, and give to the poor, and thou shalt have treasure in heaven: and come and follow me.
>
> But when the young man heard that saying, he went away sorrowful: for he had great possessions. —Matthew 19:20–22

Jesus, out of the great understanding that he possessed, saw at once that the young man worshipped his wealth, and that before he could find the inner peace, he must be willing to give up the material possessions which he was putting before God. Many of us have been rich young men, not necessarily rich in money but rich in pride, in willfulness, in supersensitiveness, in attention-getting, etc. Anything that stands between you and your God is a false god and sooner or later must be sacrificed.

Abraham Shows Us the Way Today

Once we have understood the deeper implication of the story of Abraham, nothing in this life can ever again confound us. For now that we know that we have right within us the invincible Power of God, we can go forth, never doubting, and possess the land, that consciousness that is sure to outpicture as everything we can ever need. We now are certain that there is nothing too hard for God within us to overcome, that nothing is impossible to God; and that even if our dearest possession is threatetned, we can trust God without knowing how it will all work out. Yes, trust the invisible Power of

God within us right up to the final challenge, knowing with assurance that the God of Abraham will provide. And afterwards we, too, will call the very memory of the place of our victory "Jehovah-Jireh"—the Lord will provide!

IX   JACOB EXPLAINS THE
MEANING OF THE TRINITY

Genesis, Chapters 25–33

The story of Jacob as it begins in the twenty-fifth chapter of Genesis seems to be the tale of a first-class heel. Here is a man who would stoop so low as to cheat his own brother out of his birthright, a mother's boy who conspires with his mother to deceive his aging father. It is no wonder that many Bible students, considering the narrative only from its literal implications, decide that Esau was by far the better man and that, by rights, he should have the honors and the authority bestowed upon Jacob. "Well, such is life!" they say. "There is no justice! The wicked always seem to flourish and cheaters prosper in this life!"

It Takes an Open Mind

We must have an open mind and be willing to accept the story of Jacob as an allegory, actually a continuation of the Abraham allegory, if we are to understand its true meaning.

Looking beneath the surface meaning at the esoteric meaning of the story reveals an understanding of the deep significance of the much misunderstood Trinity of Life. The story

105

of Jacob is the unfolding in consciousness of man's mental growth whereby he is able to take dominion over the material world through the use of his mind, evolving finally after a struggle between the two sides of his dual nature into the spiritual being he was meant to be.

The Power of the Mind

This dramatic episode really starts with grandfather Abraham. The history of Abraham, you will remember, is the story of the unfoldment of faith in the invisible Power of God. Abraham shows us that faith coupled with obedience can accomplish all things, that nothing is impossible to God.

Abraham is called the *father of the multitude* and it is said that *his seed shall inherit the earth.* This is true. Jacob is that *seed,* and you will see that ideas springing from the Abraham consciousness do "inherit the earth"; that is, faith takes dominion over the earth through Jacob. Faith is the beginning of everything. Through faith, the soul evolves until at last it is revealed as Israel, *the prince of God,* heir to all that God is.

The link between Abraham and Jacob is Isaac, the child who was miraculously born to Abraham and Sarah in their old age. "And Abraham gave all that he had unto Isaac." [1]

To be sure, Abraham gave all that he had to Isaac for Isaac represents a thought springing from the consciousness of faith, established faith, faith that has been proved and found effective. Isaac is *that thought of laughter and inner joy, the laughter of God within us, an exultant God, the awareness of eternal good.* It follows that Isaac is joined with Rebekah, whose name stands for *the beauty in life.* Together they form the perfect marriage.

1. Genesis 25:5.

And Isaac intreated the Lord for his wife, because she was barren: and the Lord was intreated of him, and Rebekah his wife conceived.

And the children struggled together within her; and she said, If it be so, why am I thus? And she went to enquire of the Lord.

And the Lord said unto her, Two nations are in thy womb, and two manner of people shall be separated from thy bowels; and the one people shall be stronger than the other people; and the elder shall serve the younger.

—Genesis 25:21–23

The union of Isaac and Rebekah (beauty and joy) is blessed with twins. Esau, the one who came first, was *red, rough, hairy, shaggy,* we discover through the Hebrew meaning of his name. Jacob's name means *the supplanter.* The twins are described as struggling together even in the womb, "Two nations," "two manner of people," and the prophecy is that one shall be stronger than the other and that the elder shall serve the younger.

These are the twins struggling within each one of us. Esau, the earthy one, represents that side of man which Paul called the *carnal mind.* It is called by some, *the human mind;* by others, *materialistic thinking.* It is that side of man which is interested primarily with the material, the physical body, the body comforts, the outer effects of life. It comes first for it is the side of life of which we are first aware; but Jacob follows close after, "his hand took hold on Esau's heel. . . ." At first, Jacob, representing *the mental side of life,* does not want to let the *mortal, material* side get away from him. He hangs on. Don't we all? Jacob is described as "a plain man, dwelling in tents" and Esau as "a cunning hunter, a man of the field. . . ." The Hebrew meaning of Jacob is *the supplanter,* that mind in each one of us which supplants the *carnal mind.* The twins, then, are the physical and mental side of each one of us.

The Mystery of the Trinity

In order to understand the story, we must look ahead and take into consideration the fact that Jacob later becomes Israel. That is, his name is changed because his nature has changed. Israel is the *spiritual side, the prince of God.* This is the story of the unfoldment of spiritual consciousness in man: how man, a triune being, first recognizes himself as a physical body, then as a mental being having intellectual powers, and finally as a spiritual being, the enlightened son of God.

Jacob Usurps Esau's Birthright

Esau, described in the Bible as "red, all over like an hairy garment . . ." was a cunning hunter. Esau was his father's favorite and Jacob, we are told, hung around his mother's tent.

One day Esau came in from hunting and was exceedingly hungry. True to form, Esau (the human mind) could not wait for his good. He must have his substance, his pottage, right now, and so he begged Jacob to give him some of the red pottage that he had made.

> And Esau said to Jacob, Feed me, I pray thee, with that same red pottage; for I am faint: therefore was his name called Edom. —Genesis 25:30

Again the Scripture tells us his nature, *of the earth, earthy,* for that is the meaning of Edom. It is interesting to note that the physical side of man is described as a glutton, interested primarily in filling his stomach. The mental side will gladly go without food to feed the mind, but, interestingly enough, it is the mental side of each one of us that provides the sustenance for the body and in this very way takes dominion over the physical.

Jacob, in the allegory, made Esau promise to sell him his birthright for the pottage. Esau said that it made no difference as he was about to die from hunger anyway, and so he promised his birthright and all that went with it as the elder son of the house. Thus Esau sold his birthright to Jacob for a mess of lentil soup.

Later on, when the eyes of Isaac grew dim with age, he called Esau to him and told him to get some venison and bring it to him and he would bless him before he died. Rebekah overheard this conversation between her firstborn and his father. She, then, plotted with Jacob, her favorite, to fool his father by pretending that he was Esau. Together they fixed some savory goat meat and dressed Jacob up in some hairy goat skins to make him hairy like Esau. At first Isaac questioned Jacob, but, finally, he was convinced and Jacob got the blessing that was intended for the firstborn. When Esau discovered what had happened, he hated Jacob and he said, ". . . Is not he rightly named Jacob? for he hath supplanted me these two times. . . ." Esau swore to kill Jacob. And so his mother, to protect Jacob, sent him to her brother Laban in Haran.

The Soul's Development

According to the literal interpretation of the Bible, Jacob has always been considered a thief who stole the birthright and the blessing from his elder brother Esau. Metaphysically, we see now, that Jacob is but the transitional state of the expanding mentality that evolves from considering itself strictly a physical being to the awareness of sonship. This is what Paul was talking about.

And so it is written, The first man Adam [human man] was made a living soul; the last Adam [the Christ man] was made a quickening spirit.

Howbeit that was not first which is spiritual, but that which is natural; and afterward that which is spiritual.

The first man is of the earth, earthy: the second man is the Lord from heaven. —I Corinthians 15:45–47

It is natural for each one of us to consider himself at first as a human, depending only upon human resources. The awakened intellect supplants this limited viewpoint and teaches us how to use the law of cause and effect, the Jacob consciousness. It is the stepping stone to the Israel, or prince of God, awareness. And so we have the trinity.

This reminds me of a motto I once saw in the office of a friend—"Little minds talk about people. Ordinary minds talk about events. Great minds talk about ideas."

This is another way of defining the steps in the unfoldment from Esau to Israel.

1. Esau was interested in venison and red pottage to fill his stomach.

2. Jacob was interested in using his mind to achieve dominion over the physical world.

3. Israel accepts the God-given dominion and is able to make peace between Esau and Jacob at last.

While the soul within us sleeps to its divine potential, we live on the animal plane and resent the mental which seeks to displace the physical. There is within each one of us the conflict between the mental and the physical that vie with one another and often hate and fear each other.

Esau swore to kill *the supplanter* (Jacob). The Esau consciousness knows only to destroy that which threatens it. And so we have wars. Whenever we feel that we must get in and fight, to physically overthrow that which opposes us, we are letting the Esau consciousness rule. The Jacob consciousness uses reason and even mental cunning to win its ends. This is ordained by the Lord (the Law) for He told Rebekah that "the one people shall be stronger than the other people; and the elder shall serve the younger." The materialistic side in us always resents the mental. This battle between Esau and Jacob continues until Jacob becomes Israel. And so it is with each one of us. The Esau nature bows to the spiritual side only. There is a continuous warfare between the materialistic and intellectual side of man until at last he is willing to accept the Grace of God which is freely given to all those who know themselves as sons of God.

A Spiritual Milestone in the Growth of Jacob

After Jacob received his father's blessing, he was sent on his way to Haran. Both his father and his mother, the consciousness of beauty and of joy, wish him Godspeed as he departs on his spiritual journey.

You will understand this allegory better if you will read the story in the Bible and translate it through an understanding of the following key words:

Padan-aram—a plateau in consciousness; a broad level place in the evolving consciousness.

Bethuel—abiding in the awareness of God.

stones—truth at any level; here it is intellectual Truth.

earth—the limited human consciousness.

heaven—the Universal infinite consciousness; divine Mind.

angels—God's messengers; divine inspiration; highest thoughts.

Bethel—house of God or God consciousness.

Haran—an exalted state of consciousness.

Laban—a white clear shining thought.

Canaan—lowlands of the mind.

The Jacob consciousness, having overcome the physical consciousness, now removes itself from the environment of the physical and departs on a spiritual journey for Haran, *an exalted state of consciousness.* He goes to be with Laban whose name means *a white, clear, shining thought.* Therefore, it is not at all strange that he goes by way of Padan-aram because Padan-aram means *a plateau in consciousness, a broad level place in man's evolving consciousness.*

Jacob, the mentality, is advised not to take a wife from Canaan, *the lowlands of the mind.* How could he? The wife of a man in the Bible always stands for the feeling or emotional nature and the Jacob consciousness has already evolved from the lowlands of the mind. Esau, the physical side, gets his wife from *the lowlands of the mind.* Canaan is Lot's country and Lot relates to *dark negative thinking.* Jacob, the ever expanding intellect, goes on to the consciousness of Abraham and Isaac, his father. He starts out for Haran. This is his goal as it must always be our goal—*an exalted state of consciousness.* His wife, *his feeling nature,* must be from the daughters of Laban, an offspring of *clear, shining thought,* an emotion only to be found in the *house (consciousness) of Bethuel,* meaning abiding in an *awareness of God.* On the way, he experiences a spiritual milestone in his journey from physical to spiritual awareness.

And Jacob went out from Beer-sheba, and went toward Haran.

And he lighted upon a certain place, and tarried there all night, because the sun was set; and he took of the stones of that place, and put them for his pillows, and lay down in that place to sleep.

And he dreamed, and behold a ladder set up on the earth, and the top of it reached to heaven: and behold the angels of God ascending and descending on it.

And, behold, the Lord stood above it, and said, I am the Lord God of Abraham thy father, and the God of Isaac: the land whereon thou liest, to thee will I give it, and to thy seed; —Genesis 28:10–13

The story tells us that "he lighted upon a certain place . . ." and lay down to sleep when "the sun was set . . ." He stopped in his spiritual journey as the light seemed to fail and there he meditated on the Truth. Stone in the Bible is always the symbol of Truth. He laid his head, his intelligence, on the Truth. As he rested on the Truth, a new understanding was revealed to him and, in a dream, he was given the illumination that he needed. He had a dream of angels ascending and descending on a ladder that reached to heaven and the Lord stood at the top of the ladder and made him a promise. The Lord said:

I am the Lord God of Abraham thy father, and the God of Isaac: the land whereon thou liest, to thee will I give it, and to thy seed;

And thy seed shall be as the dust of the earth, and thou shalt spread abroad to the west, and to the east, and to the north, and to the south: and in thee and in thy seed shall all the families of the earth be blessed.

And, behold, I am with thee, and will keep thee in all places whither thou goest, and will bring thee again into this land; for I will not leave thee, until I have done that which I have spoken to thee of. —Genesis 28:13–15

The great lesson here is that there is an interplay between the higher and the lower, the thoughts of God and the thoughts of man. This is an experience one may attain in deep meditation. To the Jacob consciousness, representing *the intellect,* this means something. The great revelation is that it is possible for the Jacob mentality to ascend step by step as on a ladder to an exalted spiritual consciousness. At the highest point on the ladder of spiritual realization, the Voice is heard giving the same promise that was given to Abraham and Isaac, "the land whereon thou liest, to thee will I give it, and to thy seed." This is the divine promise that all that we can conceive of, believe in, and accept for ourselves will be ours. The blessing that Jacob receives in this vision is the realization, the glad knowing, that God is in charge. This is the release that comes when our thoughts ascend as on a ladder upward to *the inner awareness of the Presence of God,* and we listen to the spiritual inspiration that comes back to us. It is the promise that our ascended thoughts will always be productive or fruitful.

The mentality that awakes to this Truth is greatly awed. "How dreadful is this place!" cries Jacob. This expression is like the *fear of the Lord* which in Bible terminology means *to stand in awe of the divine Law and the way it works.* It is a Power so formidable that one might well fear it if he misuses it. What an awesome thought this is to every one of us. To think that we house the living God and that our minds are the gateway to spiritual dominion. The mind of man is the mouth of God. It is here that God speaks to man. It is here that we receive the omnipotent Power. We are almost afraid to think of the Power that indwells us.

"And Jacob awaked out of his sleep, . . ." out of the darkness. The awakened mentality perceives that it makes no difference where one is, God is there; yes, even though we do not know it, God is right where we are. Jacob gives us a perfect affirmation in time of stress: ". . . Surely the Lord is in this place; and I knew it not." This is that wonderful realization of the mind that recognizes the Omnipresence of the divine Law. It is "My Father worketh hitherto, and I work" of Jesus. It is finding that even in darkness, God is there.

If I say, Surely the darkness shall cover me; even the night shall be light about me.

Yea, the darkness hideth not from thee; but the night shineth as the day: the darkness and the light are both alike to thee. —Psalms 139:11, 12

The recognition "surely the Lord is in this place . . ." is the beginning of the way out in any problem. The superstitious separate themselves from God, but this is false. God is everywhere present even though we know it not.

Jacob was greatly awed when he realized that he was in the house of God and said:

How dreadful is this place! this is none other but the house of God, and this is the gate of heaven.

And Jacob rose up early in the morning, and took the stone that he had put for his pillows, and set it up for a pillar, and poured oil upon the top of it.

And he called the name of that place Beth-el: but the name of that city was called Luz at the first.

And Jacob vowed a vow, saying, If God will be with me, and will keep me in this way that I go, and will give me bread to eat, and raiment to put on,

So that I come again to my father's house in peace; then shall the Lord be my God:

And this stone, which I have set for a pillar, shall be God's house: and of all that thou shalt give me I will surely give the tenth unto thee. —Genesis 28:17–22

Now, how could anyone take this literally. What literal meaning could there be to pouring oil on a rock and how could that rock be considered a house of God. Let's see what it means according to our secret code.

Annointing with oil in the Bible means to consecrate, to identify with God. The pillar is a new awareness of God that will always be consecrated or dedicated to God. As the expanding mentality awakes to Truth, it sets Truth upright and consecrates it; that is, it gives great emphasis to Truth.

This place in mind is Bethel, the conscious awareness of the Presence of God. Here Jacob makes a vow that he will trust God from now on and will look to God for spiritual ideas and inspiration. The bread by which we live is the word of God, our spiritual substance, and the clothes are the divine thoughts with which God surrounds us.

Jacob wants to be sure that he will come back again to the "father's house," this same wonderful realization of the eternal Presence, God. Here the "father's house" has the same meaning as the "father's house" in the parable of the prodigal son. In the "father's house" there is enough and to spare. My son, "all that I have is thine."

We have here the unification of Spirit, Mind, and Body which might be called one of the earliest instances of Cosmic Consciousness, the awareness that Jesus called "I and my Father are one."

The Jacob mentality has not yet fully arrived at Christ Consciousness, *Israel,* but it has glimpsed this higher awareness and is on its way.

The promise to give a tenth represents a great spiritual victory. Jacob is not the only one in the Bible who arrives at this point of spiritual growth. It is a milestone that sooner or later all of us reach as we grow in consciousness. The Esau consciousness wants only to get, to fill the belly with pottage, but the enlightened Jacob consciousness has recognized its true Source and so can afford to be generous in giving back to God a tenth of all that God gives so abundantly. Tithing is an act of faith that comes with spiritual growth.

Consciousness Unfolding

Then Jacob went on his journey, and came into the land of the people of the east.

And he looked, and behold a well in the field, and, lo, there were three flocks of sheep lying by it; for out of that well they watered the flocks: and a great stone was upon the well's mouth. —Genesis 29:1, 2

Jacob consciousness in its unfolding process comes into a land (consciousness) of inner awareness. The East always stands for the inner experience and the people in the Bible are always the thoughts of that particular land or consciousness. Jacob's well is the deep well of inspiration that comes to Jacob consciousness at this stage of its unfoldment. Out of this inspiration, the flocks (thoughts) were watered (inspired). Guarding every well of inspiration there is a great stone (Truth). It is returned to protect the well lest it become adulterated or contaminated.

Jacob's romance with Rachel begins at the well. Rachel keeps her father's sheep, *pure thoughts of Laban whose name means white, shining thought.* Therefore, Rachel, who appeals to Jacob on sight, is the pure feeling that springs from the glorious Laban consciousness and it is not surprising that she guards the sheep, *thoughts of Laban.* Rachel's name means *a lamb* and in its illumined state, such purity is immediately appealing to the Jacob consciousness.

Jacob must have fallen in love with Rachel at first sight, for the Bible tells us that he kissed her at that first meeting and "lifted up his voice, and wept." Rachel ran and told her father that Jacob was here and Laban came at once and greeted him and took him home with him for a month's visit. At the end of the visit, Laban asked Jacob what he wanted for wages. Now it seems that Laban had two daughters, Leah, the elder, and Rachel, the younger. Rachel was beautiful and well favored, and Jacob loved Rachel. Jacob offered to serve Laban for seven years for Rachel.

> And Jacob served seven years for Rachel; and they seemed unto him but a few days, for the love he had to her.
>
> —Genesis 29:20

The number seven means finished, completed, and signifies a completed time in the unfolding process. Apparently the unfolding Jacob consciousness was not yet ready to receive the purity represented here by Rachel. So many times we think that we are ready to receive the answer to our prayers. It seems that we have served *seven years* and yet there is spiritual growth still required of us before we are able to accept our good. So it must have been with Jacob.

Laban Tricks Jacob

At the end of the time when he came to collect his "wages," Laban pulled a sleight of hand and gave him the elder daughter, Leah, instead. He substituted Leah in such a way that Jacob did not know it until the next morning. This annoyed Jacob who felt that he had been tricked. When he confronted Laban, he was told that it was the custom to marry off the firstborn daughter before the younger. Laban offered to give him Rachel also if he would serve him another seven years. Jacob agreed to this and they were married. All told, Jacob had twelve sons by Leah and Rachel and their handmaids Zilpah and Bilhah. These twelve sons became the founding fathers of the twelve tribes of Israel.

The number twelve, as used throughout the Bible, is the symbol of spiritual fulfillment. Ultimately the offspring of Jacob are to stand for the very highest in spiritual consciousness representing the twelve aspects of complete spiritual fulfillment. Israel is the *awareness of being a son of God*. The twelve tribes are the inherited spiritual attributes within the perfect man of God. This is the high goal that Jacob was eventually to attain, but the journey was long and oftentimes disappointing. This is portrayed by the fact that after he had faithfully served the seven years for Rachel, he was tricked by Laban who substituted Leah whose name (nature) means *weary, faint, exhausted*. So Jacob served Laban, *those clear shining thoughts* with which he was associated, for seven more years in exchange for the two daughters Leah and Rachel. They stand for the two sides of his feeling or emotional nature.

Jacob Faces Esau

Jacob is still afraid of Esau, the unfolding Jacob consciousness is still uneasy about its relationship with the physical side of its nature as portrayed by its twin, Esau. However, at this point of awareness, it seeks to make peace with the physical side, to be reunited.

> And Jacob went on his way, and the angels of God met him.
> And when Jacob saw them, he said, This is God's host: and he called the name of that place Māhanāim.
> —Genesis 32:1, 2

Mahanaim means *two camps, two hosts*. This is very interesting. Here we have Jacob on his way to meet Esau who represents body. On the way, he meets up with God's host of angel thoughts representing spirit. Jacob, who represents the mentality, recognizes that he is *a house divided, two camps*, if he continues to fear Esau. Spirit working through mind must unify with body to become the trinity—*spirit, mind, and body, the perfect balanced Life*. At Mahanaim, duality raises its ugly head as it does whenever God's thoughts are not acceptable to man's mentality. It is interesting to note that as Jacob goes forth to meet his twin, Esau, he actually does divide his household into two camps.

And Jacob sent messengers before him to Esau his brother unto the land of Seir, the country of Edom.

And he commanded them, saying, Thus shall ye speak unto my lord Esau; Thy servant Jacob saith thus, I have sojourned with Laban, and stayed there until now:

And I have oxen, and asses, flocks, and menservants, and womenservants: and I have sent to tell my lord, that I may find grace in thy sight.

And the messengers returned to Jacob, saying, we came to thy brother Esau, and also he cometh to meet thee, and four hundred men with him.

Then Jacob was greatly afraid and distressed: and he divided the people that was with him, and the flocks, and herds, and the camels, into two bands;

And said, If Esau come to the one company, and smite it, then the other comapny which is left shall escape.

—Genesis 32:3–8

At this point, Jacob is still trying to appease the worldly consciousness, trying to impress it with possessions, still judging by appearances. He has stooped to the level of the physical and seeks on that level to meet and be reconciled with Esau. Until the mental becomes spiritual, it always caters to the physical side, to worldly possessions and worldly power. The four hundred men, like the symbols of a dream, represent what Jacob considers to be the worldly strength of Esau. "Then Jacob was greatly afraid and distressed. . . ." Approaching the problem this way, he has reason to be afraid. He has nothing to fall back on. He is trying to impress the world with his mental powers. He is not willing to trust God all the way and so, a house divided, he puts his household (*thoughts*) into *two camps*. As long as the mentality has not completely accepted the fact that all power belongeth unto God, it will continue to bow down to that which represents worldly strength and what the world calls power. We all do this over and over again until at last we come to realize that all power belongs to God. Almost all of the Bible stories bring out this same great lesson—the choice that man is given is to trust in the invisible Power of God or to trust in the seemingly obvious power of the material. Until God's Power has been proven in our experience, we are afraid to put all of our eggs in one basket and often vacillate between trusting in God and trusting in outer appearances.

Jacob's Prayer

Fortunately, in his moment of dire need, Jacob turns to God in prayer and remembers the promises that God had made to him about the continuation of the race through him and his progeny. He prays for his deliverance from Esau.

> And Jacob said, O God of my father Abraham, and God of my father Isaac, the Lord which saidst unto me, Return unto thy country, and to thy kindred, and I will deal well with thee:
> I am not worthy of the least of all the mercies, and of all the truth, which thou hast shewed unto thy servant; for with my staff I passed over this Jordan; and now I am become two bands.
> Deliver me, I pray thee, from the hand of my brother, from the hand of Esau: for I fear him, lest he will come and smite me, and the mother with the children.
> And thou saidst, I will surely do thee good, and make thy seed as the sand of the sea, which cannot be numbered for multitude. —Genesis 32:9–12

This is the surrender that must precede every answered prayer. This is letting go and letting God take over. This is the admission that man cannot survive trusting solely on human mentality. In referring to the "God" of "Abraham," he is confessing that he is willing to place the same radical reliance on the God Power as did his grandfather Abraham. This is Jacob's confession of faith. When he says "I am not worthy, . . ." he is saying as did Jesus, "of myself I can do nothing." When Jacob says ". . . I passed over this Jordan, . . ." he means that he is willing to face the judgment of his own thoughts and take the consequences. He is willing to face up to the fact that he has become "two bands," a house divided. Realizing that if he allows himself to be taken over by Esau (materialistic thinking), not only is his mind threatened but "the mother with the children," his feelings, emotions, and all of *the thoughts springing from them* which are now part of his mental household, he is now willing to trust God alone for his deliverance from the threat of Esau. And now begins the greatest experience of all in the unfolding Jacob consciousness.

Jacob's Supreme Moment

And Jacob was left alone; and there wrestled a man with him until the breaking of the day.

.   .   .

And he said, Let me go, for the day breaketh. And he said, I will not let thee go, except thou bless me.

And he said unto him, What is thy name? And he said, Jacob.

And he said, Thy name shall be called no more Jacob, but Israel: for as a prince hast thou power with God and with men, and hast prevailed.

And Jacob asked him, and said, Tell me, I pray thee, thy

name. And he said, Wherefore is it that thou dost ask after
my name? And he blessed him there.

And Jacob called the name of the place Peniel: for I have
seen God face to face, and my life is preserved.

                                        —Genesis 32:24, 26–30

This experience, the supreme moment in the life of Jacob,
appeared to take place with a man, which—as in many Bible
allegories—was God taking form as man to illustrate a great
Truth. Jacob was faced with a problem, in this case, his great
fear of Esau, but as with all of us, the adversary that he
wrestled with was the Truth that he was loathe to accept.
"Agree with thine adversary quickly," Jesus advised, "whiles
thou art in the way with him."

The adversary is ready to break off the action at any time.
The continuation of the struggle depends entirely upon the
seeker. When the adversary suggests to Jacob that they stop
because the day was breaking, Jacob replies: ". . . I will not
let thee go, except thou bless me." This was the overcoming.
There is Truth to be revealed in every problem and when
we are willing to accept it, the entire picture changes.

Now the Truth reveals the true name (nature) of Jacob:
"Thy name shall be called no more Jacob, but Israel: for as
a prince hast thou power with God and with men, and hast
prevailed." It is only at this point that Jacob accepts his divine nature and realizes that he has encountered divine
Truth. ". . . I have seen God face to face. . . ."

Something wonderful had happened to Jacob. He was not
afraid of Esau anymore. He went forth to meet him and they
greeted each other with open arms. They kissed each other.
They offered each other presents. All was forgiven.

Esau went back to Seir. Jacob went to Shalem and bought
a parcel of land and on it he built an altar and called it El-
elohe-Israel, which means, *God, the God of Israel.*

It is only when man becomes aware of his true nature as a son of God that he is able to embrace the material side and make peace with it, putting things in their rightful place.

This is what Jesus meant when he taught:

> But seek ye first the kingdom of God, and his righteousness; and all these things shall be added unto you.
>
> —Matthew 6:33

When we realize that the visible world is but the outpicturing of the invisible world of Mind, we are no longer in awe of it. Since we have dominion over the physical existence through the creative process of life we can afford to make peace with it.

The Three Levels of Consciousness Which Make Up the Trinity of Life

1. The Esau consciousness which depends upon physical force and material power.

2. The Jacob consciousness which supplants the Esau consciousness. It is continually fearful that it will be overtaken and destroyed by the Esau consciousness because it has only the mental to rely on.

3. The Israel consciousness is the Christ consciousness, or awareness of sonship. It emerges after the Jacob consciousness has faced every possible adverse situation and has overcome them all by finding God's blessing in each one, a realization that all is good because God is everywhere present.

What This Story Means to Us—a Summary

This is one of the most revealing allegories in the Bible. It reveals the unfoldment in the life of every man as he seeks to discover his true nature. Each one is seeking spiritual understanding. Each person has an innate desire to fulfill his true nature. The great psychiatrist, Dr. Carl Jung, has said that any man over the age of thirty-five who came to him for help was seeking God.

Jacob and Esau are the twins who vie within each one of us. Esau, the carnal mind, centers its attention on the things of the flesh, the material side of life. Sometimes this is called the animal in us. Jacob represents the intellectual side that seeks to overcome the animal or physical side. As man's understanding develops, the mental does supplant the physical; but the mental cannot stop for now it becomes apparent that there is further growth to be made. Jacob must become Israel.

At first, a person discovering the intellectual side of life thinks that surely this is all there is. There is such a vast storehouse of knowledge to be explored, books to be read, laws to be tried and tested. There are moments when such a little turning to the Infinite in prayer has transcended the mental and psychological laws, wiped out the sins of the past, over-ruled the laws of the mental and performed miracles. The trend is onward and upward now, out of the mental into the spiritual life. These are the steps in the divine evolution.

The Esau consciousness judges everything by appearances. It is concerned wholly with materialistic thinking. It deals not with causes, but with effects. It lives by force, pushing the effects of life around, trying to appease personalities, trying to heal bodies with medicine, being concerned over drafts, diets, and physical hygiene. At this level, we need the Ten Commandments and the civil laws of the land. There is some Esau in all of us.

And then one day we discover that there are mental laws that control the physical. "For as he thinketh in his heart, so is he." At this moment, the Jacob in us supplants Esau. The Jacob consciousness lives by the law of cause and effect. For every effect, there is a cause exactly like the effect. If you think you are poor, you will be. If you think you have poor health, you will have it. If you think that sitting in a draft will give you a cold, this will happen to you.

The Jacob consciousness is never quite sure of itself. The Jacob consciousness is fearful of what Esau can do to it. It still fears destruction by the elements, or by accidents. It fears old age. It does not entirely trust itself even though it knows that all is mind. The Jacob consciousness, discovering how the mind controls the body, applies the law of cause and effect to mental activities. It seeks to push life around through mental manipulation. It takes upon itself a great weight of responsibility. Since it has discovered this newfound power, it must now play God in the lives of men, making things happen through their own mental powers. In the mental stage, the Ten Commandments are translated into the mental meanings. One dare not even commit adultery in his mind, nor covet or steal in his mind. He must watch his thoughts constantly lest he be overcome by the Esau in himself. He divides his forces in the subconscious mind under the Leah and the Rachel consciousness. Leah is a step in the mental unfoldment, a step that has to be taken before Jacob is ready for Rachel. Rachel is a higher step along the way. Their children represent the thoughts proceeding out of the various stages of the mental growth.

Divine evolution begins with mental dominion and evolves into spiritual dominion. The Israel stage is living by Grace. This is "a more excellent way" that Paul spoke of in his letter to the Corinthians. Israel means *the awareness of the sonship, the inheritance of a prince of God.* In my father's house there is enough and to spare. The Israel consciousness no longer has to make life happen by thinking things into manifestation. It centers the attention on God and lets Life unfold through Grace into its own perfect unfoldment. Living by

Grace is going back to the Garden of Eden, that state of bliss where we eat of the fruits of the Spirit, the fruits of the "tree of life." It is rising out of human judgment into Righteous Judgment. It is being through with duality, that old seesaw of good and evil.

So it is that after Jacob wrestles with God and receives the blessing and the new name (nature) Israel, he is no longer afraid of Esau. He goes forth to meet him. Materiality is no longer an enemy, but an instrument of good. The physical world is no longer something to struggle against. God is One —Spirit, Mind, and Body. Thus there is harmony at last between Jacob and Esau. Man is a triune being and when be becomes spiritually enlightened, the three sides of his nature are in perfect balance.

X   IS EVIL NECESSARY?

JOSEPH PROVES THE POWER OF GOOD

Genesis, Chapters 37–50

The question of good and evil has perplexed philosophers and theologians down through the ages and continues to be a major issue in religious doctrine today.

Is there good and evil? What about original sin? Is man forever cursed because of Adam's fall? The Bible does not mention original sin as such. The term was devised by theologians. An understanding of this major point will help us understand the entire Bible.

Bear in mind, Adam and Eve were not the original ancestors of mankind. The story is an allegory designed to convey a Truth. The downfall of Adam had nothing to do with sex. The discovery that they were naked indicated that whereas they were formely free of judgment and condemnation, now, having partaken of the knowledge of good and evil, they began to judge themselves. They used the fig leaves to make aprons because now they had entered into human judgment.

Church doctrine may be quite impressive and can rule the thinking of many people, but it does not make a thing true. Just as there are those today who seek to lighten the load of their own guilt by finding someone whom they can brand with a greater guilt, so did our forebears find in Adam a scapegoat for their own heavy burden of sin. It is fascinating to picture the drama surrounding the birth of that famous dogma —original sin. Church politics are responsible for the age-long suffering brought about by the doctrine of original sin.

To us, this question of good and evil may seem vexing. To Pelagius, the early British theologian, it became a question of life and death—his life or his death as a heretic. Coming to Rome early in the fifth century from the monasteries of Scotland and Ireland, Pelagius found a scandalously low tone of morality prevalent. His remonstrances were met by the plea of human weakness. To remove this plea by exhibiting the actual powers of human nature became his first object. He held the following tenets to be true:

1. That Adam would have died even if he had not sinned.

2. That the sin of Adam injured himself alone, not the human race.

3. That newborn children are in the same condition in which Adam was before the fall.

4. That the whole human race does not die because of Adam's death, or sin, nor will the race rise again because of the resurrection of Jesus.

5. That the law (of the Old Testament) gives entrance to heaven as well as the gospel.

6. That even before the coming of Christ, there were men who were entirely without sin.

7. That infants, though unbaptized, have eternal life.

While it is evident that Pelagius was looking at Adam as an historic character, still it is clear that Pelagius did not consider that man was condemned by Adam's sin. The Pelagian theory was that each person was born without condemnation to sin and that each person had complete freedom of will at each moment of life to chose good or evil. Man was therefore uninjured by the sin of Adam.

It all began back at the beginning of the fifth century, as a great controversy between Pelagius and Augustine. Pelagius believed that each child was born with a clean slate. Augustine, influenced by his own doubtful past, sought to pin the blame for his own sins on Adam claiming that Adam's original sin was inherited by all who came after him and that mankind could only be saved by divine favor. Thus it all began. Augustine, the bishop of Hippo (later canonized as St. Augustine), sought to have Pelagius condemned as a heretic because he held the contrary to be true.

Augustine won, not by a competent decision, but through his ability to influence the synods of the church. So well did he play his church politics that poor Pelagius was declared a heretic. Although the Pelagian view was never proved to be erroneous the declaration was made and Augustine's self-invented view of original sin became law. From that time on, no one bothered to question whether it was right or wrong.

Every Sin Is a Mistake

Is there good and evil or is there perfect Life? When the young man came to Jesus and said, "Good master, what good thing shall I do, that I may have eternal life?," Jesus said unto him, "Why callest thou me good? There is none good but one, that is God: but if thou wilt enter into life, keep the commandments." [1] Life is whole and perfect; sin, which actually means *missing the mark,* is but a turning away from Life. Sin means *mistake,* a misuse of the divine Law of perfect Life. There are no comparisons in God for God is Absolute, unchanging Life. Good and evil have to do with the relative or the world of comparisons.

1. Matthew 19:16, 17.

Every Healing Is a Recognition of Perfect Life

Every healing of Jesus was a turning away from the illusion of good and evil to the recognition of the perfect Life of God as the only Reality. Because he understood this, he could speak with authority. He could order the man with the withered hand to stretch forth his hand because Jesus did not see a withered hand. He saw only the wholeness of Life. "Then saith he to the man, Stretch forth thine hand. And he stretched it forth; and it was restored whole, like as the other." [2]

The late Dr. Emmet Fox called this the Golden Key, to turn away from the problem, whatever it may be, and at once towards the infinite Power within which knows only divine perfection:

> As for the actual method of working, like all fundamental things, it is simplicity itself. All that you have to do is this: *Stop thinking about the difficulty, whatever it is, and think about God instead.* This is the complete rule, and if only you will do this, the trouble, whatever it is, will presently disappear.[3]

The Christ in Action

Jesus lived the Christ, divine Spirit individualized as man. He portrayed God as man as no other human being has before or since. He judged righteous judgment. His God was of "purer eyes than to behold evil . . ." and could not look upon iniquity.[4] He was the "pure in heart" [5] who see only God and healing as the inevitable result.

2. Matthew 12:13.
3. Emmet Fox, *Power Through Constructive Thinking*, New York and London: Harper & Brothers, 1940, p. 138.
4. Habakkuk 1:13.
5. Matthew 5:8.

I can of mine own self do nothing: as I hear, I judge: and my judgment is just; because I seek not mine own will, but the will of the Father which hath sent me.

. . .

Ye judge after the flesh; I judge no man.

And yet if I judge, my judgment is true: for I am not alone, but I and the Father that sent me. —John 5:30; 8:15, 16.

In each instance where the dead were raised Jesus told them to *arise*. There was the widow's son whom all believed to be dead. He was already in his casket and on his way to the burial ground when Jesus touched the casket and said, "Young man, I say unto thee, Arise." [6] Jesus refused to "eat" of the "tree of the knowledge of good and evil." To him there was no death for Life was all in all. Since Life is omnipresent, where is there room for sin, sickness, or suffering of any kind? Is it not a belief in good and evil that needs to be healed?

Joseph Refuses to Accept Evil

Joseph was the favorite son of Jacob, the son of his old age. Perhaps the mystical experiences of Jacob, now called Israel, made him appreciate Joseph more than all the rest for Joseph was also a dreamer of dreams.

Now Israel loved Joseph more than all his children, because he was the son of his old age: and he made him a coat of many colors.

And when his brethren saw that their father loved him more than all his brethren, they hated him, and could not speak peaceably unto him.

5. Luke 7:12–14.

And Joseph dreamed a dream, and he told it his brethren: and they hated him yet the more.

And he said unto them, Hear, I pray you, this dream which I have dreamed:

For behold, we were binding sheaves in the field, and, lo, my sheaf arose, and also stood upright; and, behold, your sheaves stood round about, and made obeisance to my sheaf.

And his brethren said to him, Shalt thou indeed reign over us? or shalt thou indeed have dominion over us? And they hated him yet the more for his dreams, and for his words.

And he dreamed yet another dream, and told it his brethren, and said, Behold, I have dreamed a dream more; and, behold, the sun and the moon and the eleven stars made obeisance to me.

And he told it to his father and to his brethren: and his father rebuked him, and said unto him, What is this dream that thou hast dreamed? Shall I and thy mother and thy brethren indeed come to bow down ourselves to thee to the earth,

And his brethren envied him. . . . —Genesis 37:3–11

Joseph Prospers

The brothers, being jealous of Joseph, conspired against him and would have killed him, put him in a pit and told his father that some wild beast had killed him. But Reuben persuaded them not to be quite so rash and they compromised by selling Joseph to some Ishmeelite merchants who took him into Egypt.

And Joseph was brought down to Egypt; and Potiphar, an officer of Pharaoh, captain of the guard, an Egyptian, bought him of the hands of the Ishmeelites, which had brought him down thither.

And the Lord was with Joseph, and he was a prosperous m__n; and he was in the house of his master the Egyptian.

> And his master saw that the Lord was with him, and that the Lord made all that he did to prosper in his hand.
>
> —Genesis 39:1–3

So we find that even in bondage, Joseph flourished. And now his ability to interpret dreams caused him to find great favor with Pharaoh, the ruler of Egypt.

Joseph Relies on Divine Intuition

> And Pharaoh said unto Joseph, I have dreamed a dream, and there is none that can interpret it: and I have heard say of thee, that thou canst understand a dream to interpret it.
>
> And Joseph answered Pharaoh, saying, It is not in me: God shall give Pharaoh an answer of peace.
>
> —Genesis 41:15, 16

Through God, the infinite Wisdom within him, Joseph was able to explain the dream to Pharaoh as meaning that there would be seven years of plenty and seven years of famine. Joseph advised Pharaoh to lay up a store during the years of plenty that should be sufficient to provide for the people during the years of famine. And Pharaoh was greatly pleased with Joseph.

> And the thing was good in the eyes of Pharaoh. . . .
>
> And Pharaoh said unto his servants, Can we find such a one as this is, a man in whom the Spirit of God is?
>
> And Pharaoh said unto Joseph, Forasmuch as God hath shewed thee all this, there is none so discreet and wise as thou art:
>
> Thou shalt be over my house, and according unto thy word shall all my people be ruled: only in the throne will I be greater than thou.
>
> And Pharaoh said unto Joseph, See, I have set thee over all the land of Egypt. —Genesis 41:37–41

Joseph's Dreams Realized

Even in bondage Joseph came into his own and found himself in a position, when the famine did come, to take care of
his father and brothers who had thought all these years that
he was dead. Because of Joseph's power, they did not know
him and were afraid of him, bowing down to him and declar-
ing themselves to be his servants, thus fulfilling Joseph's early
dreams. But Joseph forgave them and said,

> Now, therefore be not grieved, nor angry with yourselves,
> that ye sold me hither: for God did send me before you to
> preserve life.
>
> .   .   .
>
> And God sent me before you to preserve you a posterity in
> the earth, and to save your lives by a great deliverance.
> So now it was not you that sent me hither, but God: and
> he hath made me a father to Pharaoh, and lord of all his
> house, and a ruler throughout all the land of Egypt.
>
> .   .   .
>
> And his brethren also went and fell down before his face;
> and they said, Behold, we be thy servants.
> And Joseph said unto them, Fear not: for am I in the place
> of God?
> But as for you, ye thought evil against me; but God meant
> it unto good, to bring to pass, as it is this day, to save much
> people alive.
> Now therefore fear ye not: I will nourish you, and your
> little ones. —Genesis 45:5, 7, 8; 50:18–21

Clues to the Hidden Meanings

To understand the hidden meaning of this story, it is necessary to know that *children* stand for *thoughts springing from
the parent thought.* The people in these Bible allegories are

all states of consciousness. Joseph means *the increaser* and stands for the imaginative faculty in man. It is always the imagination that is the dreamer and interpreter of dreams. The Bible calls Joseph "a fruitful bough" and this is truly the part that imagination plays in our lives. It is through imagination that we are able to conceive of our good, accept it, and let it be created through us.

Therefore, *Joseph,* the imaginative faculty born of *Israel, the highly developed spiritual awareness,* was confident in his awareness of sonship and dared to reveal his dreams. He saw himself in a position of dominion, as indeed he should, for through imagination we are given dominion over thoughts of lack and bondage. We are clothed by our consciousness and so Joseph, imagination that is always colorful, is splendidly clothed in a coat of many colors.

The brothers of Joseph, the mundane thoughts not yet spiritually awakened resent Joseph, the dreamer of dreams, and persecute him. In the story, Joseph is sold into bondage to some traveling merchants, *thoughts concerned with materiality,* and taken down into Egypt, which means *bondage in the subconscious mind.* It is interesting to note that of these eleven other brothers, mental faculties in man, only Reuben was soft-hearted and did not want Joseph killed. Reuben is the *faculty of faith through discernment.* His name has to do with *vision.*

Egypt Always Means Bondage

Egypt denotes subconscious bondage that we create for ourselves by our own false beliefs. These old patterns of wrong thinking sink down deep into the subconscious mind and often lie dormant for long periods of time. At length they are triggered through association and give us trouble. The Bible in many different stories speaks of going "down to Egypt...."

Through Joseph, the imaginative faculty in each one, we are given dominion over the past thinking and the bondage that it has produced in our lives. Joseph, *the imaginative faculty that is undefeated*, refuses to accept bondage, feeds all of its brother thoughts and even its father thought, Jacob. Joseph, the thought of affirmative imagination springing from the mental that has been lifted up into a new spiritual dimension (Israel), is the thought that takes dominion and provides for the whole family of thoughts. Pharaoh makes him the ruler over his *house* and over all the *land* of Egypt, *dominion through consciousness*.

Why Joseph Was Given Dominion

To find dominion, Joseph must have a realization of the omnipresent Good. He cannot think of himself as being in bondage. In the story, divine Love went before him and pre-pared the way, spoke through him to Pharaoh and gave him the answers to Pharaoh's dreams. Joseph is called *the increaser,* because God, through imagination, gives the increase. Imagination is an attribute of God. All that we can conceive of, believe in, and accept for ourselves, must become our experience. Through imagination, we are liberated, cleansed of old negative patterns, and provided for richly. Like Joseph in the allegory, we, in consciousness, live in the palace of the ruler and are given dominion. Joseph saw only Good and was able to expand his consciousness of Good wherever he found himself. This was the key to his dominion, as it is to ours.

One of the interesting lessons that is brought out in this story is that Joseph never diminished his powers through hu-man judgment. No matter what adversity came to him, no matter how unjust were the circumstances that befell him, he refrained from saying *this is good or that is bad.* Only good flowed from him and only good came to him because he had a consciousness of good. He knew that even though others tried to do evil to him, they could not succeed unless he accepted evil for himself.

Pharaoh, *the sun,* is that light that we have, even in bondage, the understanding that looks to the imaginative, intuitive faculty to interpret its dreams and makes this faculty ruler over all the house, *consciousness.*

There are so many hidden Truths in this story that we cannot possibly cover them all here. Each name, each situation, has a meaning of importance. But the lesson that will be of most benefit to us is found in the words of Joseph, "But as for you, ye thought evil against me; but God meant it unto good. . . ." [7]

This is the key verse in this story of Joseph. Joseph, the constructive thought, springing from an awakened spiritual consciousness, *Israel,* refused to diminish its creativeness by judgment of good and evil. He refused to have any part of evil—". . . God meant it unto good. . . ." Because of this, everything that happened to him turned out to be for good. Each experience blessed him and, in the end, blessed his father and his brothers and all who came in contact with him. If we can take this one thought with us, it will deliver us from many a tough spot as we go through life. ". . . All things work together for good to them that love God. . . ." [8] Joseph, living by divine Law, was given his rightful heritage, dominion even in the consciousness of bondage. He was set "over all the land of Egypt."

Is evil necessary? To suppose that evil is a reality is to deny that God is omnipresent. To believe in good *and* evil is to believe in two powers and we are clearly told by the illumined of the ages that God is the only Power.

7. Genesis 50:20.
8. Romans 8:28.

There Is Nothing Good or Evil

If you spell evil backwards, the letters spell l-i-v-e. Evil is simply live turned backwards. It is the reverse of life or the misuse of the Law of Life. "There is nothing either good or evil, but thinking makes it so" is attributed to Shakespeare. It was Epictetus who said, "There is nothing good or evil save in the will." Evil, so-called, is relative. It depends upon man's judgment. What man judges evil at one time may become great good to him at another time in his experience. The experiences that he labels evil are evil solely because of the way he relates to them at the moment.

Everything must remain in harmony with God Life. The only thing that is not in harmony with perfect Life is our own reaction to it, our own imperfect judgment. *One man's meat is another man's poison.* It is considered evil to murder; yet, the same act in time of war is rewarded with medals and high acclaim. To cause suffering is considered an evil thing and we have Humane Societies for the protection of animals; yet a man who goes out into the woods and shoots or traps animals for their meat or their fur is honored as a good hunter and a good provider. The knowledge of good and evil is human judgment.

"This Also Is for Good"

An old legend from the Talmud,[9] again an example of allegorical writing, gives unusual insight into this question.

The story is about Nahum of Gamzo. He was called Nahum of Gamzo because whatever happened to him, he used to exclaim, "This also (Gamzo) is for good!"

One time the Rabbis wished to send a gift to the emperor and discussed by whom they should send it. "Let us send it

9. Rev. Dr. A. Cohen, *Everyman's Talmud, op. cit.,* p. 80.

by Nahum, the man of Gamzo," they said, "because he is used to miracles happening to him."

So they summoned Gamzo and explained the mission to him. He gladly accepted the responsibility and started on his journey. One night he slept at an inn. During the night, some men entered his room and took out of his bag the gift intended for the emperor and, in its stead, they filled the bag with dust. The next morning Nahum continued on his journey and late that day arrived at the palace of the emperor. The emperor was elated to hear that Nahum had brought him a gift, and he gathered around him all the people of the court for the celebration of the great event. We can imagine their faces when the bag was opened and was found to contain only dust. The emperor, publicly humiliated, cried, "The Jews are making a laughing-stock of me!"

He ordered Nahum to be put to death. But Nahum was noted for his unshakable faith in God and for always blessing everything for good. He said over and over, "This also is for good."

Now in the Old Testament, there are several prophets who did not die a physical death but were taken up to heaven. One of them was Elijah whose name. *Eli* plus *Jah,* means *God within is God Himself,* or *God right where you are.* Since Nahum blessed everything for good, God was right where he was. In the Talmudic stories, Elijah often appeared to help someone in great need. In this story Elijah, or *God Himself,* appears in the guise of one of the emperor's attendants and says, "Perhaps this dust is part of the dust used by their patriarch, Abraham. Whenever he threw some of it at his enemies, it turned into swords."

The emperors of those days were always waging war somewhere. At that time there happened to be a province which the emperor had been unable to conquer. So the emperor took some of the dust in the bag and threw it in the direction of his enemies, and, behold, it turned into swords and they were subdued! The emperor was overjoyed, and he took Nahum to his treasury and filled his bag with precious stones and bestowed great honor upon him.

Elijah is actually ever present, God Himself, right where we are. If we follow the technique of Nahum, the Power and Intelligence that we need will always be right where we are, ready to bless us. This is why positive thinking is so effective. Whenever we direct our thinking toward the affirmative, we are letting Elijah work in our lives. We are letting omnipresent Good express Its nature.

God Is All There Is

The entire Jewish tradition is based upon the idea that there is only One God, "The Lord our God is one Lord." [10] There is only one God, one Good, one Life, one Law. It blesses us in proportion to our acceptance of Its blessing.

Jesus pointed out that there was only one Good, God. Since God is omnipresent, all in all, over all, and through all, all is Good. God is not good as good is contrasted by the evil that man judges evil. God is Absolute Good. I love what Emerson says:

> Essence, or God, is not a relation or a part, but the whole. Being is the vast affirmative, excluding negation, self-balanced, and swallowing up all relations, parts and times within itself. [11]

When people do things to us which inconvenience, hurt, or take from us something which seems to belong to us, it is easy to blame them and to condemn life in general. Nahum

10. Deuteronomy 6:4.
11. Ralph Waldo Emerson, "Compensation," *Essays*, Boston and New York: Houghton Mifflin Company, p. 176.

had a good explanation or excuse for what had happened to the emperor's gift. He could have said, "I don't deserve the blame, really it was not my fault," but this was not his nature. He did not waste any time with negation. Instead of explaining or complaining, he said, "This also is for good." Because he blessed the situation for good, it blessed him. The loss of the emperor's gift caused him to be able to do something greater for the emperor than had first been planned by his people. As the Apostle Paul admonished his followers, "Be not overcome of evil, but overcome evil with good." [12]

Nahum overcame evil with good and his system always works for us when we remember to use it. Again and again our problems turn out to be blessings in disguise.

Among the meager possessions of the great Ghandi was a little statuette of three monkeys. One of the little monkeys covered his eyes with his hands, another his ears, and the third his mouth. Underneath is the inscription, "See no evil, hear no evil, speak no evil." Ghandi called the little monkeys his three gurus (teachers).

The only evil there can ever be is our interpretation of what we see and hear and the way we feel about it. When we see, hear, and speak only good, we are then in tune with the Infinite, the infinite Goodness of God.

It is so important that we not go back into old negative thoughts and situations of the past. To do so is to go "down to Egypt . . ." where we may experience seven years of famine.

12. Romans 12:21.

XI HOW MOSES LEADS US OUT OF BONDAGE

Exodus, Chapters 1–14
Numbers, Chapter 20

Historically, intellectually, spiritually—anyway you look at it —Moses is one of the most important characters in the Old Testament. The life and teachings of Moses form the foundation upon which is built the whole of the teaching and tradition of Judaism and Christianity. All that preceded Moses contributed stones of Truth, but it was Moses who laid the foundation. His life provided definite steps for us to follow while the words that he spoke, as recorded in the first five books of the Old Testament, provide the teaching of the Truth. Moses gave us a map for the spiritual journey and a vast array of symbolic meanings that provide the rituals and accoutrements, even the vestments for the Christian and Judaic religions today.

He drew it all together. How interesting that his name means *drawn out of!* His life was an example of living God's Truth, his words of teaching God's Truth. God did speak through Moses, just as God spoke through the prophets before him and after him, just as He speaks through those today who have ears to hear and are willing to take on the responsibility of teaching His Word. This, Moses was willing to do.

Even the teaching of Jesus depended to a large extent upon his predecessor, Moses, whom he often quoted. Thus the teaching of Moses becomes important to the Christians, as well as the Jews.

It All Started with Moses

Without Moses there would be no Judaic or Christian religions. It all started with Moses. He was the great lawgiver. From Moses came the Torah, or Pentateuch, which is the first five books of the Old Testament. All of the teaching of Judaism and Christianity stems from these first five books of the Bible. Even the teaching of Jesus which is so fresh and spontaneous can be traced verse by verse to these five books. Jesus, being a Jewish Rabbi, was a great student of the Torah. Moses gave us the Great Commandment which Jesus repeated when questioned by the Pharisees.

> Hear, O Israel: the Lord our God is one Lord:
> And thou shalt love the Lord thy God with all thine heart, and with all thy soul, and with all thy might.
> —Deuteronomy 6:4, 5; see also Matthew 22:37

And when Jesus said, "the second is like unto it," he was also quoting from Moses:

> Thou shalt not avenge, nor bear any grudge against the children of thy people, but thou shalt love thy neighbor as thyself: I am the Lord. —Leviticus 19:18

Moses gave us, as you can see, what Jesus called the Great Commandment, as well as the Ten Commandments, each one a further extension of the Great Commandment.

The great teaching of Moses is that God is one. He strongly

advocated radical reliance upon God and he proved by his own life that God could be all things to man.

The Genealogy of Moses

There is no doubt in my mind that Moses was a very real man who made real history. At the same time, it is not strange to me that everything he did and said, everything he stood for, provides us with an inner meaning, a depth of understanding that we can use today. There is nothing contradictory about this. I believe that every single thing in our lives has an inner and an outer meaning. Usually we are well aware of the outer meaning, but only begin to catch glimpses of the inner significance as we become spiritually illumined enough to comprehend it. Nothing in our lives is insignificant. Each lesson, each point of growth, is part of the whole. Little by little we see the pattern of our lives unfolding before our inner vision. This is the way we grow in spiritual understanding.

Everything in the life of Moses is significant—not only was it significant to Moses, but also to us, as we view it from this vantage point—a panorama spread before us.

Just as all of the Bible people stand for various states of awareness when we discover the meaning of their Hebrew names, so Moses is a state of consciousness springing from two parent thoughts. We are not at all surprised to find that his parent thoughts are:

Father—Amram—kindred of the Lofty one, exalted people.
Mother—Jochebed—whose glory is Jehovah.

We see at once that his parents represent the uniting of the masculine and feminine, the conscious and subconscious thinking, of a highly uplifted awareness, an awareness that communed with the Most High. It follows that they should produce a son like Moses. Moses stands for the Christ Consciousness in the Old Testament, just as Jesus stands for the Christ Consciousness in the New Testament.

Going back to the great great grandfather of Moses, we find a man who became known as Israel, *the prince of God, rulership with God*. Great grandfather Jacob had overcome the flesh and the temptations of intellectual reasoning and had prevailed with God.

> And he said, Thy name shall be called no more Jacob, but Israel: for as a prince hast thou power with God and with men, and hast prevailed. —Genesis 32:28
>
> For Jacob my servant's sake, and Israel mine elect, I have even called thee by thy name: I have surnamed thee, though thou hast not known me. —Isaiah 45:4

Great Grandfather Levi's name means *joining together, uniting, loving*. When Leah, his mother, brought him forth she said, "Now will my husband be joined unto me." The descendents of Levi became the priests of Israel. Grandfather Kohath's name means *assembly* or *uniting* as does Levi.

It is plain to see that Moses had pretty fine ancestors. The lineage of spiritual man must be spiritual; spiritual thinking produces spiritual thinking. In the Biblical writings, name truly means nature. There is never a discrepancy. The families are found to continue true to their nature.

How Moses Got His Name

At the time of Moses' birth, Pharaoh had given orders that all of the male children born of the Israelites were to be cast into the river in order to reduce the population of the Israelites.

And the children of Israel were fruitful, and increased abundantly, and multiplied, and waxed exceeding mighty; and the land was filled with them.

.   .   .

And Pharaoh charged all his people saying, Every son that is born ye shall cast into the river, and every daughter ye shall save alive. —Exodus 1:7, 22

Pharaoh was afraid that the people of Israel would become so mighty that they might join in with his enemies and fight against Egypt. He figured that if there were no young men left, the girls would have to marry Egyptians and would thereby become Egyptians. This has a very interesting significance. The women in the Bible always represent the feeling or emotional side of life. Sometimes emotional thinking leads us astray, adulterating our spiritual thoughts, our children of Israel thoughts, by drawing our feelings into the enemy camp.

When Moses was born, his mother hid him for three months and then she made an ark for him out of bullrushes and hid him by the river banks. You will remember that Pharaoh's daughter, who had come down to the river with her handmaidens to bathe, found him there and had compassion for him. His sister Miriam, watching nearby to see what would become of the child, came forward at once and offered to fetch a nurse for the child from among the Hebrew women. Thus Moses was nurtured by his own mother.

It was Pharaoh's daughter who named Moses. "And she called his name Moses: and she said, Because I drew him out of the water." [1]

We have seen, according to our secret code, that water stands for consciousness, the fluidic substance of the Mind. Moses is the awareness of Truth, hidden in the fluidic substance of the Mind, there watched over and protected until

1. Exodus 2:10.

it is discovered by the feeling that comes through the illumined intellect (Pharaoh's daughter). At first, the infant Truth is upheld by the ruling intellect, but at the same time nurtured by its true mother, the spiritual Truth from which it came.

> Moses—drawn out of; the Truth that leads us out of bondage.

Moses is the Truth, in each one of us, that eventually leads us out of bondage, the Truth that leads us into that land flowing with "milk and honey," [2] the Promised Land, which, being interpreted, is the consciousness of divine fulfillment. We are constantly being drawn out of bondage by the Moses in us.

A Drama in Three Acts

Protection and guidance go hand in hand. They are always inseparable. The story of Moses, as given in the books of Exodus, Leviticus, Numbers and Deuteronomy, is a story of constant protection and guidance. The life of Moses unfolds like a play in three acts:

> Act I.........Moses in Egypt
> Act II........Moses in Midian
> Act III.......Moses in the Wilderness

Each act consists of forty years, a period of time which is used in Bible symbology to mean an indefinite but completed period.

The three acts, the three phases in the life of Moses, represent the Trinity of Life. As we have seen in Chapter IX, Esau, Jacob, and Israel represent man's evolvement in three levels of awareness from sense consciousness to spiritual consciousness. Moses in Egypt represents the life that is lived accord-

2. Exodus 3:17.

ing to material concepts. Moses in Midian represents the mental or intellectual stage of man's development. Moses in the wilderness represents the life that relies upon spiritual guidance.

Man Reenacts the Drama

This is the story of everyman on his journey out of self-imposed bondage into the freedom of a life that is lived as a son of God. This same course of action takes place in the life of every individual. First, man struggles to gain dominion over his physical and material environment. Believing that his happiness lies in gaining worldly power, prestige, and possessions, he strives to gain these ends. Finding that these things do not bring him the happiness he seeks, he then believes that power lies in the mental or intellectual side. He is glad to destroy his old belief in the false security of the physical or material life. But again he becomes dissatisfied. Always he is heading toward the ultimate—reliance upon the Presence and Power of God.

The Significance of Forty Years

It is interesting to note that each phase is said to be forty years. Forty years represents, in Bible language, an indeterminate but completed period.

The flood was forty days upon the earth.
Isaac was forty years old when he took Rebekah for his wife.
Esau was forty years old when he took Judith for his wife.
Moses was *in the mount* forty days and forty nights.
The children of Israel ate manna for forty years.

Jesus fasted in the wilderness for forty days and forty nights.

Goliath defied the armies of Israel for forty days.

These are only a few examples of the use of the number *forty* in the Bible. It is clearly seen that these are not necessarily actual periods of time, but a symbol of completion.

Act I—Moses in Egypt

So we have man in his journey from bondage to ultimate freedom. We all start out in Egypt, the bondage to our physical environment. There may seem to be a measure of security in this bondage, even wealth and dominion, such as Moses enjoyed in the royal household, but sooner or later there comes the desire to escape from bondage. The first step is the killing of the Egyptian, *the thought of bondage*. This is the erasing of the thought that tends to enslave.

> And he looked this way and that way, and when he saw that there was no man, he slew the Egyptian, and hid him in the sand. —Exodus 2:12

After this step is taken, there is no longer any security in the land of bondage. Moses, the Truth that draws us out of bondage, must take a stand and move out of that bondage toward the goal of ultimate freedom.

> Now when Pharaoh heard this thing, he sought to slay Moses. But Moses fled from the face of Pharaoh, and dwelt in the land of Midian: . . . —Exodus 2:15

Once we have put our hand to the plow, there is no turning back.[3] Sooner or later we must all come to the conclusion

3. Luke 9:62.

that when we give our attention to the outer effects, we are in bondage to possessions and this means that instead of possessing our possessions, they possess us. Jesus understood this so clearly.

> Lay not up for yourselves treasures upon earth, where moth and rust doth corrupt, and where thieves break through and steal:
> But lay up for yourselves treasures in heaven, where neither moth nor rust doth corrupt, and where thieves do not break through nor steal:
> For where your treasure is, there will your heart be also.
> —Matthew 6:19-21
> Labour not for the meat which perisheth, but for that meat which endureth unto everlasting life. . . . —John 6-27
> Jesus answered and said unto her, Whosoever drinketh of this water shall thirst again:
> But whosoever drinketh of the water that I shall give him shall never thirst; but the water that I shall give him shall be in him a well of water springing up into everlasting life.
> —John 4:13, 14

A modern mystic put it this way:

> For what are your possessions but things you keep and guard for fear you may need them tomorrow?
> And tomorrow, what shall tomorrow bring to the overprudent dog burying bones in the trackless sand as he follows the pilgrims to the holy city?
> And what is fear of need but need itself?
> Is not dread of thirst when your well is full, the thirst that is unquenchable? [4]

Act II—Moses in Midian

Sooner or later we all discover that we have been laboring in vain.

4. Kahlil Gibran, *op. cit.*, p. 19.

Except the Lord build the house, they labour in vain that build it: except the Lord keep the city, the watchman waketh but in vain. —Psalms 127:1

For as he thinketh in his heart, so is he: . . .

—Proverbs 23:7

We come to see the utter futility of working with effects, continually struggling with conditions. The first step out of this bondage to effects is one of intellectual enlightment, discovering the law of cause and effect. It is an important day when we discover that that which we think produces our experience. To find that changing our thinking alters the effects is a great step forward. No longer are we at the mercy of conditions and circumstances. No longer do our possessions possess us. Now we have dominion over them. This is the second step of our unfoldment, or Moses in Midian.

For a while this seems to be the answer to everything. With mounting excitement, we experience what we come to believe is personal power. Until we are ready to take the third step, we spend our *forty years, some indeterminate but completed period,* in *the middle land of mind over matter* (Midian). We have made some progress, but we have yet to experience true freedom.

It all seems so right to suppose that psychologically, we can take control. For a time it seems to work, but in the Midian stage, one can get into a rut, the rut of thinking that it all depends upon the little human mind. We see that there are mental answers to many things. We have a certain amount of dominion in the Midian stage through auto-suggestion. That which we claim for ourselves becomes our experience. We use this mental law in our relationships with each other and teach it to our children. Living by the law of cause and effect is seen to be helpful. It is good as far as it goes.

Like Moses, we discover the power of our own *I am,* but it

is still the limited individual *I am.* This is a recognition of our existence at this level of consciousness. We find that if we say *I am sick,* we can expect to become ill. If we say *I am well,* we expect to become well. If we identify ourselves with riches we can prosper, but if we identify ourselves with poverty, we can expect to be poor. Whatever we identify ourselves with, through the use of our own *I am,* becomes the law of our experience. Everything from seeds to thoughts reproduces after its kind.

In Midian, we live according to judgment, judging each thing whether it be good or whether it be evil. It is an example of eating of the "tree of the knowledge of good and evil . . ." and, as in the Garden of Eden allegory, we *become as gods* because we accept the awful responsibility of gods. The person who never goes beyond mental science tends to feel that he *is* God. He thinks that it all depends upon him, forgetting that God lives through him and that God is the only Power. After awhile, this responsibility becomes a tremendous burden, almost too much to bear.

In Midian, Moses kept the flocks of Jethro, content to dwell with Jethro, living off the land (consciousness).

> And Moses was content to dwell with the man: and he gave Moses Zipporah his daughter.
> And she bare him a son, and he called his name Gershom: for he said, I have been a stranger in a strange land.
> —Exodus 2:21, 22

Moses kept the flocks of Jethro, that is, Moses kept the thoughts of abundance and even unified with the feeling of abundance by marrying the daughter of Jethro. Jethro means *his abundance* and his daughter, the feminine side, stands for *the feeling of abundance.* Through this union with Zipporah, whose Hebrew name means *free winged thoughts,* he is uplifted. A son is born named *Gershom* and Moses discovers that he is a stranger in a strange land. This is not surprising, since the children in the Bible always stand for thoughts springing from parent thought. This is the beginning of the evolvement of Moses into the third phase. It starts with the Moses consciousness experiencing divine discontent. Gershom, the son of Moses, *a thought springing from Moses,* means *I have been a stranger in a strange land.*

The first glimmer of spiritual consciousness makes us realize that we are no longer completely at home in the mental realm. The spiritual thoughts, *our children of Israel,* cry out to be delivered out of their bondage. In the mental stage, the spiritual thoughts are still oppressed under Pharaoh, *the self-assumed light of the intellect.* They are not only oppressed but completely stifled. Unless there is a strong Moses thought to lead them out of their bondage, they go unrecognized and unredeemed—sometimes remaining forever in their captivity.

One day we awaken to the realization that there is *a still more excellent way* (I Corinthians 12:31) and we reach out toward the third phase, the life that is lived by Grace where all that we need is provided easily and effortlessly without our taking anxious thought in the matter of its creation.

Act III—Moses in the Wilderness

The Moses consciousness, having become dissatisfied with the purely mental dominion, provides a vacuum which draws to it the spiritual experience. Out of the burning bush, the voice of the angel of the Lord speaks to him, ". . . Moses, Moses," and the Moses consciousness says, ". . . Here am I," meaning, *I am ready.* This is the indication that Moses is ready to be drawn out of the limiting experience of Midian into the greater experience. The guidance and protection through the Power of God comes only after Moses is ready to listen for it and receive it.

> And the angel of the Lord appeared unto him in a flame of fire out of the midst of a bush: and he looked, and, behold, the bush burned with fire, and the bush was not consumed.
>
> And Moses said, I will now turn aside, and see this great sight, why the bush is not burnt.
>
> And when the Lord saw that he turned aside to see, God called unto him out of the midst of the bush, and said, Moses Moses. And he said, Here am I. —Exodus 3:2–4

The angel of the Lord is *the messenger of the divine Law, the spiritual idea that comes* when we are ready to receive it. The flame is the Spirit. Anything that comes from Spirit is from an infinite Source, therefore it cannot be diminished or consumed. It was the burning bush, the spiritual phenomenon, that first caught Moses' attention, causing him to "turn aside. . . ." It is interesting to note that so often in man's experience it is a spiritual phenomenon that first attracts his attention. God speaks to him out of the experience. The Moses consciousness, ready now to leave the mental realm, listens and answers, ". . . Here am I."

God tells Moses to take off his shoes for the ground on which he stands is holy ground (Exodus 3:5). This is one of the key verses in the entire Bible. ". . . Put off thy shoes, . . ." put off anything that stands between you and your complete and perfect understanding. *The ground upon which you stand is holy ground—right where you are is the consciousness of wholeness and perfection.* Let nothing separate you from the Truth of being. This is what we stand upon. Here is Moses, the consciousness of Truth, being instructed that everything he needs is right where he is. And God said unto Moses:

Come now therefore, and I will send thee unto Pharaoh, that thou mayest bring forth my people the children of Israel out of Egypt.

And Moses said unto God, Who am I, that I should go unto Pharaoh, and that I should bring forth the children of Israel out of Egypt?

And he said, Certainly I will be with thee; and this shall be a token unto thee, that I have sent thee: When thou hast brought forth the people out of Egypt, ye shall serve God upon this mountain. —Exodus 3:10–12

The thought of Truth, newly awakened out of the mental realm does not feel that it is qualified. It has not yet proven itself. Moses is still in the mental realm where he feels that it all depends upon him. He has not yet emerged. It is like a person who feels that he, of his human self, is expected to be the healer and create all that he needs. To such a one the burden is very great, and the sense of inadequacy strong. The mental can become a second bondage until he finds the Great I AM—"I can of mine own self do nothing . . .," "the Father that dwelleth in me, he doeth the works." [5]

The first step toward spiritual unfoldment comes when the Moses consciousness hears the voice of God call him by name and answers ". . . Here am I." Like Samuel, who said, "Speak Lord, for thy servant heareth," [6] the Moses consciousness now awaits the Word that holds the Power. This is true humility, always the beginning of Divine Power in and through man. It is the *of myself I can do nothing* of Jesus. No prophet is a prophet in *his* right but in God's right. Before any battle is won or any progress made there is always *God spake* and the Word of God goes forth in Power to accomplish that whereunto it is sent. Moses has fulfilled the mental cycle and moves

5. John 5:30; 14:10.
6. I Samuel 3:9, 10.

into the spiritual cycle because he has "ears to hear." But still Moses doubts his capacity to be the one to take on the enormous job of leading the children of Israel out of bondage.

> And Moses said unto God, Behold, when I come unto the children of Israel, and shall say unto them. The God of your fathers hath sent me unto you; and they shall say to me, What is his name? what shall I say unto them?
>
> And God said unto Moses, I AM THAT I AM: and he said, Thus shalt thou say unto the children of Israel, I AM hath sent me unto you.
>
> And God said moreover unto Moses Thus shalt thou say unto the children of Israel, The Lord God of your fathers, the God of Abraham, the God of Isaac, and the God of Jacob, hath sent me unto you: this is my name for ever, and this is my memorial unto all generations. —Exodus 3:13–15

Doubt appears to be such a strong factor in our lives. We have many evidences of the Power of Truth, but doubt undermines and weakens the human consciousness. Doubt was still in the mind of Moses even though he had been told by the Power of Truth within that he could do the things that needed to be done. Again he expressed doubt. Like all of us, he wants to know the nature of this Power. And so the Spirit of Truth within him explains Its nature to him. It is necessary that the Moses consçiousness become one with the Spirit of Truth. "I and my Father are one" but "my Father is greater than I." [7]

"I AM THAT I AM. . . ." This is the secret of the ages. It is the Self within each one of us, *the Father who doeth the works*, it is *Jehovah God*, the *indwelling Christ, omnipotent Power individualized in and through man*. This was the God of Abraham and Isaac and of Jacob for they had discovered that with men it is impossible but with God all things are

7. John 10:30; 14:28.

possible. In this one statement, "I AM THAT I AM, . . ." is contained all that God is—infinite Power, omnipresent Love, and divine Intelligence. *And beside Him there is none other.* This is the only Power there is. *Is anything too hard for God?*

The Jehovah God of the Old Testament and the Christ of the New Testament are the same. In the New Testament we have Peter saying to Jesus, "Thou art the Christ, the Son of the living God." Why did Peter recognize this? Because Jesus understood that he was the Christ, "the Son of the living God." He understood that the God Power lived and worked through him. This is the Truth that God is giving to Moses. This is the *Christ in you, the hope of glory.* God Power in man is Christ in man. It is the only Power. To use it, man must recognize it. This Moses is willing to try to understand.

And now there are *signs following.* Moses is told to throw down his rod and it becomes a serpent. He is frightened and flees from it. Now God tells him to pick it up and it becomes a rod again. Then the Lord told him to put his hand in his bosom and draw it out and when he did, it was "leprous as snow." Then he was told to put it back into his bosom and it was restored. Like all of us, he was not easily convinced. "Could the miracle not be a coincidence?" we ask.

Still Moses lacks confidence in the Power of God within him. He pleads that he is not eloquent but slow of speech and slow of tongue.

> And the Lord said unto him, Who hath made man's mouth? or who maketh the dumb, or deaf, or the seeing, or the blind? have not I the Lord?
> Now therefore go, and I will be with thy mouth, and teach thee what thou shalt say. —Exodus 4:11, 12

God promises Moses that if he insists he will give him Aaron to be his mouthpiece and he shall tell Aaron what to say and God will be with them both. Aaron's name indicates *his* nature, *the executive Power of divine Law, Christ in action.* It is fitting and proper that he and Moses go hand in hand to lead the spiritual thoughts (children of Israel) out of bondage to materialistic thinking.

Moses is now ready to take spiritual dominion of the situation. In the third act, the Moses consciousness and the other spiritual thoughts represented by the children of Israel are constantly provided for through the miracle working Power of the divine Law. They are guided by a cloud by day and a pillar of fire by night, there is manna for each day and water gushes forth from the rock at the touch of the rod.

As we get into Act III, we see that it allegorically describes the life that is lived by Grace, that every man who is willing to trust God all the way is given the divine guidance that he needs, and that the rod symbolizes the *dominion through the Word of divine Inspiration that touches the rock of Truth causing ideas to gush forth. Ideas are the water of Life that are freely given to us.* The manna that comes day by day stands for *whatsoever we may need. It is the meat to eat ye know not of, the meat that does not perish, the treasure that does not rust. Manna means "what is it?" Manna can mean anything that is needed. It is the divine Substance out of which all that man needs is made.*

Every Thought Has Meaning

Everything that happens in the life of Moses has some pertinent significance for each one of us. For instance, take the plagues which God sent to the Egyptians. After the Lord spoke to Moses out of the burning bush, telling him that he would give him Aaron to be his mouthpiece, he told him that he should get going with the project of freeing the children of Israel. So Moses and Aaron went to Pharaoh and demanded that he free the children of Israel. Instead, he increased the load that was placed upon the Israelites by commanding that they increase the number of bricks that they produce each day, maintaining the same quality. Moreover, he refused to provide the straw with which to make them. So the people went out and gathered stubble and when they did not meet the standards set by Pharaoh, they were flogged. Things were worse than before. This baffled Moses who returned to the Lord and said,

> . . . Lord, wherefore hast thou so evil entreated this people? why is it that thou hast sent me?
> For since I came to Pharaoh to speak in thy name, he hath done evil to this people; neither hast thou delivered thy people at all. —Exodus 5:22, 23
> Then the Lord said unto Moses, Now shalt thou see what I will do to Pharaoh: for with a strong hand shall he let them go, and with a strong hand shall he drive them out of his land. —Exodus 6:1

When our spiritual thoughts, our Moses consciousness, try to reason with the Pharaoh in each one of us, *the intellect that attempts to rule,* we often feel that we have stirred up a hornet's nest within ourselves. Our burden then seems heavier than ever to bear, for we have challenged the ego and it doesn't like to be challenged. Then the Moses thought must go back to the Lord, the divine Law of all goodness, and ask *what shall I do next?* It is only when the human situation becomes thoroughly impossible that man, in his stubbornness, is willing to surrender his human will and rely solely upon God. "Man's extremity is God's opportunity" [8] might well have been said the first time by Moses.

8. Attributed to John Flavel, 1691.

The Lord Proves His Power to Moses

And now the Lord tells Moses to go before Pharaoh and put on a demonstration of his Power. This took real courage on the part of Moses who had been brought up in the King's palace and knew what the magicians and sorcerers were capable of doing. It was truly radical reliance upon the Omnipotent.

> "When Pharaoh says to you, 'Prove yourselves by working a miracle,' then you shall say to Aaron, 'Take your rod and cast it down before Pharaoh, that it may become a serpent.'" So Moses and Aaron went to Pharaoh and did as the Lord commanded; Aaron cast down his rod before Pharaoh and his servants, and it became a serpent. Then Pharaoh summoned the wise men and the sorcerers; and they also, the magicians of Egypt, did the same by their secret arts. For every man cast down his rod, and they became serpents. But Aaron's rod swallowed up their rods. Still Pharaoh's heart was hardened, and he would not listen to them; as the Lord had said. —Exodus 7:8–13 R.S.V.

The intellect seems to be powerful and capable of great accomplishment, but it is found to be swallowed up by the Almighty Power of God. As a lawyer, writer and lecturer, I can vouch for this. Reasoning intellectually, I can do fairly well, but when I trust completely in the Spirit within, everything is accomplished with ease; the ideas flow freely from an endless Source. The Power of God includes and completely consumes all else which seems to have power.

The Plagues of Egypt and the Trials of Human Nature

The plagues of Egypt represent the tests that come to man as he attempts to leave his bondage. Here we must remind ourselves that both the Egyptians and the Israelites are within each one of us. The Egyptians are the ignorant thoughts, the thoughts of bondage that we let enslave us. Human arrogance resists as we start to move out of our bondage until it seems that we have stirred up a hornet's nest. The Law is at work, however, and eventually we are delivered out of the hands of Pharaoh, out of the house of bondage. This explains the symbolism of the plagues which the Lord sent to the Egyptians; such as, water turned into blood; frogs; dust became gnats; flies; the killing of the live stock; boils; hail and fire from the sky; locusts; darkness for three days; and the killing of the firstborn. And haven't we felt as if we had experienced them all! How long it takes, what endless suffering must be endured, before our limited thinking is finally willing to trust spiritual inspiration.

The last and final plague was the killing of the firstborn. The Scripture tells about it in this manner:

> For I will pass through the land of Egypt this night, and will smite all the firstborn in the land of Egypt, both man and beast; and against all the gods of Egypt I will execute judgment: I am the Lord.
>
> And the blood shall be to you for a token upon the houses where ye are: and when I see the blood, I will pass over you, and the plague shall not be upon you to destroy you, when I smite the land of Egypt.
>
> And this day shall be unto you for a memorial; and ye shall keep it a feast to the Lord throughout your generations; ye shall keep it a feast by an ordinance for ever.
>
> —Exodus 12:12–14

The Passover, still celebrated by the Jews today, was the final step in the freeing of man's spiritual thoughts (the children of Israel) from the bondage of ignorance (Egypt). At last, there is a clarification, and the higher consciousness is released after having been held so long in bondage. The Israelites had been instructed to borrow jewels of gold and silver from their Egyptian neighbors so that they would be provided for upon their journey. Taken literally, this seems like a pretty tricky things for God to advise them to do. Taken figuratively, it means that when we are finally ready to be released from bondage, even the negative experiences provide rich jewels of understanding that we carry with us into the new land.

The Sojourn in the Wilderness

It is interesting to note here that the Lord did not lead the children of Israel through the land of the Philistines, but took them instead into the wilderness. The Philistines stand for the thoughts that are foreign to Spirit, and we are told:

> And it came to pass, when Pharaoh had let the people go, that God led them not through the way of the land of the Philistines, although that was near; for God said, Lest peradventure the people repent when they see war, and they return to Egypt:
> But God led the people about, through the way of the wilderness of the Red Sea. . . . —Exodus 13:17, 18

The newly liberated spiritual thoughts are not up to any more battles with negation. The land of the Philistines is always near us, for it is negative thinking. But each man must take his new spiritual enlightenment into his own wilderness of unenlightened thinking and there prove it for himself. The Red Sea stands for race consciousness, those fixed beliefs of reality in evil that are ever with us in our journey to the freedom of the Promised Land. Before we can pass through to the other side, the divine Law must divide the water of race consciousness. The Power of the Spirit makes the way clear to let the spiritual thinking through. The final barrier that each one must overcome is a Red Sea to him. It is the barrier of, *What will other people think? Is this the smart thing to do? Am I making a big mistake? If it's going around, I'll get it! Business is poor these days.*

Pharaoh was so sure that the Red Sea would stop them that he took after them to bring them back into slavery. And so it is with us as we go through that last period of rationalizing with erroneous thinking, that point when we say to ourselves, *maybe I have been too idealistic, maybe there is power in germs, maybe there is power in matter after all.*

> When Pharaoh drew near, the people of Israel lifted up their eyes, and behold, the Egyptians were marching after them; and they were in great fear. And the people of Israel cried out to the Lord; And they said to Moses, "Is it because there are no graves in Egypt that you have taken us away to die in the wilderness? What have you done to us, in bringing us out of Egypt? Is not this what we said to you in Egypt, 'Let us alone and let us serve the Egyptians'? For it would have been better for us to serve the Egyptians than to die in the wilderness." And Moses said to the people, "Fear not, stand firm, and see the salvation of the Lord, which he will work for you today; for the Egyptians whom you see today, you shall never see again. The Lord will fight for you, and you have only to be still." —Exodus 14:10–14, R.S.V.

Isn't this what we all do when the going gets rough? Sometimes we think it would be easier to go back into our old bondage and make peace with negative thinking. Sometimes when we find ourselves *between the devil and the deep blue sea,* we are tempted to wonder if the battle is worth it. And then, the Moses in us, that strong spiritual thought that leads us out of our old negative patterns, tells us, "Fear not, stand firm, and see the salvation of the LORD."

The children of Israel were led out of bondage, but they lacked the security that comes through an understanding of the Grace of God. On the journey they carried with them their old prejudices, their old dependence upon idols and false symbols. They had been willing to follow Moses, a man with a dream, but they murmured among themselves against Moses even as they followed him. They were not yet ready to accept that dream for themselves.

How like the children of Israel we are, each one murmuring in the wilderness of his own unenlightened thinking. We start out to escape our bondage following in the wake of a great spiritual idea and then we let doubt and false idols undermine us.

Moses, it must be kept in mind, is that leading spiritual thought in us that gathers together a great congregation of spiritual thoughts, encourages them, teaches them, disciplines them, and leads them safely out of bondage. As the Moses thought brings our lesser thoughts through the wilderness of our own undisciplined thinking, they sometimes are pursued by the enemy—our own materialistic thinking, and almost overcome by the Red Sea of doubt.

How wonderful it is that we have Moses, the Christ Truth, to lead us out of bondage and safely through the wilderness. On the way, our Moses consciousness beholds God and is transfigured by the experience. Moses, in us, goes to God with every need and thus is able to provide for the lesser spiritual thoughts until they reach the border of the Promised Land— that ultimate goal of spiritual awareness that we are all seeking.

More about Manna

I have known many people to be fed by manna in our time. Manna literally means *what is it?* It is anything that is needed at the moment. It can be food, or ideas, or anything else that is needed. It is the symbol of spiritual supply, the all-purpose Substance that takes form as we have specific needs and desires. Like the children of Israel in the wilderness, we are fed by manna only when we are willing to trust in God for our supply. Daily food for daily needs is manna for today. To hoard is to doubt that there will be more for the morrow and through the Bible story, we are cautioned that we must gather fresh manna each day. Manna comes to us today as ideas, fresh ideas, that should be used promptly if we would retain their vitality. When hoarded something goes out of them, they seem to become stale and even decay. The Bible, always dramatic, tells us that the manna that was left until morning, stank.

Manna, that miraculous food that fed thousands, was just what was needed at the moment, and every man got just what he required, no more, no less. ". . . He that gathered much had nothing over, and he that gathered little had no lack; they gathered every man according to his eating." [9]

Truly, manna is the symbol of spiritual supply. One who hoards his wealth, fearfully hiding his savings under the mattress, finds that he is poor; but he who trusts in manna for today is miraculously provided for, having all that he needs. Such a one is rich.

In the Psalms, manna is called the "corn of heaven" and "angels' food." [10] Since angels are the messengers of God, their food must be divine ideas. The "hidden manna . . ." of Revelations is the *bread of life,* food for the soul that is hidden from all who have not ears to hear.

He that hath an ear, let him hear what the Spirit saith unto the churches; To him that overcometh will I give to eat of the hidden manna. . . . —Revelation 2:17

9. Exodus 16:18.
10. Psalms 78:24, 25.

He who lives by the "hidden manna . . ." need never hunger again for he knows the everlasting Source of his supply. To him is given "power to get wealth" [11] if wealth is what he needs. ". . . They that seek the Lord shall not want any good thing." [12] There is always enough and to spare.

Manna is always from heaven, stepped down from absolute Good into the relative experience. It may be a box of groceries miraculously delivered at the door of need. It may come through a check in the mail; be an unexpected call from a friend; just the idea that is needed; or a book falling open at just the right place. "Meals for Millions" or surplus grain could be manna to many today or it could be "C" rations dropped from a plane to a raft in the sea. Manna is all things to all people. It is the ". . . God is able to make all grace abound toward you . . ." of Paul.[13] It is Good made manifest in human experience where we can see it and touch it and feel it. Each one receives manna according to his need, but to each one it is a very real thing.

Moses Spoke with God—So Can We

Moses was a mystic. All of the prophets were mystics. Believe it or not, there are quite a few today. Mysticism is a belief that direct knowledge of God, or spiritual truth, is attainable through immediate intuition or insight. It differs from ordinary sense perception by believing in the possibility of attaining knowledge or power through faith or spiritual insight. The mystic is one who has mystical (spiritual) experiences. He hears God speak to him. Sometimes it seems to be a voice from outside himself, like the voice that spoke to Moses from the burning bush. More often it is a still, small voice that

11. Deuteronomy 8:18.
12. Psalms 34:10.
13. II Corinthians 9:8.

speaks within the heart. In the Bible stories, such an experience is reported as "the Lord spake," "the Lord said," "God called," etc. Moses heard God many times. Aaron did not. Moses was told to tell Aaron what God said. Aaron was the mouthpiece of Moses. He had what would be called a *gift of gab* today. Since his approach was on the intellectual level he did not receive his instructions directly from God.

The first time God spoke to Moses was from the burning bush. Up until then, he too, had been living in the mental realm. It took the spectacular phenomenon of the burning bush to cause him to "turn aside." Sometimes it takes a miracle to make us turn aside. First, Moses had to recognize the Power of God. This is the first step in scientific prayer. During the sojourn in the wilderness we find Moses going to God with every need; when they needed water, when they needed food—Moses never took a step without getting his direction from God. Throughout the experience of getting the children of Israel out of Egypt and leading them through the wilderness, the faith of Moses never wavered. He had, what we might call, radical reliance upon God, and God did not fail him. Only once did Moses fail to give God the credit for a miracle, and this act seems to have kept him out of the Promised Land. It always seems rather sad that one who had been so faithful should have paid so dearly for one single mistake. It does, until one understands, through the use of the secret code, the hidden meaning.

Moses Makes His Great Mistake

When the children of Israel had camped in Rephidim, meaning *place of rest,* and had needed water, Moses, by God's direction, smote the rock and produced water whose streams had followed them during nearly all of the forty years in the wilderness. Now as they came to the desert of Zin, which stands for *the last thorny wilderness to be overcome,* and are almost ready to enter the Promised Land, there is again no water—*no flow of spiritual Inspiration.*

> And there was no water for the congregation: and they gathered themselves together against Moses and against Aaron.
> And the people chode with Moses, and spake, saying, Would God that we had died when our brethren died before the Lord! —Numbers 20:2, 3

The children of Israel seem to have such short memories! But, so do we. When we come to the arid places in our spiritual journey, don't we murmur against the Lord, finding it hard to remember the times when we were sure that God would lead us safely through? But again Moses went to the Lord, and again the Lord told him to take his rod up and bring the water forth out of the rock—rock, you will remember, means *Truth;* rod, *the word of God, the divine authority.* Moses gathered the congregation together. This means what we do in meditation when we gather our spiritual thoughts together. But this time Moses took the credit for himself and Aaron. The divine Law is impersonal and "will not hold him guiltless that taketh his name in vain." To God alone belongs the Power to do the mighty works and when we try to assume that Power as belonging to the human self we get into trouble.

> . . . Hear now, ye rebels; must we fetch you water out of this rock?
>
> .   .   .
>
> And the Lord spake unto Moses and Aaron, Because ye believed me not, to sanctify me in the eyes of the children of Israel, therefore ye shall not bring this congregation into the land which I have given them. —Numbers 20:10, 12

Moses died, at one hundred and twenty years old, before he reached the Promised Land. He could look across the Jordan and see it but he could not go in. Aaron was taken up into the mount (a high state of consciousness), where his clothes were removed in front of all the congregation of Israel and given to Eleazar, his son; and Aaron died there in the top of the mount. This means that the Aaron consciousness of *llumined intellect* was stripped of its thought garments that they might be inherited by Eleazar, whose name tells us that this allegorical drama indicates a step upward in consciousness. Eleazar carried on with help from God.

> Aaron—the illumined intellect.
> Eleazar—whose help is God.
> Hor—the mountain of mountains; exalted
>   state of consciousness.

With men it is impossible; but with God all things are possible.

> And Moses did as the Lord commanded: and they went up into mount Hor in the sight of all the congregation.
> And Moses stripped Aaron of his garments, and put them upon Eleazar his son; and Aaron died there in the top of the mount: and Moses and Eleazar came down from the mount.
> —Numbers 20:27, 28

Is the Promised Land a Place?

The Promised Land is *a place in consciousness, a state of mind which we are always seeking, a spiritual Utopia in consciousness where there is no more suffering, a state of bliss where everything is taken care of for us. It represents the life that is lived entirely by Grace, Paradise Regained, back to the Garden of Eden—a land flowing with "milk and honey."*

We are all seeking the Promised Land. We, too, send out Joshua and Caleb, *bold spiritual thoughts,* as scouts, to take a look at that consciousness we seek; thus we glimpse the Promised Land through meditation. When we understand that Moses and Aaron represent to us states of consciousness within ourselves, and that Joshua and Eleazar pick up the thread of the story as higher states of consciousness within ourselves, we are able to comprehend the meaning hidden here for us. Moses, Joshua, and Jesus represent three degrees of Christ Consciousness. Moses was a degree of Christ Consciousness: as the great lawgiver, he paved the way. Joshua represents still greater illumination, trusting still more in Jehovah. Jesus represents the true Christ that finally is able to say, "I have overcome the world."

Like Moses, there are times when all of us forget that our Power was only borrowed from God, that our inspiration must ever be renewed, that it is not our human word that holds the Power to strike the rock of Truth and bring the water of divine Inspiration forth, but the word of God that is spoken through us. It does not matter then what faith we exercised in the past, what heights we reached *up in the mount* of spiritual realization. When we fall back upon our old materialistic thinking, it counts for naught. There seems to be seasons of doubt for all of us, as night follows day. There are arid times when the water does not gush forth freely. Then the Promised Land seems far away, indeed. It is like the ebb and flow of the tide. But when the dark night of the soul is over, there is a flowing back into the spiritual life stronger than before. In between times, we struggle at the border of Edom (materiality), and this the Bible portrays so beautifully in these allegorical verses from Numbers.

And Moses sent messengers from Kadesh unto the king of Edom, Thus saith thy brother Israel, Thou knowest all the travail that hath befallen us:

How our fathers went down into Egypt, and we have dwelt in Egypt a long time; and the Egyptians vexed us, and our fathers:

And when we cried unto the Lord, he heard our voice, and sent an angel, and hath brought us forth out of Egypt: and, behold, we are in Kadesh, a city in the uttermost of thy border:

Let us pass, I pray thee, through thy country: we will not pass through the fields, or through the vineyards, neither will we drink of the water of the wells: we will go by the king's high way, we will not turn to the right hand nor to the left, until we have passed thy borders.

And Edom said unto him, Thou shalt not pass by me, lest I come out against thee with the sword.

And the children of Israel said unto him, We will go by the high way: and if I and my cattle drink of thy water, then I will pay for it: I will only, without doing any thing else, go through on my feet.

And he said, Thou shalt not go through. And Edom came out against him with much people, and with a strong hand.

Thus Edom refused to give Israel passage through his border: wherefore Israel turned away from him.

—Numbers 20:14–21

This represents the struggle with materiality (Edom) that goes on in each one of us when we seem to lose our spiritual contact. We think we can go through the land of Edom without looking to the right or the left, and, goodness knows, if we drink any of the water there (take any ideas there) we do have to pay dearly. We try to go through *on our feet* (our own understanding), but without the Lord to guide us, the ruling thought of materiality (the king of Edom) will not let us pass. During these periods we must pray diligently that we may get our children of Israel thoughts *up into a mountain* of high consciousness again. "And they rose up early in the morning, and gat them up into the top of the mountain. . . ." [14]

14. Numbers 14:40.

of spiritual awareness where man is able to commune with the Divine. After Moses had raised his consciousness to where he could hear God, God called to him out of this high awareness. The "house of Jacob . . ." stands for the consciousness of Jacob, *the inspired mind that was renamed Israel,* and *the children of Israel* are *those spiritual thoughts that spring from this state of mind.* It is a moment of great faith. At such a time one is willing to admit that God has been able to destroy those thoughts which have held man in bondage and to carry him "on eagles' wings . . ." unto his Presence. The covenant is God's promise to man—that if they will cleave to Him, He will cleave to them. That the land (consciousness) and everything that goes with it, blessings unlimited, will be given to those who put God first in their lives, "for all the earth is mine." The "kingdom of priests, and an holy nation," has to do, of course, with the consciousness of the individual—the dominion that comes through a unified consciousness that serves the Lord exclusively.

When Moses rehearsed this to the people, they professed their readiness to do whatsoever the Lord should command them. When Moses returned to the mount and represented their ready compliance with the divine will, God ordered him down to direct the people to sanctify themselves, and wash their clothes, as on the third day God would descend on the mountain and enter into a covenant with them.

The Israelites (spiritual thoughts), are teachable at this time, willing to follow divine inspiration. They now are willing to do whatever the Lord should command them. When our thinking is comparable, we say that we have surrendered to the will of God. It is the *let Thy perfect will be done in and through me* consciousness. The washing of the clothes simply means to keep the thoughts pure, wholly free from error. The "third day," that mystical number three, refers to wholeness of spirit, mind, and body. You will remember that

Jesus rose from the dead on the "third day." Three represents the raising of mind and body from sense to spiritual consciousness.

The Ten Commandments

In Bible symbolism, the events leading up to the presentation of the Ten Commandments were dramatic and awe-inspiring. The children of Israel were frightened at the lightning and thunder and dared not look upon God themselves. In fact, Moses was directed by the Lord to rope off the entire mount so that no man or animal could come near. When we commune with God, we must exclude all sensual or human thoughts. Moses, himself, was so transfigured by his experience in meeting with God that he had to put a veil over his face when he came down from the mountain for his face shone so that the children of Israel could not look upon it.

When Moses was up in the mount, *this high state of exalted consciousness,* he received from God the Ten Commandments, also called the Decalogue. The Decalogue is a moral miracle in ancient legislation and retains its power to this day; it is used by Jews and Christians alike.

On the surface, the Ten Commandments are wonderfully thought through, containing moral and ethical rules that cover every possible situation that man might ever encounter. If a person would always abide by the Ten Commandments, he could do no wrong. It would be impossible to offend God or man in any way. The first five of the Commandments have to do with man's relationship to God. In their obvious or literal meaning, they seem to cover everything; but as a person's spiritual understanding grows, he comes to see that they conceal deep, hidden truths.

The Hidden Meaning of the Ten Commandments

[I.] Thou shalt have no other gods before me.

[II.] Thou shalt not make unto thee any graven image, or any likeness of any thing that is in heaven above, or that is in the earth beneath, or that is in the water under the earth:

Thou shalt not bow down thyself to them, nor serve them: for I the Lord thy God am a jealous God, visiting the iniquity of the fathers upon the children unto the third and fourth generation of them that hate me;

And shewing mercy unto thousands of them that love me, and keep my commandments.

[III.] Thou shalt not take the name of the Lord thy God in vain; for the Lord will not hold him guiltless that taketh his name in vain.

[IV.] Remember the sabbath day, to keep it holy.

Six days shalt thou labour, and do all thy work:

But the seventh day is the sabbath of the Lord thy God: in it thou shalt not do any work, thou, nor thy son, nor thy daughter, thy manservant, nor thy maidservant, nor thy cattle, nor thy stranger that is within thy gates:

For in six days the Lord made heaven and earth, the sea, and all that in them is, and rested the seventh day: wherefore the Lord blessed the sabbath day, and hallowed it.

—Exodus 20:3–11

When the Lord again gave Moses the Ten Commandments, they were summed up by what Jesus later called "the Great Commandment":

Thou shalt love the Lord thy God with all thy heart, and with all thy soul, and with all thy mind.

—Matthew 22:36, 37; see also Deuteronomy 6:4, 5

It is plain to see that this is a summing up of the first four of the Ten Commandments. Each of the first four has to do with a little different aspect of keeping the Great Commandment. Truly, the one Great Commandment includes the Ten and any other rule of good conduct that one could ever conceive of. If we could understand that "God is One"—one perfect Life, shared by all, one Mind used by all, one infinite Intelligence available to all, illimitable Love everywhere present, poured out upon all alike—and if we were to love this all inclusive God—which is over all, and through all and in us all, with all the heart and with all the soul (deep subconscious mind) and with all the might—how could we make any mistakes? Would we not keep the mind and heart so full of Love that Love would manifest everywhere in our experience? It was St. Augustine who said, "Love and do what you will." If the mind and heart is filled with God (Love), it is impossible to sin (make a mistake). As we examine the first four of the Ten Commandments, we see at once that they constitute a breakdown of the Great Commandment: [1]

1. "Thou shalt have no other gods before me." [2]

There are so many things that we make gods of. Do many not worship the golden calf of monetary riches today? Do we, any more than the rich young man who came to Jesus, dare to give all that we have to the poor that we may follow him? How great a god is financial security! And how about fame and prestige and social acclaim? If you would understand the first commandment in its deepest sense, ask yourself the following questions and meditate for at least an hour upon the answers that you find in the secret place within your heart. You will find this meditation to have a deep cleansing effect upon your soul. When you have finished with it, make a promise to God within you that you keep the covenant—have no other gods before Him.

1. Deuteronomy 6:5.
2. Exodus 20:3.

Am I being true to my divine Self?
Am I putting other things before God?
Am I making a god of money? success?
Am I insisting that I be important in other people's eyes?
Am I making a god of trying to please personality?
What am I letting occupy most of my attention?
What do I think about day and night?
What am I making so important that it causes me sleepless nights?
What am I making so important that it causes me anxious moments?
Am I remembering that God is the only Power in my life?
Am I remembering that God is everywhere present?
Is there anything that I put before God?

II. "Thou shalt not make unto thee any graven image...." [3]

Now the second commandment is a way of backing up and taking a second look as we focus the white light of Truth upon the hidden places of the heart. A graven image is more than a picture engraved upon metal or stone. It can be an image engraved upon the mind of man—anything that causes us undue concern, anything to which we give undue importance. What about those neurotic patterns that keep rearing their ugly heads? What about people who remind us of some old enemy and rock the boat of our mental poise? These deep negative patterns need to be erased before we can keep the second commandment. Few people today worship images of stone, but all of us need to work on the second commandment. Perhaps we are not consciously aware that we have set up graven images to which we assign great worth. Worship means *to assign great worth to*. The graven image to which we assign great worth can be any kind of false thinking that has become entrenched, any pattern, or sequence of thinking, which has become habitual to us.

3. Exodus 20:4.

The second part of the commandment gives us still further insight. This thinking can be "in heaven above, . . ." "the earth beneath, . . ." or "in the water under the earth." This means that it can be hidden in what we think to be exalted thinking, it can be in our responses to the outer world, or it can be hidden away deep within our subconscious reactions. How do we react to the situations in our experience? Are we reacting only to the eternal Good, or are we giving power to some old memory of evil? Ask yourself these questions and meditate upon the answers that come to you, and you will discover where much of your trouble lies:

What are some of the graven images that I make for myself?

Am I giving power to my ailments. Am I proud of being a "difficult case"? eccentric?

Am I giving power to my weaknesses? my rages? my depressions?

Do I brag about my sleepless night? my ill health? my fatigue?

Do I egotistically set up my personality as a graven image?

Do I insist upon being pleased by others?

Am I trying to please an image of mother or father, superimposing this image onto others I meet?

What about the image that I hold of myself? Must it be kept inviolate? Do I pride myself on being hard to please?

Am I making a graven image of pride? pride of family? pride of accomplishment? and finally, spiritual pride?

Am I worshipping a false image of myself? of a loved one?

III. "Thou shalt not take the name of the Lord thy God in vain; for the Lord will not hold him guiltless that taketh his name in vain." [4]

In order to fully understand the third commandment, we must again define our terms. The word *name*, in the Bible,

4. Exodus 20:7.

always stands for nature. Are we taking the nature of God in vain? To better grasp this idea, try asking yourself these questions:

What is my idea of the nature of God?

Do I really believe that God is all-powerful, all-knowing, and everywhere present? Am I willing to abide by my concept of God?

How big is my God? Am I limiting God in my thinking?

Am I remembering that God is the only Power in my life?

Am I remembering that the divine Law of infinite Goodness that brought me out of the land of Egypt, out of the house of bondage of false thinking, is all powerful today to meet my problem?

Am I remembering that the Lord my God is one and that this oneness includes me?

When I pray, "Thine is the kingdom and the power, and the glory forever"—do I really mean it?

The divine Law, which is completely impersonal, will not hold him guiltless that taketh his name in vain. The Law is always just, giving to each one exactly what he invests in Life *through his thinking*. ". . . As thou hast believed so be it done unto thee."

IV. "Remember the sabbath day, to keep it holy. Six days shalt thou labour, and do all thy work: but the seventh day is the sabbath of the Lord thy God: in it thou shalt not do any work, thou, nor thy son, nor thy daughter, thy manservant, nor thy maidservant, nor thy cattle, nor thy stranger that is within thy gates." [5]

The fourth commandment is still sound on every level. On the obvious level, how wonderful it would be to rest one day in every seven, letting go of all of the hurry and stress of the

5. Exodus 20:8–10.

other six! What peace and quiet we could all enjoy. Suppose all of the stores and other activities were to be closed one day of the seven and we all spent our time thinking about the nature of God, releasing our problems into His loving care. Right on the face of it we see that we wouldn't have to rely on tranquilizers and headache pills, nor would the mental institutions be crowded. If we continued to respect the sabbath, there soon would be no one there at all! Physically and mentally, observing the fourth commandment would be highly therapeutic. Now, let's take a look at the mystical meaning which the secret code reveals to us. The keys that unlock the hidden meaning here are to be found in these words:

six—the working period in the cycle of creation.

seven—it is finished, perfection, that which is finished, completed and perfect.

the family (son, daughter, manservant, maidservant, cattle, the stranger within thy gates)—the thought family, both conscious (male) and subconscious (female), the objective thoughts, the subjective thoughts and feelings, those that serve, and even the animal or sensual thoughts, and the thought that is new and strange to your usual pattern of thinking, that stranger within the gates—all human thinking shall rest.

Here we are instructed in how to cooperate with the Creative Process of Life. It is so very important to *let go and let God*. Only when we let go can God take over and do the real work. It is in the resting period when we have done all that we can do and are willing to turn the problem over to God that the real work takes place. The seeds (ideas) have been planted in Mind and the Creative Medium begins to work on them. It is so important that we do not dig up the seeds and worry them to death. It is during the seventh day, the period when we rest our case with God and trust God to bring us our highest good, that we find the greatest activity takes place. The unseen fingers of the subconscious mind go to work and, at the end of the seventh day, it is done, finished, complete, sometimes in ways we knew not of. Ask yourself:

Am I able to let go and let God? Do I understand the meaning of the word release?

Why did Jesus tell Martha that Mary had chosen the best part?

Do I sometimes keep a thing from happening by trying to make it happen?

Can I trust enough to surrender my problem completely?

Can I say with Jesus, of myself I can do nothing, the Father within me doeth the works?

v. The fifth commandment is: "Honour thy father and thy mother: that thy days may be long upon the land which the Lord thy God giveth thee." [6]

At first glance, it would seem that we could stop here. Surely this one has no hidden meaning—but wait, how does it check out when we let it be interpreted by the Bible itself. The key words here are:

father—the masculine, or directive aspect of Mind.
mother—the feminine, feeling side, subjective aspect.
days—day as contrasted to night, divine illumination.
land—the land which God gives is the consciousness that we
    are one with Him, spiritual awareness.
Lord, thy God—the divine law of infinite Goodness.

Examining the subtle meanings here, we come up with something like this: *Honour thy true Source, thy Father-*

6. Exodus 20:12.

Mother God, and give no Power to that which is not of God, that you may walk in the Light in the true consciousness of being one with God.

People must have thought it pretty harsh words when Jesus said, "And call no man your father upon the earth: for one is your Father, which is in heaven." [7]

If we are to call no man upon this earth father, then this must apply to mother also, and commandment number five must refer to the Father which is in heaven, the Father-Mother concept of Life. Then, ask yourself:

Am I dishonoring my divine Parent, my Father-Mother God, by giving power to outside conditions?

Am I looking to my true Source, or giving false power to effects?

Am I dishonoring my divine Parent by bowing down to fears? judgments of myself and others? old conditioning and associations?

Am I dishonoring the feminine side of Life by putting feeling into thoughts about myself and others that I would not want to see outpictured in my life? by letting feelings and emotions rule me?

Having been told to take dominion, am I dishonoring the directive aspect of Mind by letting my thoughts take dominion of me?

VI. "Thou shalt not kill." [8]

To properly evaluate the deeper meaning of the sixth commandment, we must consider the way in which mortals bring about death and destruction. Murder is only the outer layer of the true meaning. The natural assumption is that the killing refers to killing people. There are so many kinds of death.

7. Matthew 23:9.
8. Exodus 20:13.

> Yet each man kills the thing he loves,
>   By each let this be heard,
> Some do it with a bitter look,
>   Some with a flattering word,
> The coward does it with a kiss,
>   The brave man with a sword.[9]

What of the parent who stifles the child's initiative? The wife or husband who nags his spouse until the other feels that it is useless to try? The obvious murderer kills only the body; the death of the soul by degrees causes far greater suffering. Criticism and condemnation are a form of killing. Have we not all been guilty of killing another's enthusiasm, of killing another man's dream?

If we really understood the meaning of Life, would we ever want to kill anything? Whenever we try to violently cross off the outer, it is only because we do not understand that there is an easier way. The proper way is to first change the mental image and then let the outer conform to the inner. Man's common thinking is that sickness or violence must precede death. In other words, that the body must be killed before there can be a transition to the next life. A real understanding of eternal life will show us that death is a "shadow" and that life is real. Therefore, at the right time, one can leave this life to go to the next without sickness or violence. He can leave the body behind as he grows into the next experience.

The same applies to a person leaving one job for another. Too often, the common thinking is that one has to hate the boss or the work as a reason for leaving it. This is not necessary. Hate will bind one to the job. Love the job and the boss and grow out of the experience. One does not have to kill the old experience to leave it. To understand this commandment ask yourself these questions:

9. Oscar Wilde, *The Ballad of Reading Gaol.*

Am I approaching my life with violence?

Am I trying to force Life to conform to my human will?

Am I trying to force the old patterns of negative and fearful thinking out of Mind, without first creating for myself a new pattern of God-centered thinking?

Do I truly understand the Creative Process that assures me of having my heart's desire without having to kill the old experience?

VII. "Thou shalt not commit adultery." [10]

In its deep meaning, this one must refer to the mystical marriage—the marriage of the soul to Christ. When the subconscious mind is filled with peace and understanding, when Love rules supreme, then we experience the mystical marriage within. "What therefore God hath joined together, let no man put asunder." [11] Physically and mentally, it is important to be true to our earthly mate, but it is far more important to be true to the spiritual marriage which is the unity of the conscious and subconscious mind in harmony with God. Every time we adulterate the Truth of Being in our thinking, we are being untrue to the marriage within. In order to understand some of the ways in which we commit mental adultery, ask yourself these questions:

How many times have I indulged in mental recrimination lately?

Am I keeping my eye single or do I give attention to both good and evil? health and disease? poverty and wealth?

Am I true to God in all of my dealings with my fellowmen?

How many times a day do I walk out on God to fool around with fear, anxiety, and despair?

Can I henceforth be true to the highest that is within me?

VIII. "Thou shalt not steal." [12]

If we truly understood the Law, we would know that it is

10. Exodus 20:14.
11. Matthew 19:6.
12. Exodus 20:15.

impossible to steal and get away with it, impossible at every
level. That which we take from another will not stay with us
long if it does not belong to us by right of consciousness. If
we have the consciousness of it, we will have no need to steal
it. Would anyone want to steal if he understood that he could
have anything he could ever desire if he would first prepare
a thought mold for it? An understanding of Truth soon convinces us, with Charles Macklin, that "every tub must stand
upon its own bottom." [13] There is only one way to acquire
our good and that is by first preparing ourselves in consciousness to receive it.

> . . . A man can receive nothing, except it be given him
> from heaven [within]. —John 3:27
> Every good gift and every perfect gift is from above, and
> cometh down from the Father of lights, with whom is no
> variableness, neither shadow of turning. —James 1:17

There are so many ways that people try to steal that which
does not belong to them. If you would know whether or not
you are keeping the eighth commandment, ask yourself these
questions:

Am I trying to steal credit that does not belong to me?

*Am I trying to claim recognition that does not belong to
me?*

*Am I trying to impress people, claiming to be something
I am not?*

Am I fooling myself?

Am I making false excuses for myself?

*Am I being dishonest with myself in a vain effort to pro-
tect my ego?*

*Am I trying to steal something from Life without first pre-
paring myself in consciousness to receive it?*

13. *Man of the World*, Act I, Scene 2.

IX. "Thou shalt not bear false witness against thy neighbor." [14]

And how do we bear false witness? Gossip is one way. Then, there is slander, and in its lesser forms, criticism—any negative story that we pass along to others. We might even go so far as to say that every time we behold another as less than the divine perfect son of God that he truly is, we are bearing false witness against him. "Oh, that poor cripple!" you exclaim—you are bearing false witness against him, giving him a negative treatment. Every word of condemnation that we utter, every thought locks the door on someone's prison. But, even more important, every unkind thought or word locks us in the same prison, for that which we behold becomes the pattern for our own experience.

We are all one. Hence every thought that blights another, blights the perfect image in ourselves. As we grow in spiritual understanding, we come to see that every unlovely thought must be corrected at the source, lest it bear children and our minds be consumed with ugly thoughts. If we behold our neighbor, and this includes all mankind, as sick, sinful, or in any way less than his true Self, then we owe it to him *and to ourselves* to correct this image at once. As you pass down a hospital corridor, bless each occupant—know the Truth about them, that, in the Mind of God they are perfect, whole and free. Healings will result. Perhaps you will never know about them, but you will be building a consciousness of health for yourself that will grow and expand until you realize a personal blessing. It is well to do a little soul searching on this one. Ask yourself these questions:

Am I bearing true witness to others by seeing them whole?
Do I criticize and condemn my neighbor?

14. Exodus 20:16.

Do I lock my neighbor in a mental cage and throw away the key?

Do I repeat things that are not the Truth about others?

Do I see God in everyone and every situation?

Do I bear false witness against myself by seeing myself as less than a divine, perfect spiritual being?

The pure in heart see only God. If we could learn to keep this commandment, we would find many side benefits. For one thing, we would soon discover that no one ever got on our nerves any more.

x. "Thou shalt not covet thy neighbour's house, thou shalt not covet thy neighbour's wife, nor his manservant, nor his maidservant, nor his ox, nor his ass, nor anything that is thy neighbour's." [15]

If we really understood the Law of Mind, would we ever need to covet? Did Jesus not tell us how to realize our desires.

> Therefore I say unto you, What things soever ye desire, when ye pray, believe that ye receive them, and ye shall have them. —Mark 11:24

As we prove this premise, we discover that we can rejoice with our neighbor over his good, for anything that is possible for him must also be possible to us. We have exactly the same opportunity. Life *is* fair. The Creative Process works through the Law of Mind. That which we believe in, accept for ourselves, and confidently expect is sure to come into our experience. Eventually, we come to see that to covet another's good only diminishes our own, for it holds up to life an image of lack for ourselves. To rejoice in another's good fortune is the best way of all to build an awareness of the very same thing for ourselves.

15. Exodus 20:17.

Beware of Judging the Self Too Harshly

To meditate on the questions I have given you concerning the Ten Commandments will provide a good mental house-cleaning, and if you take the time, even the basement will shine, for you can neutralize the darkest corners of the subconscious mind by such meditation. But just a word of warning—we have all broken the Ten Commandments when we consider their deeper meanings. Do not be too harsh with yourself. Forgive yourself for past sinning (missing the mark) and start over with a clean slate!

Other Laws and Covenants

Through Moses, the Lord gave laws and covenants governing every facet of man's existence.

ORGANIZED GOVERNMENT:

This time the instructions came through Jethro (divine preeminence). When Jethro came to see Moses in the wilderness to bring him his wife and children, he was concerned to find Moses working so hard in governing such a vast number of people.

> And when Moses' father in law saw all that he did to the people, he said, What *is* this thing that thou doest to the people? why sittest thou thyself alone, and all the people stand by thee from morning unto even?
>
> And Moses said unto his father in law, Because the people come unto me to enquire of God:
>
> When they have a matter, they come unto me; and I judge between one and another, and I do make them know the statutes of God, and his laws.
>
> And Moses' father in law said unto him, The thing that thou doest is not good.
>
> Thou wilt surely wear away, both thou, and this people

that is with thee: for this thing is too heavy for thee; thou art not able to perform it thyself alone.

Hearken now unto my voice, I will give thee counsel, and God shall be with thee: Be thou for the people to God-ward, that thou mayest bring the causes unto God.

And thou shalt teach them ordinances and laws, and shalt shew them the way wherein they must walk, and the work that they must do.

Moreover thou shalt provide out of all the people able men, such as fear God, men of truth, hating covetousness; and place such over them, to be rulers of thousands, and rulers of hundreds, rulers of fifties, and rulers of tens:

And let them judge the people at all seasons: and it shall be, that every great matter they shall bring unto thee, but every small matter they shall judge: so shall it be easier for thyself, and they shall bear the burden with thee.

.   .   .

So Moses hearkened to the voice of his father in law, and did all that he had said.

And Moses chose able men out of all Israel, and made them heads over the people, rulers of thousands, rulers of hundreds, rulers of fifties, and rulers of tens.

And they judged the people at all seasons: the hard causes they brought unto Moses, but every small matter they judged themselves. —Exodus 18:14–22, 24–26

Here we have organized thinking on the mystical level, and organized government on the mental and physical level. *Order,* it is said, *is the first rule of Heaven.*

HEALTH

And thou shalt love the Lord thy God with all thine heart, and with all thy soul, and with all thy might.
—Deuteronomy 6:5

And the Lord will take away from thee all sickness, and will put none of the evil diseases of Egypt, which thou knowest, upon thee. . . . —Deuteronomy 7:15

WEALTH

But thou shalt remember the Lord thy God: for it is he that giveth thee power to get wealth, that he may establish his covenant which he sware unto thy fathers, as it is this day.

—Deuteronomy 8:18

GUIDANCE

Besides the various lessons of guidance which came to us through the story of how God led the children of Israel through the wilderness, we are given the story of the Urim and the Thummim.[16] The Urim and the Thummim were objects placed in the breastplate of the high priest of the Israelites; by them, in some way, the high priest obtained divine guidance for the people. Take a look at the Hebrew meanings of Urim and Thummim.

Urim—light.
Thummim—truth.

The Urim, then, means light; the Thummim, truth. It is clearly seen that they are the mystical symbols of divine guidance that are continually worn as a breastplate of protection by the high priest within us, that conscious awareness of the Presence of God that is our everlasting guidance and protection.

The shield and breastplate are often used throughout the Bible in this way. Since, in this instance, the original Hebrew words were retained in the English translation, we are able to see the original significance.

Our soul waiteth for the Lord: he is our help and our shield. —Psalms 33:20

For the Lord God is a sun and shield: the Lord will give grace and glory: no good thing will he withhold from them that walk uprightly. —Psalms 84:11

16. Exodus 28:30; Deuteronomy 33:8.

For he put on righteousness as a breastplate, and an helmet
of salvation upon his head. —Isaiah 59:17

It is amazing how thoroughly the needs of man have been
met at every level of existence, from physical needs, such as
sanitation, to the highest needs of the soul, through the teaching of Moses as directly revealed to him by God. Through it
all runs the admonition to obedience. It is only through obedience that any of us reach the Promised Land and reap the
rich rewards that have been promised.

All the commandments which I command thee this day
shall ye observe to do, that ye may live, and multiply, and go
in and possess the land which the lord sware unto your
fathers.

And thou shalt remember all the way which the Lord
thy God led thee these forty years in the wilderness, to
humble thee, and to prove thee, to know what was in thine
heart, whether thou wouldest keep his commandments, or no.

And he humbled thee, and suffered thee to hunger, and
fed thee with manna, which thou knewest not, neither did thy
fathers know; that he might make thee know that man doth
not live by bread only, but by every word that proceedeth
out of the mouth of the Lord doth man live.

Thy raiment waxed not old upon thee, neither did thy foot
swell, these forty years.

Thou shalt also consider in thine heart, that, as a man chasteneth his son, so the Lord thy God chasteneth thee.

Therefore thou shalt keep the commandments of the Lord
thy God, to walk in his ways, and to fear him.

For the Lord thy God bringeth thee into a good land, a
land of brooks of water, of fountains and depths that spring
out of valleys and hills;

A land of wheat, and barley, and vines, and fig trees, and
pomegranates; a land of oil olive, and honey;

A land wherein thou shalt eat bread without scarceness,

thou shalt not lack any thing in it; a land whose stones are iron, and out of whose hills thou mayest dig brass.

When thou hast eaten and art full, then thou shalt bless the Lord thy God for the good land which he hath given thee.

Beware that thou forget not the Lord thy God, in not keeping his commandments, and his judgments, and his statutes, which I command thee this day:

Lest when thou hast eaten and art full, and hast built goodly houses, and dwelt therein;

And when thy herds and thy flocks multiply, and thy silver and thy gold is multiplied, and all that thou hast is multiplied;

Then thine heart be lifted up, and thou forget the Lord thy God, which brought thee forth out of the land of Egypt, from the house of bondage;

Who led thee through that great and terrible wilderness, wherein were fiery serpents, and scorpions, and drought, where there was no water; who brought thee forth water out of the rock of flint;

Who fed thee in the wilderness with manna, which thy fathers knew not, that he might humble thee, and that he might prove thee, to do thee good at thy latter end;

And thou say in thine heart, My power and the might of mine hand hath gotten me this wealth.

But thou shalt remember the Lord thy God: for *it is* he that giveth thee power to get wealth, that he may establish his covenant which he sware unto thy fathers, as it is this day.

And it shall be, if thou do at all forget the Lord thy God, and walk after other gods, and serve them, and worship them, I testify against you this day that ye shall surely perish.

As the nations which the Lord destroyeth before your face, so shall ye perish; because ye would not be obedient unto the voice of the Lord your God. —Deuteronomy 8:1–20

Moses here gives us a review of his entire teaching and you will find it an excellent opportunity to apply your knowledge of the secret code. You will find here the covenant between God and his creation, man; that those who are obedient to the commandments shall prosper but those who forget the Lord and walk after other gods shall surely perish.

XIII A LITTLE PEBBLE AND
A LOT OF GOD!

I Samuel, Chapter 17

How You Can Slay the Giants in Your Life

Just a little pebble—and a lot of God! You've heard the story of David and Goliath. Usually we think of this story in connection with the idea that it isn't always the big man who wins. There is a lot more to it than that. The Bible tells it this way:

And there went out a champion out of the camp of the Philistines, named Goliath, of Gath, whose height was six cubits and a span.

And he had an helmet of brass upon his head, and he was armed with a coat of mail; and the weight of the coat was five thousand shekels of brass.

And he had greaves of brass upon his legs, and a target of brass between his shoulders.

And the staff of his spear was like a weaver's beam; and his spear's head weighed six hundred shekels of iron: and one bearing a shield went before him.

And he stood and cried unto the armies of Israel, and said unto them, Why are ye come out to set your battle in array?

am not I a Philistine, and ye servants to Saul? choose you a man for you, and let him come down to me.

—I Samuel 17:4–8

Judging by appearances, as we all do, this giant would frighten anybody. Goliath had succeeded in defying the "armies of Israel. . . ." He had invited out any warrior but no warrior came. For "forty days" he had gone out and set up the challenge and no one had accepted him. Every time he strode upon the battlefield, the Israelites quaked.

We all face giants now and then, fearful thoughts that threaten to overwhelm us. Sometimes they take on tremendous proportions, seeming to be as well protected as Goliaths, and we, too, are afraid. Then we must choose a *man* from our understanding of Truth that is able to go out and meet this thought. We know that if we don't meet it in Truth, it will overcome us and we will have to serve it.

And Goliath threatened them:

If he be able to fight with me, and to kill me, then will we be your servants: but if I prevail against him, and kill him, then shall ye be our servants, and serve us.

—I Samuel 17:9

David Is Not Afraid

But there was a young chap named David who heard about this giant and was not terrified. He was the youngest son of Jesse and had been taking care of his father's sheep in Bethlehem while his three older brothers were with Saul at the battlefield. David had been asked by his father to take some provisions to his brothers at the camp and had arrived just in time to hear Goliath make his proud boast and see the terrifying effect on the Israelites. He watched the men run away when they saw the giant. David inquired what it was all about. ". . . Who is this uncircumcised Philistine, that he should defy the armies of the living God?" he said. His brothers were annoyed with him. They told him that it wasn't his business at all and that he should get back to his sheep. Finally Saul sent for David and David said to Saul, ". . . Let no man's heart fail because of him; thy servant will go and fight with this Philistine."

When we understand the meaning hidden in their Hebrew names, we can understand why, in this drama, the brothers of David were annoyed with him. The brothers have impressive names, Eliab means *God is Father*, Abinadab means *my father is noble,* and Shammah means *fame and renown.* It would seem that they had everything, enough behind them to qualify them to face the enemy, but here is their young brother, considered too young to go to battle, and the keeper of his father's sheep (pure thoughts). Now, the father's name is Jesse and his name in Hebrew means *Jah* (Jehovah) *is*. His children, according to the undeviating accuracy of Bible symbolism, must be thoughts springing from this basic premise. They all come from Bethlehem—Judah. Bethlehem means *house of bread, the spiritual substance of all life* and Judah means *praise* or *spiritual recognition*. What a family! But even with this heritage, the elder brothers seem to be hesitant to face the giant. Little brother David, *the beloved,* has been *keeping his father's sheep,* the pure thoughts that spring from the Source of all Life, *God is*. David, *the beloved,* is the *awareness of sonship*—"This is my beloved Son, in whom I am well pleased," [1] ". . . Son, thou art ever with me, and all that I have is thine." [2] He may be young but to him is given the Power. Even a new awareness of sonship introduces Power into a situation.

1. Matthew 3:17.
2. Luke 15:31.

Saul Accepts David's Offer

Saul's name means *asked.* It is Saul that makes the demand of life and life has sent him this young man, a new, fresh approach to the problem; one who is courageous to say the least, a young man who tells him that he is not even afraid of dangerous animals, *thoughts relating to physical power,* that threatened his father's sheep (pure thoughts).

And David said unto Saul, Thy servant kept his father's sheep, and there came a lion, and a bear, and took a lamb out of the flock:

And I went out after him, and smote him, and delivered it out of his mouth: and when he arose against me, I caught him by his beard, and smote him, and slew him.

Thy servant slew both the lion and the bear: and this uncircumcised Philistine shall be as one of them, seeing he hath defied the armies of the living God.

David said moreover, The Lord that delivered me out of the paw of the lion, and out of the paw of the bear, he will deliver me out of the hand of this Philistine.

—I Samuel 17:34–37

O! if we could only remember that *we* are *the beloved,* heir to all that God is, and that the same God that has delivered us in the past from our fearful thoughts will deliver us again from the present terror that confronts us.

Now Saul was in a tight spot. He was willing to accept anything. So he accepted the offer of this brazen young man to go out and do battle with the giant Goliath, who had terrified the whole army of the Israelites.

"Go," he said, "and the Lord be with thee."

Saul dressed David in his own armor, "put a bronze helmet upon his head and clad him in a coat of mail. David buckled his sword over his coat and tried to walk, but in vain, for he was not used to such armor." [3] Then David made a decision which he expressed with these words, ". . . I cannot go with these; for I have not proved them." He took off the armor and put it aside. Now that certainly was not the accepted thing to do. In any battle, one wore the traditional armor. Not this boy. He went over to a little brook and chose "five smooth pebbles" which he put into a sack at his belt. He had a sling. He was arrayed for battle. And Goliath drew near, hurling remarks at the youth, such as: ". . . Come to me, and I will give thy flesh unto the fowls of the air, and to the beasts of the field." But David was not afraid. He hurried forward to meet the Philistine saying, ". . . I come to thee in the name of the Lord of hosts . . ." "for the battle is the Lord's, and he will give you into our hands."

No Man Can Wear Another's Armor

Each man must wear his own armor, that is, be clothed and protected by his own thoughts. This armor may seem scant in the eyes of the world for the world cannot see the invisible armor of Truth. Paul, in his letter to the Ephesians, described the armor of Truth.

Finally, my brethren, be strong in the Lord, and in the power of his might.

Put on the whole armour of God, that ye may be able to stand against the wiles of the devil.

. . .

Wherefore take unto you the whole armour of God, that ye may be able to withstand in the evil day, and having done all, to stand.

Stand therefore, having your loins girt about with truth, and having on the breastplate of righteousness;

3. I Samuel 17:38, 39 (Moffatt Translation).

And your feet shod with the preparation of the gospel of peace;

Above all, taking the shield of faith, wherewith ye shall be able to quench all the fiery darts of the wicked [thoughts].

And take the helmet of salvation, and the sword of the Spirit, which is the word of God: —Ephesians 6:10, 11, 13–17

No one can grow for you. Your armor must be your own spiritual inspiration expressed from the inside out. This is the only armor that you can wear with assurance. Saul, the human will, may give you some pretty fancy ideas, but they will not belong to the son of God within you. David, *the beloved within you,* has not proved them, but he has great confidence in the "five smooth pebbles," Truth ideas, with which he selects to defend himself.

What a Wonderful Allegory

This is an allegory, a wonderful lesson in metaphysics, a lesson for you and for me. The Philistines are the wanderers; the word, in the Hebrew, actually means *migrating, transitory, wandering.* People in the Bible stand for thoughts in our consciousness and here the Philistines indicate wandering thoughts in our minds, thoughts deviating from the true course of the Spirit. Goliath means in the Hebrew *the exile, a soothsayer.* It is that tremendous, sorrowful thought that we have that tells us that we cannot face life and live it as we really want to. It makes us think we have to conform, to be influenced by appearances. "Bigness counts," it argues. "To be arrayed with material goods causes one to be secure," it rationalizes.

Goliath is *of Gath* meaning fortune. The Goliath thought has about as much value as a soothsayer basing his predictions on chance or fortune. Such a thought is *an exile, foreign to our True nature.* Goliath represents to us the artificial forces of human power, striding, bellowing, trying to act like something strong and invincible.

The *Metaphysical Bible Dictionary*, in discussing the metaphysical meaning of Goliath says:

> Ideas are not all of the same importance. Some are large and strong, and some are weak and small. There are aggressive, domineering ideas, like Goliath, that parade themselves prominantly, brag about their power, and with fearful threats of disaster keep us frightened into submission to their unrighteous reign. These domineering ideas of error have one argument that they impress upon us at all times: fear of results should we dare to meet them openly and oppose their reign in consciousness.[4]

Doesn't that sound just like old Goliath as he terrorized Israel, the *children of God, the thoughts that would be God-like or spiritual?*

David is interpreted from the Hebrew to mean *the beloved, the beloved of God, that inner Self that is within the very depth of us.* It is powerful to meet the enemy no matter how large he (it) may seem to be. Nor does this true Self need the armor of superstition that we so often think necessary in life. We have only to think a thought in love, believing and trusting in it. Releasing it to the Lord, the Divine Law of Life, we are delivered gloriously out of the hand of the *enemy* no matter how imposing this *enemy* may be. As David told Goliath, *the battle is the Lord's.*

The Battle Is the Lord's

Then said David to the Philistine, Thou comest to me with a sword, and with a spear, and with a shield: but I come to

4. *Metaphysical Bible Dictionary, op. cit.,* p. 240.

thee in the name of the Lord of hosts, the God of the armies of Israel, whom thou hast defied.

This day will the Lord deliver thee into mine hand; and I will smite thee, and take thine head from thee; and I will give the carcases of the host of the Philistine this day unto the fowls of the air, and to the wild beasts of the earth; that all the earth may know that there is a God in Israel.

And all this assembly shall know that the Lord saveth not with sword and spear: for the battle is the Lord's, and he will give you into our hands. —I Samuel 17:45–47

This is the way that we should meet every problem that confronts us, this is the courage it takes to kill the giants that appear from time to time. They can look terrifying. They hurl insults at us just as Goliath hurled insults at David; but when we remember that the battle is not ours but the Lord's, we take on the armor of Almighty God. His Truth shall be "thy shield and buckler," [5] "our refuge and strength, a very present help in trouble." [6]

And David put his hand in his bag, and took thence a stone, and slang it, and smote the Philistine in his forehead, that the stone sunk into his forehead; and he fell upon his face to the earth.

So David prevailed over the Philistine with a sling and with a stone, and smote the Philistine, and slew him; but there was no sword in the hand of David.

Therefore David ran, and stood upon the Philistine, and took his sword, and drew it out of the sheath thereof, and slew him, and cut off his head therewith. And when the Philistines saw their champion was dead, they fled.

—I Samuel 17:49–51

5. Psalms 91:4.
6. Psalms 46:1.

How to Kill the Giants in Your Life

So David, the beloved son of God within each one of us, paying no attention to outer appearances, needing no protection from the wealth or power of materiality, takes just one little pebble, one little thought of Truth, and hits Goliath right in the center of his forehead, right at the point of the giant's self-styled intellectual knowledge. This was the one place where he was not protected. He was vulnerable there to Truth. The Bible tells us that he "fell upon his face. . . ." I love that. So many of our present-day colloquialisms come from Bible stories. This is an expression that we use today—*he literally fell on his face!* Just one little pebble, one little Truth thought released, was all that it took!

The power of Truth is tremendous. Once we use it, in love, to overcome what seems to be a tremendous problem, we find that the problem has a vulnerable point for love to work through. As Jesus said, "Love is the fulfilling of the Law." [7]

Dare to Be Yourself

David dared to cast aside the armor that was offered him. He dared to be himself, the beloved of God, to use what he had, the omnipotent Power of God.

You, too, are *the beloved, a unique individual, a perfect child of God, made in the image and likeness of God.* You have abilities, skills, an infinite Source of Power to call upon. You are the individualization of the Source of All Good, All Power. When you can trust Infinite Love working in and through you, when you can truly say with David, "the battle is the Lord's, . . ." then the problems which seem to be impregnable, solid, fixed obstacles, veritable giants, will give

7. Romans 13:10.

before the Divine Self of you. They will *fall on their faces* and be no more. You will be reminded of David as you, figuratively speaking, cut off their heads with their own swords. The very thing that seemed so terrifying to you will prove to be the thing that convinces you of its nothingness. Love takes dominion, puts the giant under its feet (understanding).

You must act in love, believing in yourself for what you are in Truth, daring to be your real Self, the beloved child of God who needs no human armor, only *a little pebble (of Truth) and a lot of faith in God!*

XIV   HOW TO WIN BATTLES
JEHOSHAPHAT'S WAY

II Chronicles, Chapter 20

The story that I am about to tell you is one of my favorites. In fact, it was King Jehoshaphat who introduced me to the secret code that unravels the hidden mystery of the Old Testament. I will never forget my mounting excitement as I checked out the Hebrew meanings of the proper names associated with this biblical character. If only they would prove to be correlative—and they did. Each name contributed to the entire story. So, as we consider some of the Bible stories that illustrate the new approach to the Old Testament, we could hardly leave Jehoshaphat out. His name gives us a clue right away.

Judge Righteous Judgment

King Jehoshaphat—dominion through divine judgment.

Upon Jehoshaphat's return to Jerusalem, he set up judges in the fenced cities, instructing them: ". . . Take heed what ye do: for ye judge not for man, but for the Lord, who is with you in the judgment." [1]

1. II Chronicles 19:6.

Right away we know that Jehoshaphat stands for the quality of *judging righteous judgment,* and we would do well to let Jesus help us clarify this meaning. "Judge not according to the appearance, but judge righteous judgment." [2]

This is a story that is designed to show us the value of righteous judgment. What appears, on the surface, to be one of the goriest battles in the Old Testament turns out to be a powerful allegory teaching us how to meet the problems of this world in which we live today. It is designed to be read when the enemies of this world threaten us; at those times when our problems seem to be like a multitude descending upon us from "beyond the sea" of consciousness. The enemies of which I speak are the enemies "of . . . [our] own household," [3] our own thought enemies who threaten Jehoshaphat (God's righteous judgment in us).

Every Battle in the Bible Is a Battle within Ourselves

Every battle described in the Old Testament has a counterpart in us. In order to fully avail ourselves of the inspiring lessons that these stories bring us, we must forget for awhile the historical significance and keep in mind that they have an allegorical meaning, a timely meaning for us today. We are speaking of battles in consciousness, battles between our own thought people. Our own confused state of mind is the battleground. As Paul puts it:

> For we wrestle not against flesh and blood, but against principalities, against powers, against the rulers of the darkness of this world, against spiritual wickedness in high places.
>
> —Ephesians 6:12

2. John 7:24.
3. Matthew 10:36.

A Highly Dramatic Play

In all of the Old Testament there is no better example of the way in which the secret code reveals the hidden meaning in the Bible than the story of Jehoshaphat overcoming his enemies. It is presented for us as a highly dramatic play in five acts, to be found in the first twenty-five verses of Chapter twenty of II Chronicles. I can just see this drama unfold in its symbolic version, like a great movie extravaganza, the Cecil B. De Mille variety! There are only two actors in the cast, but like the Bible movies, Hollywood version, there are many extras—real mob scenes.

THE CAST

Jehoshaphat, King of Judah.
Jahaziel, one of the priests.
The enemy; children of Moab, the children
    of Ammon, the children of Mt.
    Seir.
The congregation of Judah.

ACT I

Jehoshaphat sees the enemy approaching. He is greatly frightened and seeks the Lord, proclaiming a fast throughout all Judah.

It came to pass after this also, that the children of Moab, and the children of Ammon, and with them other beside the Ammonites, came against Jehoshaphat to battle.

Then there came some that told Jehoshaphat, saying, There cometh a great multitude against thee from beyond the sea on this side Syria; and, behold, they be in Hazazonta-mar, which is En-gedi.

And Jehoshaphat feared, and set himself to seek the Lord, and proclaimed a fast throughout all Judah.

—II Chronicles 20:1–3

ACT II

In Act II, Jehoshaphat and his people gather together in the house of the Lord and find their guidance through prayer.

And Jehoshaphat stood in the congregation of Judah and Jerusalem, in the house of the Lord, before the new court,

And said, O Lord God of our father, art not thou God in heaven? and rulest not thou over all the kingdoms of the heathen? and in thine hand is there not power and might, so that none is able to withstand thee?

Art not thou our God, who didst drive out the inhabitants of this land before thy people Israel, and gavest it to the seed of Abraham thy friend for ever?

And they dwelt therein, and have built thee a sanctuary therein for thy name, saying,

If, when evil cometh upon us, as the sword, judgment, or pestilence, or famine, we stand before this house, and in thy presence, (for thy name is in this house,) and cry unto thee in our affliction, then thou wilt hear and help.

And now, behold, the children of Ammon and Moab and mount Seir, whom thou wouldest not let Israel invade, when they came out of the land of Egypt, but they turned from them, and destroyed them not;

Behold, I say, how they reward us, to come to cast us out of thy possession, which thou hast given us to inherit.

O our God, wilt thou not judge them? for we have no might against this great company that cometh against us; neither know we what to do: but our eyes are upon thee.

—II Chronicles 20:5–12

ACT III

As the curtain comes up on Act III, the congregation of Judah is still standing in hushed silence around their King awaiting an answer from the Lord. Like an unprogrammed Quaker meeting, the answer come through Jahaziel.

Then upon Jahaziel the son of Zechariah, the son of Benaiah, the son of Jeiel, the son of Mattaniah, a Levite of the sons of Asaph, came the Spirit of the Lord in the midst of the congregation;

And he said, Hearken ye, all Judah, and ye inhabitants of Jerusalem, and thou king Jehoshaphat, Thus saith the Lord unto you, Be not afraid nor dismayed by reason of this great multitude; for the battle is not yours, but God's.

To morrow go ye down against them: behold, they come up by the cliff of Ziz; and ye shall find them at the end of the brook, before the wilderness of Jeruel.

Ye shall not need to fight in this battle: set yourselves, stand ye still, and see the salvation of the Lord with you, O Judah and Jerusalem: fear not, nor be dismayed; to morrow go out against them: for the Lord will be with you.

And Jehoshaphat bowed his head with his face to the ground: and all Judah and the inhabitants of Jerusalem fell before the Lord, worshipping the Lord.

And the Levites, of the children of the Kohathites, and of the children of the Korhites, stood up to praise the Lord God of Israel with a loud voice on high. —II Chronicles 20:13–19

ACT IV

The congregation of Judah goes out to meet the enemy singing songs of praise. Singers are appointed that go out to meet the enemy singing: ". . . Praise the Lord; for his mercy endureth for ever."

And they rose early in the morning, and went forth into the wilderness of Tekoa: and as they went forth, Jehoshaphat stood and said, Hear me, O Judah, and ye inhabitants of Jerusalem; Believe in the Lord your God, so shall ye be established; believe his prophets, so shall ye prosper.

And when he had consulted with the people, he appointed singers unto the Lord, and that [they] should praise the beauty of holiness, as they went out before the army, and to say, Praise the Lord; for his mercy endureth for ever.

—II Chronicles 20:20, 21

ACT V

In Act V, a very wonderful thing happens. The children of Israel behold the miracle working Power of God. The Lord sets ambushments in the midst of the enemy, and the children of Moab and the children of Ammon set upon the children of mount Seir. The enemies destroy each other so that none escape. The people of Judah have only one thing left to do—gather in the spoils. The play ends with the people of Judah gathering up the precious jewels that they strip from the dead bodies.

And when they began to sing and to praise, the Lord set ambushments against the children of Ammon, Moab and mount Seir, which were come against Judah; and they were smitten.

For the children of Ammon and Moab stood up against the inhabitants of mount Seir, utterly to slay and destroy them: and when they had made an end of the inhabitants of Seir, every one helped to destroy another.

And when Judah came toward the watch tower in the wilderness, they looked unto the multitude, and, behold, they were dead bodies fallen to the earth, and none escaped.

And when Jehoshaphat and his people came to take away the spoil of them, they found among them in abundance both riches with the dead bodies, and precious jewels, which they stripped off for themselves, more than they could carry away: and they were three days in gathering of the spoil, it was so much. —II Chronicles 20:22–25

What drama! What a motion picture this would make! Can't you just see the people going forth to battle arrayed in glorious color, banners flying, trumpets playing, beautiful blue sky overhead! Behold their surprise as they discover the riches and jewels that are there to be gathered in at the last. What an opportunity for the scenario writer, the color expert, the costumer, and think of the possibilities for appropriate musical background to accompany these dramatic scenes. Truly, the Bible never does anything in halfway measures. It almost overdramatizes so that we will be sure to catch the hidden meaning there for us.

What the Play Means to Us Today

Before we go into the hidden meaning in Act I, let's see what some of the proper names mean.

Jehoshaphat—divine judgment; righteous judgment; the government of Jehovah.

Jehaziel—Jehovah reveals; Truth revealed; divine Inspiration.

Children of Moab—thoughts springing from dark, negative thinking. (Moab was the son of Lot and Lot stands for dark, negative thinking.)

Children of Ammon—thoughts springing from the Ammon parent thought; careless, disorderly thinking; thoughts based upon race consciousness; world opinion.

Children of mount Seir—thoughts springing from the mount Seir consciousness; sense consciousness; emotional, stormy thinking. The Hebrew meaning of mount Seir (parent thought) is bristling; shaggy; hairy; rough; shaking; shuddering; fearful; stormy; tempestuous; he-goat.

Turning now to Act I, we have this great multitude of enemy thoughts threatening Jehoshaphat, *our divine judgment,* and the thought people of Judah and Jerusalem, *our thoughts of praise (Judah) and peace (Jerusalem).* We've all been there and, like Jehoshaphat, we've been afraid. Sometimes the enemy takes the guise of *what will people say?* At other times it may be *what will happen to our country? Will there be enough to go around? Will the bank account cover the bills? What will happen to me in my old age?* The children of Moab and Ammon and mount Seir come against all of us and generally we think that no one ever had such enemies before; but always they are thoughts that threaten our inner security, thoughts based on *judging by appearances, judging by world opinion, fearful, shaking, shuddering, stormy, tempestuous thoughts.* Often they wake us up in the night when our spiritual resources seem to be at lowest ebb. We are afraid and sometimes we wouldn't give a nickel for our Jehoshaphat's chances of survival.

It is interesting here to note where the enemy comes from:

beyond the sea—outside of our usual consciousness.
Hazazontamar—the victory divided; a divided mind.
Engedi—fountain of fortune; the wilderness of making a decision.
Syria—the level of thinking that has no understanding of spiritual Truth.

They surely do seem like a multitude, these clamoring thoughts that threaten our spiritual peace. We are tempted to vacillate; we can't make a decision. Jehoshaphat is afraid. But Jehoshaphat, *divine judgment in us,* is King—he has dominion—so he proclaims a fast from negation, a fast throughout all Judah, *spiritual consciousness that praises God.* This is the moment of overcoming when the battle could go either way. As we stick by Jehoshaphat, we judge righteous judgment. Turning away from appearances, we and all of our spiritual thought people go into the house of the Lord and there we have a good prayer. There is no more beautiful prayer in all of the Bible than the one here attributed to Jehoshaphat. It recognizes the Almighty Power of God, the dominion of God over all, including the seeming evil. It remembers past spiritual victories to build up faith in the invincible Power of God. It looks to the faith of Abraham, the faith that endures, and then it states its need—deliverance from the enemy. It is a prayer that places radical reliance upon God while maintaining complete humility. ". . . For we have no might against this great company that cometh against us; neither know we what to do."

"For when I am weak, then am I strong," said Paul. It is through this prayer of complete surrender to God Power that Power is realized. The spiritual thoughts stand in the house of the Lord; *consciousness of divine Protection,* before the new court; *a new attitude of mind,* with all of their attention focused on Good. And this includes their little ones, their wives, and their children—all of the thoughts and feelings, even the little thoughts that branch off from the big thoughts. It is a wonderful moment of standing firm in the Truth.

And now Jahaziel, *divine Inspiration,* speaks. At first glance, it seems strange that we are given the ancestors of Jahaziel, but upon researching them we see that they are all a part of Jahaziel's nature.

Jahaziel—Jehovah reveals; Truth revealed; divine Inspiration.
Zechariah—the Lord is remembered.

Benaiah—son of Jehovah; prospered by Jehovah; restored by Jehovah.
Jeiel—treasure of God; God collects; God unifies.
Mattaniah—gift of Jehovah.
Asaph—collector; assembler; collective spiritual thinking.

It is clear that Jahaziel is God-endowed to give the people the right advice. Through this high consciousness comes "the Spirit of the Lord in the midst of the congregation." This is the divine Inspiration that comes to all of us when we remember to turn away from false conditions, negative thinking, wild, stormy, emotional thoughts that fill us with fear. When we take our stand for the Lord, we, too, are told that "the battle is not yours, but God's." The word that comes through Jahaziel is that they do not need to hurry. This takes all anxiety out of the situation. Tomorrow is time enough to think about the enemy. Moreover, they are told just where to find the enemy. The human mind lays such store by the reflected light of the intellect when all the time divine Intelligence knows the answers.

Ziz—reflected light; the reflected light of the intellect.
Jeruel—God points the way—even in the wilderness of human thought.

O, if we could always remember these wonderful words of Jahaziel:

Ye shall not need to fight in this battle: set yourselves, stand ye still, and see the salvation of the Lord with you, O Judah and Jerusalem: fear not, nor be dismayed; to morrow go out against them: the the Lord will be with you.
—II Chronicles 20:17

With one mind, they all praise the Lord. In such unified consciousness, the battle is won in a Bible story or in any challenging situation today. We might say that it is a foregone conclusion that tomorrow will bring the victory.

So in Act IV, it seems perfectly logical that the enemy be met in song. All resistance has gone out of the situation. Singers are appointed to go out to meet the enemy singing: ". . . Praise the Lord; for his mercy endureth for ever." There is no fear, no resistance, no antagonism. Early in the morning, they go forth singing. With the new fresh light they meet the enemy unafraid even in the wilderness of Tekoa. Tekoa stands for *pitching a tent or putting up a new house, a new stand in consciousness.* It is a wonderful moment. Nothing has happened to the enemy, but the battle is won. How often we have had it proven to us that once the battle is won in consciousness, the events fall into place in an orderly fashion.

In Act V, we see the demonstration, the signs following, the orderly conclusion of the whole matter. First, the Lord sets ambushments in the midst of the enemy. This is the cutest part of all. Ambushments mean *protected strength within.* How well this word *ambushments* relates to the allegory. Every time we lift our consciousness through prayer to the point where we are unified in faith and praise, we do have *protected strength within,* the strength that can move mountains or accomplish anything that needs to be accomplished. But the part I love most of all is what happens next—the enemies destroy each other! Those old negative thoughts cross each other out. Nothing can stand in the face of Truth, but error destroys itself.

And when Judah, used here interchangeably with children of Israel, *the spiritual awareness of being sons of God,* comes toward the watch tower in the wilderness, they behold that none has escaped. The enemy is all dead. Was this a gory battle? No, a nice clean job of cleaning up some negative thinking that threatened to destroy the good thinking.

watch tower—that high place in consciousness where the vision is extended.

Summary

This is really the story of how Scientific Prayer is victorious over all problems. It was Emmet Fox who said:

> Scientific Prayer will enable you, sooner or later, to get yourself, or anyone else, out of any difficulty on the face of the earth. It is the Golden Key to harmony and happiness.
>
> All that you have to do is this: *Stop thinking about the difficulty, whatever it is, and think about God instead.*[4]

The Jehoshaphat story explains so beautifully what scientific prayer really is. It is refusing to look at the great multitude of negative thoughts that seem to be coming against us. It is being still in the recognition of the Presence of God that is right where we are. It is listening for divine Inspiration and hearing the Jahaziel, in us, tell us the Truth about the situation; that we do not have to fight in this battle, that we do not have to be frightened or dismayed; that we can calmly await the salvation of the Lord (divine Law of infinite Goodness) knowing that God is with us at all times. It is, then, obeying the instructions of Jehoshaphat, in us, acting upon these instructions by fearlessly going out into the midst of the enemy, praising the divine Law. It is being so sure that God has ordained Wholeness, perfect Life, divine Right Action everywhere present that we can praise the mercy of God that endures forever. It really does not matter what kind of enemy may have beset us—children of Moab, children of Ammon, or children of Mt. Seir. They are only children—little thoughts springing from parent thoughts of fear and negation. The enemy we face may call itself lack, sickness, unhappiness. Like

4. Emmet Fox, *op. cit.*, pp. 137, 138.

the enemies of Jehoshaphat, our enemies usually come in bunches; but they are not the things that seem to come at us, but are our own responses to them. With Jehoshaphat (divine judgment) ruler of our kingdom within, with this new up-lifted consciousness, we, too, have protected strength within. Our enemies, too, destroy themselves. We do not have to do a thing but praise the Lord and carry away the precious jewels of spiritual growth, the added blessings that come with the victory within.

Truly, Jehoshaphat teaches us how to win all battles, the only way, God's way of divine judgment.

The riches and jewels are more than can be carried away. This is a very clever way of saying that out of the trials and tribulations that we meet in Truth, overcoming them through a recognition that the Lord is with us, praising and worshipping the Truth that endures right in the midst of the situation, come rich rewards. How often we look back and say we are actually grateful for the problem that made us stretch for without it we would never have had the rich spiritual growth that came with it.

XV   JOB—THE MAN WHO
MADE A COMEBACK

The Book of Job

History is full of stories of men who lost everything that they possessed and then, starting out all over again, recouped their losses and went on to undreamed of success. It is often said, "You can't keep a good man down." We have all known failures who have made a comeback. Such a man was our friend Job. His name in Hebrew means, *returning or coming back.* So real does Job become to us, as we read of him, that long before we reach the end of the story, we come to know him intimately. How Job suffers! How he complains! What well-meaning friends! And that nagging wife—oh, the patience of Job! What a story! Job—the man who made a comeback— presents a lesson everyone should heed today.

The Book of Job is a dramatic poem, a philosophical drama, in which the characters represent attitudes of mind or states of consciousness. Job is everyman struggling self-righteously to prove that his troubles are not his fault. The choices offered to him in meeting adversity are the choices offered to each one of us.

The play is presented in three acts, plus a prologue and an epilogue. So well organized is this drama that it could easily be presented today with little revision. The program would line up something like this:

PROLOGUE

Act I . . . . JOB IS CURSED
Act II . . . . . . JOB ARGUES WITH HIS WIFE AND HIS FRIENDS
Act III . . . . . THE TRUTH IS REVEALED TO JOB

EPILOGUE

THE CAST

Job	Job's wife
Satan	Eliphaz the Temanite
The Lord	Bildad the Shuhite
Sons of God	Zophar the Naamathite
Messengers	Elihu

Voice from the whirlwind

The Prologue

In the prologue, we learn quite a bit about Job. Here the narrator informs us just what kind of a man Job was—God-fearing, self-righteous, abiding by the letter of the law.

> There was a man in the land of Uz, whose name was Job; and that man was perfect and upright, and one that feared God, and eschewed evil. —Job 1:1

The first five verses of the Book of Job, you might say, give us a portrait of Job, his character, and his position in the world.

Job is described as a rich man with vast holdings, property, thousands of sheep, camels, cattle, a great household of servants at his beck and call. Almost at once we are told that he is a good man, perfect and upright, one who fears God and has no use for evil. Moreover, we are told that he has seven sons and three daughters and that he is "the greatest of all the men of the east."

> And there were born unto him seven sons and three daughters.
>
> His substance also was seven thousand sheep, and three thousand camels, and five hundred yoke of oxen, and five hundred she asses, and a very great household; so that this man was the greatest of all the men of the east.
>
> And his sons went and feasted in their houses, every one his day; and sent and called for their three sisters to eat and to drink with them.
>
> And it was so, when the days of their feasting were gone about, that Job sent and sanctified them, and rose up early in the morning, and offered burnt offerings according to the number of them all: for Job said, It may be that my sons have sinned, and cursed God in their hearts. Thus did Job continually. —Job 1:2–5

Job wasn't taking any chances. So "downright upright" was he that he even made up for the sins of his sons (*thoughts springing from a parent thought*), lest inadvertently one of the family might make the mistake of cursing God in their hearts. In the very beginning, we learned that Job considered cursing God in one's heart to be a sin that must at all costs be avoided.

The stage is set. The narrator has given us a character sketch of Job. The drama is about to begin. We can almost hear the orchestra performing a very dramatic overture. As we wait for the curtain to go up on Act I, let us see what we can discover by applying our secret code to some of the key words in the Prologue.

Uz—(Hebrew) well settled, firmness.
Job—(Hebrew) persecuted, afflicted, returning, a coming back.

seven sons—perfect masculine or conscious thoughts.

three daughters—unified subconscious mind.

sheep—pure, innocent thoughts.

camels—patient thoughts given to forbearance.

cattle—thoughts more on the materialistic side, relating to sensation.

east—the within; the inner life.

servants—thoughts that serve Job, thoughts subject to his dominion.

The Job consciousness is quickly identified as being "in the land of Uz. . . ." This indicates that it is settled thinking, a firm state of mind. In the mystical terminology of the Scriptures, we are told that Job represents a very important state of mind, a dominant attitude in the thinking or inner life (the east), "the greatest of all the men of the east." This is a state of mind that is made up of many *pure innocent thoughts*. Job's holdings are heavy in sheep. He had seven thousand sheep (pure innocent thoughts). His next largest holdings are in camels. The camel has been called *Job's beast* because of its nature. It is noted for its patience and forbearance. The camels, then, stand for his patient nature. Job represents a good state of mind except for his self-righteousness. Like many good men and upright, he apparently believed that his goodness set him up above other men and entitled him to special consideration.

The seven sons represent thoughts springing from the parent thought in the directive or conscious mind; the three daughters represent the subconscious thinking. Going back briefly to our chapter on the mystery of numbers, we see that his thinking was very well-balanced—rather perfect in the conscious mind and unified in the feeling nature or subconscious mind.

Like all self-righteous men, Job lived by the letter of the law. It was of this type that Paul was thinking when he said:

Not that we are sufficient of ourselves to think any thing as of ourselves; but our sufficiency is of God;

Who also hath made us able ministers of the new testament; not of the letter, but of the spirit: for the letter killeth, but the spirit giveth life. —II Corinthians 3:5, 6

To summarize: Job is the self-righteous human self of each one of us that tempts us to place our security in our possessions, our self-righteous attitudes, our human thought-taking. Like all self-righteous thinking, Job thinking lays great store by outer form. Job continually made sacrifices lest his thinking go astray; but this was not enough. He who puts his faith in the world of appearances will sooner or later be disappointed.

Act I—Job Is Cursed

SCENE 1

As the play opens, we discover that trouble is brewing for Job. I rather picture this scene as a ballet sequence. High in the center of the stage the Lord sits upon his throne while the sons of God present themselves in beautiful pageantry. Heralded by trumpets, they dance in, Satan in their midst. The sons of God are dressed in white satin, Satan in red with a long tail that is continually threshing back and forth like a flexible harpoon. An intricate bit of choreography brings them to the foot of the throne. The music stops on a dramatic note. After a hushed moment filled with expectation, the Lord says:

Whence comes thou? —Job 1:7

The spotlight shifts to Satan. Satan:

From going to and fro in the earth, and from walking up and down in it. —Job 1:7

The conversation between the Lord and Satan continues:

And the Lord said unto Satan, Hast thou considered my servant Job, that there is none like him in the earth, a perfect and an upright man, one that feareth God, and escheweth evil?

Then Satan answered the Lord, and said, Doth Job fear God for nought?

Hast not thou made an hedge about him, and about his house, and about all that he hath on every side? thou hast blessed the work of his hands, and his substance is increased in the land.

But put forth thine hand now, and touch all that he hath, and he will curse thee to thy face.

And the Lord said unto Satan, Behold, all that he hath is in thy power; only upon himself put not forth thine hand. So Satan went forth from the presence of the Lord.

—Job 1:8–12

Scene 2

In Scene 2, we find Job receiving the news from the three messengers. The play would probably include a little ballet here, too. Job is told that his oxen and asses, sheep and camels, sons and daughters have all been taken.

And there was a day when his sons and his daughters were eating and drinking wine in their eldest brother's house:

And there came a messenger unto Job, and said, The oxen were plowing, and the asses feeding beside them:

And the Sabeans fell upon them, and took them away; yea, they have slain the servants with the edge of the sword; and I only am escaped alone to tell thee.

While he was yet speaking, there came also another, and said, The fire of God is fallen from heaven, and hath burned up the sheep, and the servants, and consumed them; and I only am escaped alone to tell thee.

While he was yet speaking, there came also another, and said, The Chaldeans made out three bands, and fell upon the camels, and have carried them away, yea, and slain the servants with the edge of the sword; and I only am escaped alone to tell thee.

While he was yet speaking, there came also another, and said, Thy sons and thy daughters were eating and drinking wine in their eldest brother's house:

And, behold, there came a great wind from the wilderness, and smote the four corners of the house, and it fell upon the young men, and they are dead; and I only am escaped alone to tell thee. —Job 1:13–19

All this trouble. Grief on every side. "Just one blow after another!" we hear people say when they find that they cannot depend upon the world of materiality. It would seem that there wasn't much more that could afflict Job. He had been hit on every side; yet he keeps his faith.

Then Job arose, and rent his mantle, and shaved his head, and fell down upon the ground, and worshipped,

And said, Naked came I out of my mother's womb, and naked shall I return thither: the Lord gave, and the Lord hath taken away; blessed be the name of the Lord.

In all this Job sinned not, nor charged God foolishly.

—Job 1:20–22

SCENE 3

In Scene 3 we have Satan again presenting himself with the sons of God before the Lord. Again the Lord asks, "Whence comest thou?"

Again Satan answers, "From going to and fro in the earth, and from walking up and down in it."

> And the Lord said unto Satan, Hast thou considered my servant Job, that there is none like him in the earth, a perfect and an upright man, one that feareth God, and escheweth evil? and still he holdeth fast his integrity, although thou movedst me against him, to destroy him without cause.
>
> And Satan answered the Lord, and said, Skin for skin, yea, all that a man hath will he give for his life.
>
> But put forth thine hand now, and touch his bone and his flesh, and he will curse thee to thy face.
>
> And the Lord said unto Satan, Behold, he is in thine hand; but save his life. —Job 2:3–6

Now Satan plays what he considers his trump card. He causes Job to have boils "from the sole of his foot unto his crown." The scene ends with Job sitting down among the ashes scraping his body with a piece of broken crockery.

> Then said his wife unto him, Dost thou still retain thine integrity? curse God, and die.
>
> But he said unto her, Thou speakest as one of the foolish women speaketh. What? shall we receive good at the hand of God, and shall we not receive evil? In all this did not Job sin with his lips. —Job 2:9, 10

Each one of us, in his journey in consciousness, is at times tempted to blame God for his afflictions not realizing that they are brought on by Satan, the lie of our own erroneous thinking. It often seems that life is testing man to make him give up. In Truth, it is man testing himself. Man is continually seeking to return to the Garden of Eden where he can partake of the fruit of the "tree of life" which means to live by Grace. But, as long as he chooses to eat from the "tree of the knowledge of good and evil," he is going to experience good and evil. It is human judgment and the results of human judgment. As long as Job thought that great possessions, a large family, and good health, were to be judged as good on the one hand, that the loss of them was to be judged as evil on the other hand, he was eating from the "tree of the knowledge of good and evil." It was inevitable that he be expelled from his Garden of Eden. The job consciousness in this answer shows that it lives by human judgment, or a knowledge of good and evil. He is not yet ready to acknowledge that all is God. His God must be the author of both good and evil. But still Job refuses to curse God and die. How often each one of us confronted with disappointments and discouragement is tempted to curse God and die to the true Selfhood. Murmuring and railing against an unkind fate seems the only outlet for our human frustration.

In order to even begin to understand this philosophical drama, we must understand the nature of Satan. The more we expand our understanding of Truth, the more we come to see that an understanding of evil is just as important as an understanding of good; for as long as we believe in evil, we cannot truly believe in omnipresent Goodness.

Satan, pictured by ancient artists of Biblical lore as wearing a red suit, complete with horns and forked tail, is given many names in the Bible. He is called the Devil, the Dragon, the Evil One, the Angel of the Bottomless Pit, the Prince of this World, the Prince of the Power of the Air, the God of this World, Apollyon, Abaddon, Beliel, Beelzebub. While he has many names, the inference is always the same—he is always pictured as the adversary of good, a belief in the power of evil.

Satan is a Hebrew word, derived from a verb which means *to oppose, to be an adversary.* Beliel is also used as evil opposition. The Hebrew word means *worthless.* It is not the name of any individual, but any man or woman who is considered wicked, worthless, lawless might be referred to as a son or daughter of Beliel. Hence it stands for that kind of thinking in man. Beelzebub, or Beelzebul, means *lord of the flies,* or *lord of filth.* Beelzebub was used to denote *the lord of the demons,* hence, the chief of erroneous thinking.

The *Metaphysical Bible Dictionary* gives, to my mind, the best interpretation of Satan.

The deceiving phase of mind in man that has fixed ideas in opposition to Truth *(adversary, lier in wait, accuser, opposer, hater, an enemy).* Satan assumes various forms in man's consciousness, among which may be mentioned egotism, a puffing up of the personality; and the opposite of this, self-depreciation, which admits the "accuser" into the consciousness. This "accuser" makes man believe that he is inherently evil.

Satan is the "Devil," a state of mind formed by man's personal ideas of his power and completeness and sufficiency apart from God. Besides at times puffing up the personality, this satanic thought often turns about and, after having tempted one to do evil, discourages the soul by accusing it of sin. Summed up, it is the state of mind in man that believes in its own sufficiency independent of its creative Source.[1]

Satan seems to have power. Satan seems to get around a lot. How simple it is when calamity strikes to blame it on Satan when all the time we invite trouble by our own mistaken thinking. Satan, in Bible stories, is always the scapegoat. But Job diagnoses his own mental malady when he says in Act II:

For the thing which I greatly feared is come upon me, and that which I was afraid of is come unto me. —Job 3:25

1. *Metaphysical Bible Dictionary, op. cit.,* p. 575.

How often we find that the very thing we fear comes into our experience—the artist who loses his eyesight, the musician who becomes deaf, the singer who loses his voice, the athlete who develops some crippling bone disease, and on and on. Could it be that they, deep within the hidden reaches of the subconscious mind, feared that just these things would deprive them of their ability to produce? When we trust in the world of effects, even when these effects are expressed as our own physical strength, we are never at rest, never *in safety*. As the Psalmist said:

> Some trust in chariots, and some in horses: but we will remember the name of the Lord our God. —Psalms 20:7

There is a subtle difference here that many never come to see. It is all right to use the chariots and horses, to use advertising and other conveniences known to man, but our trust must first be in God.

> Thine, O Lord, is the greatness, and the power, and the glory, and the victory, and the majesty: for all that is in the heaven and in the earth is thine; thine is the kingdom, O Lord, and thou art exalted as head above all.
> Both riches and honour come of thee, and thou reignest over all; and in thine hand is power and might; and in thine hand it is to make great, and to give strength unto all.
> —The Prayer of David, I Chronicles 29:11, 12

Job did not listen to his wife. He did not *curse God and die;* but he still had some lessons to learn before he could "dwell in the land . . ." in confidence.

> Trust in the Lord, and do good; so shalt thou dwell in the land, and verily thou shalt be fed. —Psalms 37:3

In Act I, the Sabeans and the Chaldeans represent the temptation to believe that intellectual power is all that one needs to find security. The Chaldeans were the soothsayers, the astrologers, the magicians of Babylon. They represent the temptation to put one's faith in fortune-telling and superstitions of all kinds. Babylon always stands for confusion in human thinking, always destruction. The *fire of God* is the *cleansing fire of Spirit,* the Truth that falls from heaven (within) to teach us through experience so that we may discover where our true values lie. The "great wind from the wilderness . . . [that] smote the four corners of the house . . ." and destroyed Job's sons represents the confusion that comes from the wilderness of our own unenlightened thinking (wilderness) and takes the house (the individual consciousness). All of the thought (sons) that reside in that house (consciousness) are destroyed.

Act II—Job Argues with His Wife and Friends

As Act II opens, we see Job's three friends who have, by pre-arrangement, come to comfort him in his great time of trial. They, too, have rent their mantles and put dust on their heads. And now they sit around the miserable Job who is on his ash heap, scratching his boils. It is not a pretty sight. They have been sitting there with Job for seven days and seven nights. Seven means *it is finished.* They are determined to stick it out, to finish the job, to find some remedy for Job's sad plight. Among them they give him every conceivable kind of advice—that is, every conceivable kind of advice on the human and intellectual level. Much of it is very good advice, too, but somehow, it just doesn't help Job too much.

The curtain opens on Scene I of Act II. Job says:

> Let the day perish wherein I was born, and the night in which it was said, there is a man child conceived. —Job 3:3

Picture Job, surrounded by his friends, sitting on the ash

heap scratching his boils. Muttering under his breath, he complains bitterly against his plight and ends with the oft-quoted words:

> For the thing which I greatly feared is come upon me, and that which I was afraid of is come unto me. —Job 3:25

In this state of mind, Job does not comprehend that he has attracted his own misfortune through fear.

Fear is the great enemy of mankind. It has been wisely said, "There is nothing to fear but fear itself." Fear is the beginning of every ill, the sin against the Holy Ghost. It is faith in the enemy. It is the sin (mistake) that cannot be forgiven because as long as it continues, it increases misery. Fear reduces us to the bottomless pit because it crowds out of consciousness the life-giving Power of Love. *What I greatly feared has come upon me* is the Biblical way of expressing the Law of Attraction. Jesus explained the Law of Attraction when he said *it is done unto you as you believe.* Fear, a belief in evil of any sort, will draw evil to the one who fears. Fear attracts the very thing that is feared.

And now, Job's friends try to comfort him.

In Scene 2 of Act II, Eliphaz speaks.

In Scene 3 of Act II, Bildad speaks.

In Scene 4 of Act II, Zophar speaks.

Each one gives Job excellent advice. There is nothing wrong with their good advice. Eliphaz starts by saying, in effect, "I hope you won't be angry, but I cannot help but tell you where you are making your mistake." He tells Job that for a man who has helped others and given them inspiration, "Where's *your* faith?" He goes on to say that if Job is innocent he will come out all right. He gives quite a sermon on the Law of Cause and Effect.

Eliphaz backs up his lecture by telling Job that his words

of wisdom came to him in a vision. He is like the person who says, "I know intuitively what is wrong with you and what you should do about it," or, "It came to me in prayer just what your problem is." Actually, all three give him excellent advice, instruction that is both intellectually sound and downright sensible. They follow the letter of the law and we can have no quarrel with what they say.

So far, we have always found that the clue to the whole matter lies in the Hebrew meaning of the proper names. Let us see, then, what the names of Job's three friends have to tell us.

Eliphaz, the Temanite—God of strength. He was a son of Esau, and Teman is Esau's country; so we know that he is still under the jurisdiction of materialistic thinking.

Bildad, the Shuhite—son of contention. Bildad signifies the intellect's love of reasoning, analyzing, contending, arguing; the Shuhite (Hebrew), depressed, tells us that this brings depression.

Zophar, the Naamathite—sparrow. Zophar seems to have the same meaning as Zipporah (wife of Moses), chirping, twittering, small bird. Naamah is an Ammonite, therefore on the human or materialistic side of thinking; but Naamah means *pleasant*. So we take it that Zophar represents agreeable human thinking, trying to be helpful in its twittering way.

Job's three well-meaning friends who tried so hard to set him straight represent phases of intellectual thinking and reasoning, that which is less than spiritual understanding. Thus, it was impossible for them to help him find any remedy for his afflictions. ". . . With men this is impossible; but with God all things are possible." [2]

2. Matthew 19:26.

There are plenty of people who will tell us what is wrong with us, point out where we have made our mistakes, but it is the one who directs us to the God Power within us who is truly helpful.

Eliphaz tells Job:

Now a thing was secretly brought to me,
And mine ear received a whisper thereof.
 In thoughts from the visions of the night,
 When deep sleep falleth on men,
 Fear came upon me, and trembling,
 Which made all my bones to shake.
 Then a spirit passed before my face;
 The hair of my flesh stood up.
 It stood still, but I could not discern the appearance
  thereof;
 A form was before mine eyes:
 There was silence, and I heard a voice, saying,
"Shall mortal man be just before God?
 Shall a man be pure before his Maker?
 Behold, he putteth no trust in his servants;
 And his angels he chargeth with folly:
 How much more them that dwell in houses of clay,
 Whose foundation is in the dust,
 Which are crushed before the moth!
 Betwixt morning and evening they are destroyed:
 They perish for ever without any regarding it.
 Is not their tent-cord plucked up within them?
 They die, and that without wisdom." [3]

On and on raves Eliphaz, pointing out the frailty of human man and advocating that Job seek unto God. "I would seek unto God, and unto God would I commit my cause. . . ." [4]

3. *The Modern Reader's Bible*, Edited by Richard G. Moulton, New York: The Macmillan Company, 1945, pp. 1042, 1043.
4. Job 5:8.

But none of these wise sayings seem to lift the spirit of Job one whit. He still has the boils, his possessions are still gone, and one imagines his wife standing over him continually nagging him to "curse God and die." Nowadays we might conclude that she was waiting for his insurance. At any rate, she was of little comfort to Job.

When the three friends have finished their excellent advice, Job is just as downtrodden, just as rebellious, just as morose as ever. Still wishing that he were dead, still protesting that it is really not his fault that he is in this sad plight.

> I will complain in the bitterness of my soul.
>> Am I a sea, or a sea-monster,
>> That thou settest a watch over me?
>> When I say, My bed shall comfort me,
>> My couch shall ease my complaint:
>> Then thou scarest me with dreams,
>> And terrifiest me through visions:
>> So that my soul chooseth strangling,
>> And death rather than these my bones.
>> I loathe my life;
>> I would not live alway;
>> Let me alone;
>> For my days are vanity.
>> What is man, that thou shouldest magnify him,
>> And that thou shouldest set thine heart upon him,
>> And that thou shouldest visit him every morning,
>> And try him every moment?
>> How long wilt thou not look away from me,
>> Nor let me alone till I swallow down my spittle? [5]

There is just no humility in Job. Self-righteousness and self-pity go hand in hand. Self-pity always contends that it is not man's fault; that God is punishing him for no good rea-

5. Moulton, *op. cit.*, p. 1046.

son. It is a long struggle for Job consciousness. The little ego self does not give up easily. The instruction that he receives from his friends makes sense. It is well worth our study, but Job claims that he knows all this. Job is like the people who say, "I've read all the books. I know all this, but it just doesn't work for me!"

> No doubt but ye are the people.
> And wisdom shall die with you.
> But I have understanding as well as you;
> I am not inferior to you:
> Yea, who knoweth not such things as these?
> I am as one that is a laughing-stock to his neighbour,
> A man that called upon God, and he answered him,
> The just, the perfect man is a laughing-stock.[6]

Job is so put upon, so resentful of this undeserved fate. He rails on and on, with Bildad and Eliphaz and Zophar interrupting him from time to time with their excellent instruction. Eliphaz gives him those beautiful words so often quoted today.

> Acquaint now thyself with him and be at peace:
>> Thereby good shall come unto thee.
> Receive, I pray thee, the law from his mouth,
>> And lay up his words in thine heart.
>>> If thou return to the Almighty,
> Thou shalt be built up;
>>> If thou put away unrighteousness far from thy tents.
>> And lay thou thy treasure in the dust,
>>> And the gold of Ophir among the stones of the brooks:
> And the Almighty shall be thy treasure,
> And precious silver unto thee.
> For then shalt thou delight thyself in the Almighty,

6. Moulton, *op. cit.,* p. 1051.

And shalt lift up thy face unto God.
　　Thou shalt make a prayer unto him,
And he shall hear thee;
And thou shalt pay thy vows.
　　Thou shalt also decree a thing,
And it shall be established unto thee;
And light shall shine upon thy ways.
　　When they cast thee down,
Thou shalt say, There is lifting up;
And the humble person he shall save.
He shall deliver even him that is not innocent:
Yea, he shall be delivered through the cleanness of thine
　　　　hands.[7]

If Job hadn't been so stubborn he would have done well to listen to this instruction. Fortunately for Job, there is an underlying thread of faith that runs throughout his negative thinking. It is so well expressed in Chapter nineteen.

For I know that my redeemer liveth, and that he shall stand at the latter day upon the earth.
And though after my skin worms destroy this body, yet in my flesh shall I see God: —Job 19:25, 26

Like all of us, Job was prone to vacillate. He wanted to trust in God. One moment he would say, "Though he slay me, yet will I trust in him," and the next moment he spunkily declared, "but I will maintain mine own ways before him." Job was a diehard—but, aren't we all? "Blessed are the meek"—blessed are the teachable—"for they shall inherit the earth." At this stage, the Job consciousness is not very teachable.

So these three men ceased to answer Job, because he was righteous in his own eyes.

7. Moulton, *op. cit.*, pp. 1064, 1065.

Then was kindled the wrath of Elihu the son of Barachel the Buzite, of the kindred of Ram: against Job was his wrath kindled, because he justified himself rather than God.

—Job 32:1, 2

Act III—The Truth Is Revealed to Job

Act III introduces a new character, Elihu, the son of Barachel, the Buzite, of the kindred of Ram. What is the hidden meaning here?

Elihu—my God is that which is; God is he; Jehovah. Elihu represents the Holy Spirit or the recognition by man that his true inner Self is Spirit.

Barachel—God doth bless; prospered of God; kneels before God.

Buzite—my contempt.

Our new character, then, is a recognition of God within and contempt for that which does not measure up to the divine phase or awareness of Spirit in man.

The very name, Elihu, suggests his message—*God is.* In this drama of wisdom, Elihu represents the Holy Spirit. He is the Spirit of Truth right within Job, that finally makes itself heard; the recognition that finally comes to man that his true Self is Spirit. The coming of Elihu signifies that, at long last, the Job consciousness is ready to look away from outer conditions and human argument and turn within to be taught of the Spirit.

It is interesting to note that Elihu waits until all the rest are through speaking because they were elder than he.

And Elihu the son of Barachel the Buzite answered and said, I am young, and ye are very old; wherefore I was afraid, and durst not shew you mine opinion.

I said, Days should speak, and multitude of years should teach wisdom.

But there is a spirit in man: and the inspiration of the Almighty giveth them understanding. —Job 32:6–8

The spiritual thought hangs back. Human thinking seems so very old, so well entrenched. It has had a head start with us. For such a long time we have thought that there is nothing beyond the intellect. It is only when all else has failed that we are willing to listen to that little newborn thought within us that tells us: *There is a spirit in men: and the inspiration of the Almighty giveth them understanding.*

Elihu cuts right through to the heart of the matter. He tells Job that he is not impressed with the man Job, that he is not given to flattering titles; but that he knows the Truth about him. He knows that no amount of talk on the outside will change the Job thinking. Well-meaning friends can point out our mistakes until doomsday but no one is ever willing to accept the wise advice until the Spirit of Truth within him whispers that which he needs to know.

Howbeit when he, the Spirit of truth, is come, he will guide you into all truth. . . . —John 16:13

Elihu represents the Spirit of Truth within Job that teaches him from within the Truth that he needs to know.

Only the Spirit of Truth within Job can show him that he may rise up out of his human self-righteousness into a new level of spiritual understanding. Once the new order of thinking is revealed, there is contempt for the old confusion. It becomes worthless babel. Elihu tells the Job thinking as it struggles with the problems of life in this world, that it has been swamped with a lot of vain words. It condemns the intellectualism of Job and his friends.

Behold, I waited for your words,
I listened for your reasons,
Whilst ye searched out what to say.
Yea, I attended unto you,
    And, behold, there was none that convinced Job,
    Or that answered his words, among you.[8]

Job's friends gave him good advice, much of it spiritual
Truth, but he would not listen.

How often we, in well-meaning concern, try to give our
friends advice only to find their ears are closed. Only the
Elihu within can give instruction which will be acceptable.
Only Elihu can speak to the heart. In the play, Elihu explains
this to Job.

For God speaketh once,
Yea twice, though man regardeth it not.
    In a dream, in a vision of the night,
    When deep sleep falleth upon men,
    In slumberings upon the bed;
  Then he openeth the ears of men,
  And sealeth their instruction,
  That he may withdraw man from his purpose,
  And hide pride from man;
  He keepeth back his soul from the pit,
  And his life from perishing by the sword.

Mark well, O Job, hearken unto me:
  Hold thy peace, and I will speak.
If thou hast any thing to say, answer me:
  Speak, for I desire to justify thee.
If not, hearken thou unto me:
  Hold thy peace, and I will teach thee wisdom.[9]

8. Moulton, *op. cit.,* p. 1075.
9. Moulton, *op. cit.,* pp. 1075, 1076, 1077.

Job holds his peace. He makes no sign. Elihu now turns to the three friends:

Hear my words, ye wise men,
　And give ear unto me, ye that have knowledge.
For the ear trieth words,
　As the palate tasteth meat.
Let us choose for us that which is right:
　Let us know among ourselves what is good.
For Job hath said, "I am righteous,
And God hath taken away my right:
　　Notwithstanding my right I am accounted a liar;
　　My wound is incurable, though I am without transgression."
What man is like Job,
　Who drinketh up scorning like water?
Which goeth in company with the workers of iniquity,
　And walketh with wicked men.
For he hath said,
"It profiteth a man nothing
That he should delight himself with God."
Therefore hearken unto me,
Ye men of understanding:
Far be it from God, that he should do wickedness;
And from the Almighty, that he should commit iniquity.
　　For the work of a man shall he render unto him,
　　And cause every man to find according to his ways.
Yea, of a surety, God will not do wickedly,
Neither will the Almighty pervert judgment.
　　Who gave him a charge over the earth?
　　Or who hath disposed the whole world?

For hath any said unto God,
　　"I have borne chastisement, though I offend not:
That which I see not teach thou me:
　　If I have done iniquity, I will do it no more?"
Shall his recompense be as thou wilt, that thou refusest it?

For thou must choose, and not I:
Therefore speak what thou knowest.
Men of understanding will say unto me,
Yea, every wise man that heareth me:
Job speaketh without knowledge,
    And his words are without wisdom.
Would that Job were tried unto the end,
    Because of his answering like wicked men.
For he addeth rebellion unto his sin,
He clappeth his hands among us,
And multiplieth his words against God.[10]

First, Elihu, playing the part of the Spirit of Truth within Job, addresses himself to the perverse Job thinking, then to the intellectual reasoning type of thinking represented by the three friends. Finding no response, it turns to the Universal Power Itself. There follows a beautiful prayer of recognition which establishes, without doubt, that God is the only Power, the only Intelligence, the only Teacher, the only Justice. Any sort of separate human thinking must give up in the face of this argument. Worldly wisdom, intellectualism, count for nothing when we stand in awe of divine Wisdom.

Elihu also proceeded, and said,
Suffer me a little, and I will shew thee that I have yet to speak on God's behalf.

I will fetch my knowledge from afar, and will ascribe righteousness to my Maker.

For truly my words shall not be false: he that is perfect in knowledge is with thee.

Behold, God is mighty, and despiseth not any: he is mighty in strength and wisdom.

       .   .   .

Behold, God exalteth by his power: who teacheth like him?

       .   .   .

10. Moulton, *op. cit.*, pp. 1077, 1078, 1079.

Behold, God is great, and we know him not, neither can the number of his years be searched out.

. . .

Touching the Almighty, we cannot find him out: he is excellent in power, and in judgment, and in plenty of justice: he will not afflict.

Men do therefore fear him: he respecteth not any that are wise of heart. —Job 36:1–5, 22, 26; 37:23, 24

The word *fear* means here, as elsewhere in the Bible, *to stand in awe of*. The divine Law has no respect for persons. The "Wise of heart" is used here to indicate those who are worldly wise, wise in their own human judgment. The argument of Truth finally prevails with the Job thinking. In Chapters thirty-six and thirty-seven, Elihu is so convincing that no amount of false thinking could resist him. It is a beautiful meditation and one that we would all do well to read when doubt assails us.

There are four key ideas that the story of Job should have shown us up to this point:

1. Intellectual reasoning is a futile pastime.
2. Persistence pays big dividends.
3. We must never renounce God.
4. Freedom comes through praying for others.

Job's saving grace was his refusal to renounce God. Because he kept coming back to God he left the way clear for Elihu to come in. Job's love for God was not conditioned by what happened to him in the earthly experience. He complained a lot about his fate; but because he deferred to God, he was finally set free from the bondage brought about through his own fear and self-righteousness.

The three friends of Job teach us a very important lesson —the futility of trying to take an imperfect human and make him over. Like Eliphaz, Bildad, and Zophar, we are all prone to argue on the level of cause and effect. This gets us nowhere.

Even ministers who should know better fall into this trap. They keep thinking that if only the troubled person could understand that he is his own worst enemy, that he is making his own troubles as fast as he can, that if only he could learn to be more loving, more forgiving, more trusting, etc., etc., then he could be helped. Well-meaning criticism always breeds resistance.

It is only the awareness of Elihu that makes any progress in helping another—"he that is perfect in knowledge is with thee." Condemning the mistakes of another will only cause him to try to justify himself. "And I, if I be lifted up from the earth, will draw all men unto me." [11]

As we lift our attention to the Christ, we lift the one whom we desire to help into an awareness of God with him. Elihu beheld the perfect man, the angel of the Presence, the Christ in Job. "Mark the perfect man, and behold the upright: for the end of that man is peace." [12]

This was the turning point for Job as it is for every man.

In the next scene, the Lord answers Job out of the whirl-wind. Right in the midst of the whirlwind of confusion comes the realization of Truth. This is the surrender of Job. It makes me think of that beautiful verse in the forty-sixth Psalm: "The heathen raged, the kingdoms were moved: he uttered his voice, the earth melted." [13]

First Job's friends tried to advise him in that which seemed so obvious. Their argument was the *quid pro quo,* this for that philosophy. It had to do with the law of cause and effect. It was a lot of futile talk that accomplished nothing. Then, the Christ consciousness, represented by Elihu, speaks Truth and something happens. Job is convinced. Now the Job think-

11. John 12:32.
12. Psalms 37:37.
13. Psalms 46:6.

ing is willing to stop struggling with conditions. In effect, it says: ". . . Speak, Lord; for thy servant heareth. . . ." [14]

The voice of the Lord, the "still small voice" within, must always wait until we have "ears to hear" before it can be heard.

For four chapters, the Voice from the whirlwind instructs Job. In beautiful verse, Job is made aware of the omnipotent Power of God. The Voice tells how all of the infinite particulars and details of Life are maintained and sustained by God.

> Where is the way where light dwelleth? and as for darkness, where is the place thereof,
>
> That thou shouldest take it to the bound thereof, and that thou shouldest know the paths to the house thereof?
>
> Knowest thou it, because thou wast then born? or because the number of thy days is great?
>
> Hast thou entered into the treasures of the snow? or hast thou seen the treasures of the hail,
>
> Which I have reserved against the time of trouble, against the day of battle and war?
>
> By what way is the light parted, which scattereth the east wind upon the earth?
>
> Who hath divided a watercourse for the overflowing of waters, or a way for the lightning of thunder;
>
> To cause it to rain on the earth, where no man is; on the wilderness, wherein there is no man;
>
> To satisfy the desolate and waste ground; and to cause the bud of the tender herb to spring forth?
>
> Hath the rain a father? or who hath begotten the drops of dew?
>
> Out of whose womb came the ice? and the hoary frost of heaven, who hath gendered it?
>
> The waters are hid as with a stone, and the face of the deep is frozen.

14. I Samuel 3:9.

Canst thou bind the sweet influences of Pleiades, or loose the bands of Orion?

Canst thou bring forth Mazzaroth in his season? or canst thou guide Arcturus with his sons?

Knowest thou the ordinances of heaven? canst thou set the dominion thereof in the earth?

Canst thou lift up thy voice to the clouds, that abundance of waters may cover thee?

Canst thou send lightnings, that they may go, and say unto thee, Here we are?

Who hath put wisdom in the inward parts? or who hath given understanding to the heart? —Job 38:19-36

Now Job is humbled as he comes to a full realization of the Spirit within. It is the realization that Jesus had, *of myself I can do nothing, the Power within me doeth its works.*

Then Job answered the Lord, and said,

Behold, I am vile; what shall I answer thee? I will lay mine hand upon my mouth. —Job 40:3, 4

What can he say? He realizes that all Power comes from God; that without God, man is nothing. It is the end of the search for Job, the beginning of divine fulfillment. Surrender is such an important part of answered prayer. It is only when we are willing to stop struggling with our futile human strengh and let the Omnipotent One take over that we get anywhere. It is as if the door is opened and all Power walks in.

Once Job gets his mind off his own troubles, he is able to take the next step—he prays for his friends.

And the Lord turned the captivity of Job, when he prayed for his friends: also the Lord gave Job twice as much as he had before. —Job 42:10

Why was all restored, and twice as much as he had before, when Job prayed for his friends? Praying for another has a wonderful effect on the one who prays. Love enters in. With the attention directed toward God, there is no time to dwell on the appearance of evil. That to which a person directs his attention in Love is sure to become his experience. Everything reproduces after its kind. When one prays for himself, there is a tendency to hang onto the problem, setting up the lack as something that is difficult to overcome. When one prays for his friends, it is easy to let go of the appearances and direct the attention to God. It is a case of "he who rows his brother across the stream gets there also," for how can one direct his attention to God without bringing God into his experience also?

> Then came there unto him all his brethren, and all his sisters, and all they that had been of his acquaintance before, and did eat bread with him in his house: and they bemoaned him, and comforted him over all the evil that the Lord had brought upon him: every man also give him a piece of money, and every one an earring of gold. —Job 42:11.

After Job, through prayer for his friends, lifted his thinking to a level higher than intellectual reasoning, there came to him the thoughts that were unified with his new enlightened consciousness: his brethren, the conscious thoughts, and his sisters, the subjective ones. These were the spiritual thoughts "that had been of his acquaintance before. . . ." He had known this thinking before. It was familiar to him. In this unified consciousness they partook of the bread of Life, the true spiritual Substance. These thoughts brought him the comfort of knowing that none of the suffering that had come to him through the law of cause and effect belonged to him. And these uplifted thoughts brought, from every man, "a piece of money . . ." and, from everyone, "an earring of gold." In other words, a wealth of treasure. There is no end to the good that comes to us through the unified consciousness.

So Job was given twice as much as before. His thoughts of Truth were multiplied. Again he had seven sons and three daughters. The names of the sons are not mentioned but the names of the three daughters are specifically given. The Hebrew meaning of their names adds the finishing touch to this story for they clearly describe the thoughts springing from the feeling side of the uplifted Job consciousness. They are:

Jemima (Hebrew)—dove, purity. This indicates that the soul is purified from fear, contention, and self-justification.

Kezia (Hebrew)—stripped off. When the soul or subconscious mind has been stripped of its mistaken thinking it has true perception and discrimination.

Kerenhappuch (Hebrew)—horn of beauty. This is the beauty of the purified soul.

The daughters of Job represent the now purified subconscious mind, the feminine side of the enlightened Job consciousness.

The story of Job is the story of everyman's experience in his search for God. God is the Principle Character in everyman's life whether he knows it or not. ". . . God was in Christ, reconciling the world unto himself. . . ." [15]

Epilogue

And in all the land were no women found so fair as the daughters of Job: and their father gave them inheritance among their brethren.

15. II Corinthians 5:19.

After this lived Job an hundred and forty years, and saw his sons, and his sons' sons, even four generations.

—Job 42:15, 16

The beautiful women, so fair, are the beautiful feelings of Job in his oneness with the Spirit within, the feeling side that inherits an abundance of every good thing when it has become unified with the conscious mind (the brethren). Our emotions so often are the "traitors in the camp" that make all the trouble, but once they are brought into alignment with our enlightened thinking, we feel balance endlessly in our experience. This is expressed by Job living another 140 years, seven doubled and multiplied by ten for emphasis—perfect everything, even to four generations. Four always indicates perfect balance.

It was a long struggle. It involved a lot of words before Job was ready to let God be expressed through him. At last he found that his security was of God, an inner state that did not depend upon outer conditions. He found it out when he stopped thinking about himself and was willing to pray for his friends. Thus do we all receive the blessing of God.

XVI   THE PSALMS—A PROVING GROUND FOR THE CODE

The Book of Psalms is the longest book in the Bible. It has been called *The Little Bible,* because it contains so much of the teaching of the Bible. It is like a review of the Old Testament and a prophecy of that which is to come in the New Testament. Much of the teaching of Jesus is to be found in the Psalms which were undoubtedly the hymnal of the Hebrew people and, as such, were not only familiar to all Hebrew boys of his time, but committed to memory by them. The Psalms offer us an excellent proving ground in using the secret code.

Some Interesting Facts about the Psalms

Inquiring into the meaning of the word *psalm,* I find that there are quite a series of words relating to this subject. The Hebrew word is *tethillim* meaning *praises.* The collection of sacred poetry received its name *Psalms* from the Greek, in consequence of the lyrical character of the pieces of which it consists which were intended to be sung to stringed, or other, instruments of music. The word means *song* as a noun, and, as a verb, it means *to pull, twitch, or play upon a stringed instrument, or to sing to the harp*. We are all familiar with the word *psalmist*, meaning *the composer of psalms;* but did you know that he was also called a *psalmodist, a psalmographer, a psalmographist,* and that he was given to practicing *psalmody, the act, practice or art of singing psalms?* A masculine *psalmographer* is called a *psalterer* and a feminine one is known as a *psaltress, a female player on the psaltery.* Things pertaining to the *psalter, a book of psalms,* are referred to as *psalterian.*

There are one hundred and fifty psalms, songs of praise mostly, but some also deal with historical events, personal and biographical incidents, and prayers and meditations. You might say that it is a sort of combined prayer book and hymnal of the ancient Hebrews with much other useful material thrown in. To this day, the Psalms are sung to music as congregational hymns and solos. They are used almost exclusively, in prayer books, as responsive readings to be used by minister and congregation.

Many of the ancients, both Jews and Christians, believed that the Psalms were written by David. Many of them were written by David, others by various poets. They were written over a period of years, some as late as 165 B.C. It is thought that they were gathered together, much as folk songs are gathered together today, after coming to expression here and there among the people.

The word, *selah,* used seventy-one times in the Psalms, has an unknown meaning. Some think that it is used to indicate a pause or timing of the musical accompaniment. In context, it often seems like an exclamation mark, a sort of dramatic emphasis.

All That We Would Ever Need

Actually, we could get along very nicely with just the Psalms for spiritual inspiration. Praising God is finding God. When we praise God, we identify ourselves with Him. The Psalms not only help us to do this, but they provide promises to comfort and sustain us in every need, assurances of protection to counteract fear, hymns of thanksgiving to aid us in the most important activity in our lives—the worship of God.

> With his whole heart he praised the Lord, and loved God that made him. . . . —Ecclesiasticus 47:10

I agree with Marchette Chute, "the Hebrew Psalter [is] the most beautiful books of poetry in the world." [1]

Judge Thomas Troward was a great lover of the Psalms. After he passed on, his comments on the Psalms were published with a foreword by Mrs. Troward who wrote:

> He [Judge Troward] was particularly attracted by the Psalms. In his opinion, these one hundred fifty pieces of beautiful prose poetry give reflection to every mood of mankind, from the depths of sadness to the spirit of the triumphal conclusion, "Let everything that hath breath praise the Lord. Praise ye the Lord." He made a practice of studying one Psalm carefully every day whatever other portions of the Bible he might also choose to read, and this accounts for the number of Notes that fill this particular part of his Bible.[2]

Our Secret Code as Used in the Psalms

Almost all of our secret code words are used in the Psalms—house, land, mountains, rivers, mystical numbers, and often-

---

1. Marchette Chute, *The Search for God*, New York: E. P. Dutton & Co., Inc., 1965, p. 225.
2. Thomas Troward, *Troward's Comments on the Psalms*, Foreword by Annie Troward, New York: Robert M. McBride & Co., 1929, pp. viii, ix.

used proper names—and they are all used here with meanings consistent to that elsewhere used in the Bible.

I find that the revised versions lose much of the beautiful cadence found in the King James Version. It is like translating poetry from a foreign language. It no longer seems to be poetry.

It would, of course, be impossible to interpret all of the Psalms here. Let us, therefore, take a few of the best known of these beautiful, lilting songs and see what they reveal when we let a few of our key words interpret for us the rich hidden meanings. Actually, the Psalms, more than any other part of the Bible, interpret themselves. There is so much feeling in them that they communicate themselves to the feeling nature rather than to the analytical mind.

In considering the Psalms, it is essential to think of them as poetry, such musical poetry that one feels at once that they should be sung, not read. It is absolutely impossible to take them literally. Like the writings of Robert Browning and Walt Whitman, the truths contained are more felt than intellectualized. It will be helpful now to consider first a few of the terms most often employed by the psalmist.

The people—thought people: the sinners; the scornful; the heathen; the ungodly; the righteous; the just; him that loveth violence; enemies; foes. The people, so called, are the thoughts that you and I entertain. When this is understood, we can understand why the Lord lifts up some and dashes others to destruction.

The Lord—the divine Law continually at work in the lives of men, lifting up, restoring, revitalizing, bringing all into harmonious balance.

The righteous—our spiritual thoughts; thoughts that trust in the divine Law; right-use-ness of the Law; living by Truth; judging righteous judgments instead of judging by appearances.

The places—places in Mind; states of consciousness. The rivers; the waters; the floods; the land; the sea; the desert; the wilderness; the waves; the mountains; the hills; the valleys all refer to the states of mind, the ups and downs that man experiences in his own consciousness. At times, he feels desolate, separated from the Truth of Being, and this is described by the Psalmist as being "in the wilderness" or "in the desert." When he looks "unto the hills," the highlands of Mind, he is sustained and uplifted.

The kings of the earth (with a small "k")—our thoughts of intellectualism, human reasoning to which man is apt to give undue importance.

The great King, the King of glory (King spelled here with a capital "k")—the dominion of God, Spirit in man. This dominion is only to be found in the "mountain of holiness," the high awareness of spiritual wholeness.

Psalms 1 and 2

Psalms 1 and 2 seem to set the stage. Understanding their deep significance, we can proceed to grasp the hidden meaning of the rest. "These two Psalms," wrote Judge Troward, "contain the teaching of the whole Bible in miniature." [3]

PSALM 1

Blessed is the man that walketh not in the counsel of the ungodly, nor standeth in the way of sinners, nor sitteth in the seat of the scornful.

But his delight is in the law of the Lord and in his law doth he meditate day and night.

And he shall be like a tree planted by the rivers of water, that bringeth forth his fruit in his season; his leaf also shall not wither; and whatsoever he doeth shall prosper.

The ungodly are not so: but are like the chaff which the wind driveth away.

3. Troward, *Troward's Comments on the Psalms, op. cit.,* p. 1.

Therefore the ungodly shall not stand in the judgment, nor sinners in the congregation of the righteous.

For the Lord knoweth the way of the righteous: but the way of the ungodly shall perish. —Psalm 1

Blessed, in the vernacular of the Bible, always means happy. *Happy* "is the man that walketh not in the counsel of the ungodly, nor standeth in the way of sinners, nor sitteth in the seat of the scornful." So, we have, *happy* "is the man, . . ." *that point of awareness in the one Mind that recognizes the Power of God in his life.* Such a man has no traffic with the "ungodly," or the mistaken thinking of "sinners." *To sin is to miss the mark, to make one mistake after another. Sinners are those who are continually missing the mark* and theirs is an unhappy lot. The "seat of the scornful" *(those who openly defy the Power and Presence of God)* is also to be avoided if one would be happy.

Three classes of people, says Judge Troward,[4] oppose Law or Truth. He describes them thus:

1. The ungodly—those who practically deny God's existence; who are without God.

2. Sinners—who wilfully transgress against their better knowledge.

3. The scornful—who scorn the idea of Law or the possibility of knowing it. —Law, however, will in the end be too strong for them and, if opposed, must crush them: while to the obedient it necessarily produces constantly increasing life.

Man is constantly being tempted to listen to the "counsel of the ungodly. . . ." The counsel of the ungodly is just as destructive today as it was when this psalm was written. To listen to any philosophy that separates us from an awareness

4. Troward, *Troward's Comments on the Psalms, op. cit.,* p. 2.

of the Presence of God is to court death and destruction. "... The wages of sin is death."

On the other hand, the happy man, the consciousness of extreme happiness, even "delight," is trust in the divine Law of infinite Goodness. To pray without ceasing; to meditate on the divine Law day and night is bliss. Such an awareness is like a tree that puts its roots down deep into the ground. Fed by rivers of water, it draws from its Source and brings forth its fruit in due season. This fruit is what man calls demonstration, the gifts that outpicture from the divine within. What more can we ask? "... Whatsoever he doeth shall prosper." When we trust in the Lord and wait patiently for him, nothing can ever again concern us. The Law of infinite Goodness brings forth the fruitage of our planting in due season. Such an approach to life brings "delight" which the dictionary terms *extreme satisfaction*.

The "ungodly," the psalmist goes on to say, "are not so. ..." This is because there is no stability in their thinking. They "are like the chaff, ..." the empty husks which the wind blows away. This kind of thinking is not productive of good. It has nothing to stand on in the "congregation of the righteous"—the aggregate thoughts of Truth. The "way of the ungodly, ..." erroneous thinking that is not founded in Truth, will perish. Sooner or later it will be done away with.

This is not the story of a God of vengeance, but an explanation of the activity of the divine Law as It relentlessly uproots and casts out every thought opposed to Truth. God could not destroy His own creation. The phantoms of man's own misdirected thinking are states of consciousness totally unknown to God. They are as unrelated to God as darkness is related to light. But, just as the light turned on in a dark room ferrets out every dark corner, so does the Light of divine Understanding expose every crack and cranny of our negative thinking. "For the Lord [divine Law] knoweth the way of the righteous: but the way of the ungodly [thoughts] shall perish."

PSALM 2

Why do the heathen rage, and the people imagine a vain thing?

The kings of the earth set themselves, and the rulers take counsel together, against the Lord, and against his anointed, saying,

Let us break their bands asunder, and cast away their cords from us.

He that sitteth in the heavens shall laugh: the Lord shall have them in derision.

Then shall he speak unto them in his wrath, and vex them in his sore displeasure.

Yet have I set my king upon my holy hill of Zion.

I will declare the decree: the Lord hath said unto me, Thou art my Son; this day have I begotten thee.

Ask of me, and I shall give thee the heathen for thine inheritance, and the uttermost parts of the earth for thy possession.

Thou shalt break them with a rod of iron; thou shalt dash them in pieces like a potter's vessel.

Be wise now therefore, O ye kings: be instructed, ye judges of the earth.

Serve the Lord with fear, and rejoice with trembling.

Kiss the Son, lest he be angry, and ye perish from the way, when his wrath is kindled but a little. Blessed are all they that put their trust in him.

It is all here, "the teaching of the entire Bible in miniature," as Judge Troward says.[5] The unenlightened thoughts of materiality will always "rage," the kings of the earth "take counsel together, . . ." and they seem mighty convincing at

5. Troward, *Troward's Comments on the Psalms, op. cit.,* p. 1.

times. Their power, however, does not frighten the divine Law. ". . . My king," *the Christ of God within,* is established upon "my holy hill of Zion," that high place of spiritual awareness where abides wholeness (holy) and perfection. In this awareness "I will declare the decree: the Lord hath said unto me, Thou art my Son; this day have I begotten thee." This is the awareness of divine sonship, the awareness of the Christ within. Let the heathen rage. In the secret place within "I will declare the decree. . . ."

In the secret place within "I will declare the decree. . . ." A decree is an order from one having authority; in this case the Highest Authority there is declares, ". . . Thou art my Son; this day have I begotten thee." This is the moment of triumph when the kings of the earth have no longer any way of frightening us—their diagnoses that seemed so convincing, their threats of old age or poverty or loneliness and all the rest, ". . . Thou shalt break them with a rod of iron; thou shalt dash them in pieces like a potter's vessel." This is the benediction, that beautiful release that comes when we return to the recognition of the Sonship to "dwell in the house of the Lord for ever." We hear the same voice within that Jesus heard, "this is my beloved Son, in whom I am well pleased." Psalms one and two describe the work of the divine Law as we align ourselves with It. We are told to "Serve the Lord with fear, and rejoice with trembling." "Fear" in the Psalms always means *to stand in awe of the Law,* and who doesn't, once he sees It working in his life. "Blessed are all they that put their trust in him," the Christ within, for all that the Father hath is his.

Applying the Secret Code

Let us trace some of the most often-used words in our secret code as they appear in the Psalms.

House—the consciousness of the individual, the habitual thinking in which one dwells.

See how this opens up the following quotations so familiar to all of us.

Except the Lord build the house, they labour in vain that build it. . . . —Psalm 127:1

Except the consciousness of the individual be established in Truth, established upon the divine Law of Goodness, it is wasted thinking.

Peace be within thy walls, and prosperity within thy palaces.
For my brethren and companions' sakes, I will now say, Peace be within thee.
Because of the house of the Lord our God I will seek thy good. —Psalm 122:7-9

Oh, to dwell in the habitual consciousness of peace, to know the prosperity of divine abundance within thy palaces. To know that God is everpresent is to know true wealth and the "peace . . . which passeth all understanding." ". . . Peace be within thee." This is the peace that no man takes from us. This is the peace of which Jesus spoke:

Peace I leave with you, my peace I give unto you: not as the world giveth, give I unto you. Let not your heart be troubled, neither let it be afraid. —John 14:27

GLOSSARY

Aaron—brother of Moses; enlightener; mountaineer; executive Power of divine Law; mouthpiece of the Truth; Christ in action; Aaron carries out the divine instructions.

Ab, Abba—Hebrew prefix meaning Father.

Abraham—father of multitudes; the name that God gave to Abram as his true spiritual nature unfolded.

Abram—father of height, exalted Father; both Abram and Abraham stand for faith in the invisible Power of God.

Abinadab—father is noble.

Absolute—complete; entire; unconditional; First Cause; pure Spirit.

Adam—generic man; the son of man; human man.

affirmation—affirming the presence of God (Good).

allegory—the veiled presentation, in a figurative story, of a meaning metaphorically implied but not expressly stated. Allegory is prolonged metaphor, in which typically a series of actions are symbolic of other actions. Bunyan's *The Pilgrim's Progress* is an example of an allegory.

ambushments—protected strength within.

Ammon—(children of Ammon) thoughts springing from Ammon consciousness; careless, disorderly thinking; race consciousness; world opinion.

Amram—father of Moses; kindred of the Lofty One; exalted people.

angel of the Lord—messenger of the Divine Law; the spiritual idea that comes when we are ready to receive it.

angels—spiritual thoughts; inspiration from God, messengers of God.

animals—thoughts relating to physical strength.

ark—inner state of wholeness.

Asaph—collector; assembler; collective spiritual thinking.

attributes of God—facets of the divine Being that describe the nature of God: Spirit, Life, Love, Truth, Light, Intelligence, and Peace.

Baal—symbol of materiality; there are many kinds of Baal in our lives—all false gods.

Babel
Babylon } —confusion; mental confusion; chaos.

beasts—sensuous or material thoughts.

Being—God, the Source of all.

Benaiah—son of Jehovah; prospered by Jehovah; restored by Jehovah.

Bethel—house of God; consciousness of all Good.

Bethlehem—house of bread; the spiritual substance of all life.

Bethuel—abiding in the awareness of God.

Beulah land—Beulah means married. Beulah land signifies a perfect union with God.

Bible—from the Greek, *Biblos,* the Book.

Bildad, the Shuhite—son of contention. Bildad signifies the intellect's love of reasoning, analyzing, contending, argument; the Hebrew meaning of Shuhite is depressed, telling us that this thinking brings depression.

birds—liberated thoughts; ideas in the conscious mind.

blood—the circulation of life; the life principle.

body—Spirit in form; the body of Life; God manifest.

bread—the substance of Life.

bread of Life—the word of God; spiritual food; divine Inspiration.

bride—soul; the spiritualized subconscious unified with the Christ consciousness.

bridegroom—the Christ consciousness; complete oneness with God Life.

burning bush—the phenomenon of Spirit; the flame, the cleansing fire of Spirit, is from an infinite Source and therefore cannot be consumed or diminished.

Caleb—a bold spiritual thought.

Canaan—lowland; material existence; the subconscious mind that is later redeemed as the Promised Land.

candles—individual spiritual insight or understanding.

cattle—thoughts based on sensation or animal strength.

cave—hidden thought; concealed thinking; pressed down into the subconscious mind.

children—thoughts springing from parent thought.

Christ—Spirit individualized in man; spiritual man; the son of God; the image of God; heir to the kingdom of God and all of the attributes of God; God Power in man.

church—the spiritual consciousness of a group of people.

circumcision—cutting off of mortal tendencies; indicative of purification; turning away from the materialistic concept.

city—a collection of thoughts or group consciousness.

city foursquare—completely balanced consciousness.

consciousness—awareness.

creatures—thoughts of various kinds, the nature of the thought implied by the kind of creature.

creeping things—subtle thoughts that tempt.

David—beloved; awareness of sonship; beloved of God.

day—a degree of unfoldment in consciousness; illumined consciousness; divine illumination.

desert—the arid waste of human thinking; looking to matter for satisfaction; a barren place in one's thinking where nothing seems to grow; thinking that is not productive of good; unillumined consciousness; the wilderness; ignorance.

devil—*the accuser* (Greek); a false belief in evil as a power.

divine—pertaining to the Divine; of God.

divine Inspiration—the inspiration of God; intuition; ideas from within.

divinity—pertaining to the divine. The divinity of man is the

True nature of man or spiritual man created in the image of God, endowed with the attributes of God.

drink—to take into consciousness.

earth—the outer manifestation; *as in heaven, so on earth* means *as within, so without.*

east—the within.

to eat—to partake of mentally and spiritually; to receive into one's consciousness.

Eden (see Garden of Eden)—delight; bliss; Garden of Eden; the beautiful, blissful awareness of being cared for by God.

Edom—red earth; materiality; synonymous with Esau and all that he stands for.

Egypt—bondage of materiality; negation; false sense of bondage.

Eleazer—whose help is God.

Eli—under God; my God, God within. Also means unity; ascent; exaltation; the most high.

Eliab—God is Father.

Elihu—My God is that which is; God is he; Jehovah. Elihu represents the Holy Spirit or the recognition by man that his true inner Self is Spirit.

Elijah—God himself—Eli (God) plus (Jehovah); therefore, the presence of God.

Eliphaz, the Temanite—God of strength. He was a son of Esau, and Teman is Esau's country; so we know that he is still under the jurisdiction of materialistic thinking.

Elisha—God is savior.

Emmanuel—"God with us"; the Christ; God in us. In the Old Testament, called Jehovah God; in the New Testament, the Christ.

Engedi—fountain of fortune; the wilderness of making a decision.

Esau—red; hairy; the material or physical side.

esoteric—from the Greek *esōterikos* meaning the *inner*. Webster defines it: "Designed for, and understood by, the specially initiated alone. . . ."

Eve—the feminine or feeling side.

exoteric—from the Latin *exotericus* and the Greek *exōterikos* meaning *outside;* Webster defines it: "External, exterior. Suitable to the imparted to the public. . . ."

family—the thought family (son, daughter, manservant, maidservant, cattle, "thy stranger . . . within thy gates"); the objective thoughts (male), subjective thoughts and feelings (female); the thoughts that serve, the animal or sensual thoughts, the thoughts that are new and strange to the usual pattern of thinking.

fast—to abstain from certain thinking, such as negative or false thinking or thoughts of separation from God.

father—the masculine, directive aspect of Mind.

Father—God; the Universal Source of all Life; Universal Mind.

fatherless—those who do not know that they have a heavenly Father; those who let themselves feel separated from the Father consciousness or universal Mind.

fear of the Lord—to stand in awe of the divine Law and the way it works.

feet—the understanding; that which we stand upon.

fire or flame—the cleansing fire of Spirit; divine energy that is never exhausted.

firmament—to make firm, to make solid, a foundation; firm unwavering place in consciousness; a firm foundation of faith.

First Cause—God; originating cause of all life.

fish—ideas drawn out of the deep.

flocks—thoughts; groups of thoughts, such as flocks of sheep, indicate pure thoughts.

food—the spiritual thought by which we are fed; such as, "I have meat to eat that ye know not of."

forty—an indefinite but completed period of time; indicates stages of spiritual growth in one's life; a finished experience.

fowl—conscious thoughts in Mind.

garden—fertile soil of the Mind.

Garden of Eden (see Eden)—garden of the soul; the kingdom of God within; living by Grace where all is provided.

Gath—fortune or chance.

Genesis—the beginning; the first book of the Bible.

Gershom—son of Moses and Zipporah; a stranger in a strange land; divine discontent.

go up into a mountain—enter into a state of high spiritual consciousness.

God—the name or nature of God; the word that refers to all that the Infinite is; Life; Truth; Love; Intelligence; Power; Omnipresent, Omnipotent, Omniscient; the only Life; the only Substance, over all and through all.

Goliath—the exile; a soothsayer.

Good—see Goodness.

Goodness—a term used to designate God; infinite Goodness. God and Good are synonymous.

gospel—good news.

Grace—the illimitable Love of God as expressed in and through man and all Creation.

graven image—any kind of false thinking or mental pattern that we have allowed to become grooved or set.

Hagar—stranger; the human side of man which flees from the spiritual side.

Haran—an exalted state of mind (consciousness).

Hazazontamar—to have a divided mind, be in a quandary.

heart—the emotional or "feeling" side of life; subconscious mind.

heaven—the divine consciousness within; the realm of divine ideas; the conscious awareness of God; bliss; divine harmony realized.

hills and valleys—the ups and downs of one's thinking; high places of thinking as contrasted with low or depressed areas of thinking.

holy city—the consciousness of divine wholeness; inner awareness of being whole, perfect and complete.

holy ground—the consciousness of wholeness; divine perfection right where we are.

Hor—the mountain of mountains; a high, exalted state of consciousness.

Horeb—the mountain of God; a state of high spiritual awareness; the realization of the Presence and Power of God. We come to the mountain of God through prayer and meditation.

house—the individual consciousness; the habitual thinking in which one *dwells*.

house of the Lord—to "dwell in the house of the Lord" is to live in an awareness of the Presence of God, the Omnipresence of God; unification with the all-Good.

I AM THAT I AM—the secret of the ages; Jehovah God; the divine Self within each one of us; the indwelling Christ.

image and likeness of God—in Genesis I we are told that man is the "image" and "likeness" of God; partaking of the very nature of God; having inherent within himself all of the attributes of God; Jesus said the son is like the Father.

immanent God—God within; God right where we are as contrasted with a God afar off or separate from man; as Tennyson put it, "nearer than breathing, closer than hands and feet"; the Spirit within man; the very Life of our life.

Immanuel—see Greek form, Emmanuel.

infinite—unlimited; unending; the Absolute; a synonym for God.

Intelligence—God is infinite Intelligence; attribute of God.

Isaac—God laughed; the miracle of God through the working of faith (Abraham); Christ consciousness; Spirit individualized through faith.

Isaiah—salvation of Jehovah; God helps man by working through him.

Ishmael—personality; judging by human standards.

island—a body of land that is apparently separate from the mainland but actually has an undyerlying connection; hence, consciousness where one feels separated from his Source; separate from the wholeness of life when actually there is underlying unity.

Israel—the awareness of sonship; the "children of Israel" are the children of God; God consciousness or spiritual thoughts that are led out of mental bondage.

Jacob—the supplanter; the mental or intellectual steps upward; Jacob through spiritual unfoldment later became known as Israel, the prince of God.

Jah—a contraction of the word Jehovah with the same meaning;

used as a prefix in proper names, it is interchangeable with Je, Jo, and Ju.

Jahaziel—Jehovah reveals; Truth revealed; divine Inspiration.

Jehoshaphat—divine judgment; judging righteous judgment; stands for dominion through divine judgment; the government of Jehovah (God in man).

Jehovah—God living in and through man; same as Christ in the New Testament.

Jeiel—treasure of God; God unifies.

Jemima—dove, purity. This indicates that the soul is purified from fear, contention, and self-justification.

Jerusalem—city of peace; the conscious awareness of the peace of God within.

Jesus—savior; deliverance through Jehovah.

Jethro—divine Abundance; his preeminence.

Job—persecuted, afflicted, returning, a coming back.

Jochebed—mother of Moses; whose glory is Jehovah.

Joseph—the increaser; the faculty of imagination in man; Joseph was called "a fruitful bough"; through divine imagination our lives bear much fruit.

Joshua—same meaning as Jesus; Jehovah saves; salvation through the Christ Consciousness; Joshua, the Christ in man, took the children of Israel into the Promised Land.

Judah—consciousness of praising God; the "land of Judah" is that place in consciousness where we recognize and praise God.

Kerehappuch—horn of beauty. This is the beauty of the purified soul.

Kezia—stripped off. When the soul or subconscious mind has been stripped of its mistaken thinking it has true perception and discrimination.

kingdom of God   ⎱ —the divine order of perfection, God real-
kingdom of Heaven ⎰ ized, which Jesus said was not "Lo here! or, lo there! for, behold, the kingdom of God is within you." The word *kingdom* stands for absolute authority, dominion or rule, therefore the kingdom of God is the absolute authority; the dominion of God in and through spiritual man, his "image" and "likeness."

kings—ruling thoughts, thoughts that take dominion.

Laban—clear, shining thoughts.

lamps—producing the light; that consciousness which uses divine understanding (oil).

land—consciousness unfolding at different levels; various stages of awareness within the individual; i.e., lowlands, highlands, fertile lands, wastelands, etc. There are many kinds of lands referred to in the Bible and all relate to states of consciousness.

law—the law of cause and effect, sowing and reaping.

divine Law—the orderly working out of the divine Principle; God manifesting Himself throughout creation; God works through Law; the process by which God works. Lord and Law in the Bible can often be used interchangeably.

Leah—weary, faint, exhausted; denotes the human soul.

Levi—the grandfather of Moses; joining together; uniting; loving.

Life—a synonym for God; God is Life everywhere present.

Light—a synonym for God denoting divine illumination; "God is light, and in him is no darkness at all."

living water—the awareness of Truth; spiritual Inspiration; streams in the desert of unenlightened thinking.

Lord—the divine Law; infinite Good unfolding in an orderly manner; the perfect Law of God; everything created by God is Good; also a title of respect.

Lot—dark, negative thoughts; thoughts based upon human judgment.

Love—a synonym for God.

male or man—the conscious or directive mind within each person; the part of the mind that reasons and analyzes.

manna—spiritual substance; ideas that take form; literally, manna means *what is it*. What is it that you need? Manna becomes whatever is needed for it is spiritual supply to fill each man's need.

marriage—the union in consciousness of the masculine and feminine mind; the union of wisdom and love; the mystical union of the soul to the Christ Consciousness.

Mattaniah—gift of Jehovah; illumination; recognition of the Self.

meat—*to eat* in the Bible means to partake of mentally and spiritually. Therefore, when Jesus said "I have meat to eat that ye know not of," he was referring to the spiritual Inspiration by which he lived. ". . . The meat which perisheth" is depending upon the outer world for our good.

Midian—the middle stage of man's unfoldment; dominion through intellectual growth; a stage of unfoldment on the spiritual journey where mind takes dominion over matter; human judgment.

mind—the individual instrument of God in action.

Mind—the infinite Mind; God in action; the great creative Medium through which Spirit creates out of Itself.

Moab—son of Lot; children are thoughts springing from a parent thought, therefore, Moab would be of the offshoot of dark negative thinking; children of Moab signify thoughts springing from the Moab type of consciousness.

moon—the reflected light of intellectual reasoning.

morning—the light (illumination) that comes to the soul after a long period of darkness; the new fresh inspiration, such as "joy cometh in the morning."

morning star—the light that endures throughout the long night of ignorance and despair.

Moses—Truth drawn out of Mind; the consciousness that draws our spiritual thoughts out of bondage to materiality (Egypt); the Truth that leads us out of bondage.

mother—the feminine or feeling side of life; subjective mind; the love side that nurtures the little new idea.

Mt. Seir—hairy; bristling; shaggy; (see Jehoshaphat story) children of Mt. Seir are thoughts springing from the Mt. Seir consciousness; stormy, emotional thinking; thoughts originating in sense consciousness.

mountain or mount—a lofty state of consciousness; *to go up into a mountain* means to lift one's thinking to a high state of spiritual consciousness.

mystical—direct communion with God through contemplation.

name—nature; the *name of God* means according to the nature of God.

night—a dark period in man's consciousness; ignorance; a period when one seeks the light of understanding.

north—the conscious mind; outer appearances.

oil—the substance of Light; understanding; i.e., the "foolish . . . took no oil."

omnipotent—all Power; Power to which nothing is impossible.

omnipresent—everywhere present in the same degree; infinite.

omniscient—all knowing; all Intelligence.

one—the number that stands for unity; wholeness; undivided; indivisible; all encompassing; "the Lord our God is one."

Padan-aram—a plateau in consciousness; a broad level place in the evolving consciousness of the soul.

parable—a short fictitious narrative from which a spiritual Truth can be drawn.

pebbles—Truth ideas; (see stone) little stones.

Peniel—the presence of God; recognition of God; "for I have seen God face to face," said Jacob, and he named the place Peniel.

people—symbolic Bible use refers to "thought people." The enemies are all those of our own household—our own thoughts. ". . . My people would not harken to my voice. . . ." (Psalms 81:11) We have "good people" and "bad people" taking sides, but always they symbolize our good thoughts overcoming evil or negative thoughts.

Pharaoh—dominion through mental power; the self-assumed light of the intellect that keeps its thought followers in bondage to materiality.

Philistines—thoughts that are foreign to Spirit; transitory, migrating, wandering thoughts.

plains and plateaus—broad level expanses in man's unfolding consciousness; a place in one's spiritual growth where there is a certain amount of vision; a time of rest before traveling on toward the mountain tops of consciousness.

Promised Land—the state of mind representing divine fulfillment; to live in the Promised Land would be to live entirely by Grace trusting in God for every need.

race consciousness—the common belief; that which the world accepts but which is not necessarily true; often false beliefs.

Rachel—a lamb; a pure thought on the feminine or feeling side.

Reality—divine Truth; that which can never be changed or improved; God.

Rebekah—beauty in life; joy.

Red Sea—race consciousness; the psychic sea of doubt.

relative—the human ever-changing side of life; that which is not Reality; not real and eternal; that which is temporal; appearances.

Rephidim—a place of rest; the plateau we reach along the way in our spiritual journey.

Reuben—faculty of faith through discernment; vision.

Reul—companion of God.

river of life—the flow of divine Truth.

rivers, streams—the movement of Truth in Mind.

rock—the Truth that endures.

rod—power of the word; authority through the speaking of the word; the inspired word of God as spoken through His servant, man.

Sabbath—time of rest; the *it is finished consciousness* that releases the prayer of God; the seventh day, meaning time of finished perfection.

Salem—consciousness of peace.

Samuel—heard of God; God hears.

sand—rock (Truth) that has been pulverized, does not hold together; unstable or shifting thought.

Sarah—princess or ruling thought; thought of dominion.

Sarai—contentious; being a feminine name it denotes the feeling nature, therefore, contentious feelings.

Satan—from the Hebrew—*to oppose, to be an adversary;* a belief in evil as a power opposed to good; (see devil) also called *the accuser.*

Saul—asked for; the human will that is displaced or given a new name (nature) through divine enlightenment (Saul becomes Paul).

sea—the vast undifferentiated Substance of Mind; universal Mind; the sea of Mind; the deep universal subconscious mind.

see—to see is to discern; to comprehend the Truth; understand-ing.

seed—ideas; thoughts springing from a parent thought; the *seed of Abraham* meaning thoughts springing from the kind of consciousness denoted by Abraham; *i.e.,* thoughts springing from faith in the invisible Power of God.

self—the little human self that must become silent if we would hear the voice of Truth.

Self—the God Self; the divine Center within each one; the Life within each one; God in man.

serpent—the temptation; the thought that tempts us to judge by false appearances; human judgment.

seven—the mystical number denoting something that is finished; complete; perfection; release; seventy times seven is used for emphasis indicating complete forgiveness—no loose ends.

Shammah—fame and renown.

sheep—pure innocent thoughts.

shepherds—keepers of the sheep; the consciousness that protects and guards the pure innocent thoughts.

shield—one is, according to Bible symbology, clothed in these thoughts, therefore a shield would be protective thinking.

sin—literally missing the mark; any mistake or misuse of the di-vine Law.

six—a period of labor; six days shalt thou labour; cycle of crea-tion.

Solomon—peace; the offspring of David (beloved) indicates the peace that comes from an awareness of Love; known for his great wisdom, the wisdom that comes through peace and love.

soul—the individual consciousness.

Soul—the universal or God Consciousness.

south—the subconscious mind.

Spirit—God; the breath of Life; the Spirit of God in man **and** throughout all of Life.

Spirit of Truth—the still small voice of divine Intelligence within; that which guides unto all Truth; God in man.

spiritual—pertaining to the Spirit; relating to the invisible world of the Spirit of God in man.

star—spiritual illumination; a bright light shining in the darkness; revelations of Truth. Jesus is called the "bright and morning star"—the light that endures through the night and is still shining when morning comes.

star of the east—the great inner Light that guides us to the newborn Christ; since east always stands for within, the star of the east must be an inner experience, a light that shines in the consciousness of man.

stone—intellectual or spiritual Truth. All forms of stone—rock, pebbles, sand—indicate various degrees or kinds of Truth. When Jacob put his head upon a stone for a pillow he put his mind on Truth. To build one's house (awareness) upon a rock is to have one's thinking stabilized in Truth. Sand is Truth that has been broken up, pulverized by the winds of time, and denote shifting thought that blows with the wind.

streams in the desert—streams of living water; Truth which flows through the desert wasteland of unenlightened thought and makes that barren wasteland of human thinking "blossom as the rose," making the consciousness beautiful. What could be more beautiful than an oasis of roses in the midst of the desert?

sun—spiritual illumination; spiritual Truth that sustains all of Life. The moon is the reflected light of the sun or intellectual illumination.

Syria—that level of thinking that has no understanding of spiritual Truth.

tabernacle of God—the abode of the Spirit; the body tabernacle; the temple of the living God "which temple ye are"; "the tabernacle of God is with men" indicates that perfect state when we shall come to know that God is in us and we in Him.

Tekoa—pitching a tent; taking a new stand in consciousness.

tent—a temporary dwelling place; a temporary state of mind which can be changed or expanded; transitional thinking; to "enlarge the place of thy tent" is to expand one's limited thinking.

three—the mystical number of unity; three in one; the trinity,

Spirit, Soul and body; the threefold nature of Being or God acting through Mind to produce manifestation.

throne—the dominion of God within; "he that sat upon the throne" is the Almighty Power of God within man taking dominion.

Thummim—Truth; whole; entire; complete; perfect; sound.

treatment—scientific prayer; the prayer that seeks not to change God but to put the one treating into alignment with the divine perfection of God which already exists.

tree—the connecting link between earth and heaven; the thinking that is rooted in the earth but reaches toward heaven.

"tree of the knowledge of good and evil"—human judgment; judging by appearances.

"tree of life"—the Truth about God and man; to eat of the fruit of the "tree of life" is to partake of the fruitage in life of a soul that is in tune with God.

trinity—Spirit, Mind and Body (Spirit, Soul and Body); the threefold nature of God as It emerges into manifestation through mind; Spirit taking form through the action of God as Law.

truth—that which one perceives to be true; intellectual truth is relative and changing.

Truth—God; Absolute Truth; Truth is the same yesterday, today and forever; eternal Truth is unchanging Truth, the final irrevocable Truth that always has been and always will be. Man discovers Truth as he awakens to Truth.

twelve—the mystical number indicating completion; spiritual fulfillment or completion.

Urim—lights; illumination; revelation; shining brilliancies; enlightenment.

watch tower—the high place in one's consciousness where the vision is extended.

water—the fluidic Mind; movement in consciousness; "face of the deep" indicates universal consciousness.

water of Life—spiritual inspiration; the Truth.

west—the outer appearances.

widow—a half-truth; one who has lost the mystical marriage with the God within; the consciousness which has let itself be separated from the unity of Life.

wilderness—the unenlightened state; the wilderness of unenlightened thought.

will of God—the perfect plan of Life for man; the will of God must conform to the nature of God (Love), therefore the will of God is always for our highest good.

wine—spiritualized thought.

wisdom—divine Intelligence revealed to man; the wisdom that guides and directs man when he is willing to listen.

word of God—divine Inspiration; the wisdom of God; Truth revealed through the Christ within.

woman—(female) the subjective or receptive side of life; the feeling side; the creative medium that follows through with the masculine direction.

worship—to assign great worth to; we worship God when we put Good first in our lives.

Zechariah—the Lord is remembered.

Zin—the last thorny wilderness to be overcome.

Zipporah—Daughter of Jethro, the wife of Moses; free-winged thoughts.

Zis—the reflected light of the intellect.

Zophar, the Naamathite—Sparrow. Zophar seems to have the same meaning as Zipporah (wife of Moses), chirping, twittering, small bird. Naamah is an Ammonite, therefore on the human or materialistic side of thinking; but Naamah means pleasant. So, we take it that Zophar represents agreeable human thinking, trying to be helpful in its twittering way.

BIBLIOGRAPHY

Anderson, Camilla M., M.D., *Beyond Freud.* New York. Harper and Bros. 1957.

Bible Encyclopaedia and Scriptural Dictionary (3 Volumes). Chicago. Howard-Severance Company. 1908.

Carrel, Alexis, *Man the Unknown.* New York. Harper and Bros. 1935.

Chute, Marchette, *The Search for God.* New York. E. P. Dutton & Co., Inc. 1965.

Cohen, Rev. Dr. A., *Everyman's Talmud.* New York. E. P. Dutton & Co., Inc. 1949.

Durant, Will, *The Story of Philosophy.* New York. Simon & Schuster, Inc. 1926.

Emerson, Ralph Waldo, *The Works of Ralph Waldo Emerson.* New York. Tudor Publishing Company.

Encyclopaedia Britannica. Chicago, London, Toronto. Encyclopaedia Britannica. 1954.

Fox, Emmet, *Power Through Constructive Thinking.* New York. London. Harper and Bros. 1940.

Gibran, Kahlil, *The Prophet.* New York. Alfred A. Knopf, Inc. 1958.

The Holy Bible. James Moffat translation. New York. Doubleday, Doran & Co., Inc.

The Holy Bible—Revised Standard Version. New York. Thomas Nelson & Sons. 1952.

The Illuminated Bible. Columbia Educational Books, Inc. 1941.

Metaphysical Bible Dictionary. Lee's Summit, Mo. Unity School of Christianity. 1953.

Moulton, Richard G., Editor, *The Modern Reader's Bible*. New York. Macmillan Co., Ltd. 1945.

The New Chain-Reference Bible (Fourth Edition). Compiled and edited by Frank Charles Thompson, D.D., Ph.D. Indianapolis, Indiana. B. B. Kirkbride Bible Co., Inc. 1964.

The New English Bible. New York. Oxford University Press, Inc. 1961.

The New Testament in Four Versions. Christianity Today Edition. New York. The Iversen-Ford Associates. 1963.

Overstreet, Harry A., *The Mature Mind*. New York. W. W. Norton & Company, Inc. 1949.

Reed, Dr. Grantly Dick, *Childbirth Without Fear*. New York. Harper and Row, Publishers. 1953.

Strong, James, *Strong's Exhaustive Concordance of the Bible*. New York. Abingdon-Cokesbury Press. 1950.

Troward, Thomas, *Bible Mystery and Bible Meaning*. New York. Dodd, Mead & Company. 1913.

Troward, Thomas, *Troward's Comments on the Psalms*. New York. Robert M. McBride & Co. 1929.

Voss, Carl Hermann, *The Universal God*. Boston. Beacon Press. 1961.

Webster's New International Dictionary. Second Edition. Springfield, Mass. G. and C. Merriam Company. 1957.

West, Morris L., *The Shoes of the Fisherman*. New York. William Morrow & Company, Inc., 1963.

Young, Robert, *Analytical Concordance to the Bible,* 20th ed. New York. Funk & Wagnalls Company, Inc.